Psalms
&
Canticles

*Meditations and Catechesis
on the Psalms and
Canticles of Morning Prayer*

John Paul II

Psalms
&
Canticles

Meditations and Catechesis
on the Psalms and
Canticles of Morning Prayer

LTP
LITURGY
TRAINING
PUBLICATIONS

Editorial Note

The catecheses and meditations on the psalms and canticles of the Liturgy of Lauds published in this volume, were given by Pope John Paul II during the Wednesday General Audiences between 28th March 2001 and 1st October 2003, after which the Holy Father extended the series to the psalms and canticles of evening prayer. The audiences were given in Italian and the texts used are the official translation released by the Holy See.

The texts of the Psalms and Canticles reproduced in this publication are those used in the Divine Office, a translation of the *Liturgia Horarium* approved by the Episcopal Conferences of Australia, England and Wales, Ireland and Scotland, published by Wm Collins Sons & Co Ltd. Psalm texts are translated from the Hebrew by the Grail, © By Ladies Of The Grail (England). Used by permission of GIA Publications, Inc., exclusive agent. All rights reserved. Canticle texts are taken from the Revised Standard Version, Common Bible © 1973 Division of Christian Education, National Council of Churches of Christ in the USA.

© Libreria Editrice Vaticana, Vatican City, 2001–2003

PSALMS & CANTICLES: MEDITATIONS AND CATECHESIS ON THE PSALMS AND CANTICLES OF MORNING PRAYER © 2004 Archdiocese of Chicago: Liturgy Training Publications, 3949 South Racine Avenue, Chicago IL 60609; 1-800-933-1800, fax 1-800-933-7094, e-mail orders@ltp.org. All rights reserved. See our website at www.LTP.org.

Front cover photo © Catholic News Service.

Printed in the United States of America.

Library of Congress Control Number: 2004109889

19   18   17   16   15   3   4   5   6   7

ISBN 978-1-56854-556-1

PSMED

CONTENTS

Introduction

———— ✖ ————

The Psalter is the ideal source of Christian prayer

1. In the Apostolic Letter *Novo millennio ineunte* I expressed the hope that the Church would become more and more distinguished in the "art of prayer", learning it ever anew from the lips of the Divine Master (cf. n. 32). This effort must be expressed above all in the liturgy, the source and summit of ecclesial life. Consequently, it is important to devote greater pastoral care to promoting the *Liturgy of the Hours* as a prayer of the whole People of God (cf. *ibid.*, n. 34). If, in fact, priests and religious have a precise mandate to celebrate it, it is also warmly recommended to lay people. This was the aim of my venerable Predecessor Paul VI, a little over 30 years ago, with the Constitution *Laudis canticum* in which he determined the current form of this prayer, hoping that the Psalms and Canticles, the essential structure of the *Liturgy of the Hours*, would be understood "with new appreciation by the People of God" (*AAS* 63 [1971], 532).

It is an encouraging fact that many lay people in parishes and ecclesial associations have learned to appreciate it. Nevertheless, it remains a prayer that presupposes an appropriate catechetical and biblical formation, if it is to be fully savoured.

To this end, we begin today a series of catecheses on the Psalms and Canticles found in the morning prayer of Lauds. In this way I would like to encourage and help everyone to pray with the same words that Jesus used, words that for thousands of years have been part of the prayer of Israel and the Church.

2. We could use various approaches to understanding the Psalms. The first would consist in presenting their literary structure, their authors, their formation, the contexts in which they were composed. It would also be fruitful to read them in a way that emphasizes their poetic character, which sometimes reaches the highest levels of lyrical insight and symbolic expression. It would be no less interesting to go over the Psalms and consider the various sentiments of the human heart expressed in them: joy, gratitude, thanksgiving, love, tenderness, enthusiasm, but also intense suffering, complaint, pleas for help and for justice, which sometimes lead to anger and imprecation. In the Psalms, the human being fully discovers himself.

Our reading will aim above all at bringing out the religious meaning of the Psalms, showing how they can be used in the prayer of Christ's disciples, although they were written many centuries ago for Hebrew believers. In this task we will turn for help to the results of exegesis, but together we will learn from Tradition and will listen above all to the Fathers of the Church.

3. The latter, in fact, were able with deep spiritual penetration to discern and identify the great "key" to understanding the Psalms as Christ himself, in the fullness of his mystery. The Fathers were firmly convinced that the Psalms speak of Christ. The risen Jesus, in fact, applied the Psalms to himself when he said to the disciples: "Everything written about me in the law of Moses and the Prophets and the Psalms must be fulfilled" (*Lk* 24,44). The Fathers add that in the Psalms Christ is spoken to or it is even Christ who speaks. In saying this, they were thinking not only of the individual person of Christ, but of the *Christus totus*, the total Christ, composed of Christ the Head and his members.

Christians were thus able to read the Book of Psalms in the light of the whole mystery of Christ. This same perspective also brings out the ecclesial dimension, which is particularly highlighted when the Psalms are sung chorally. We can understand, then, how the Psalms came to be adopted from the earliest centuries as the prayer of the People of God. If in some historical periods there was a tendency to prefer other prayers, it is to the monks' great credit that they held the Psalter's torch aloft in the Church. One of them, St Romuald, founder of Camaldoli, at the dawn of the second Christian millennium, even maintained, as his biographer Bruno of Querfurt says, that the Psalms are the only way to experience truly deep prayer: "*Una via in Psalmis*" (*Passio sanctorum Benedicti et Johannis ac sociorum eorundem*: MPH VI, 1893, 427).

4. With this assertion, which seems excessive at first sight, he actually remained anchored to the best tradition of the first Christian centuries, when the Psalter became the book of Church prayer *par excellence*. This was the winning choice in view of the heretical tendencies that continuously threatened the unity of faith and communion. Interesting in this regard is a marvellous letter that St Athanasius wrote to Marcellinus in the first half of the fourth century while the Arian heresy was vehemently attacking belief in the divinity of Christ. To counter the heretics who seduced people with hymns and prayers that gratified their religious sentiments, the great Father of the Church dedicated all his energies to teaching the Psalter handed down by Scripture (cf. *PG* 27, 12ff.). This is how, in addition to the Our Father, the Lord's prayer by antonomasia, the practice of praying the Psalms soon became universal among the baptized.

5. By praying the Psalms as a community, the Christian mind remembered and understood that it is impossible to turn to the Father who dwells in heaven without an authentic communion of life with one's brothers and sisters who live on earth. Moreover, by being vitally immersed in the Hebrew tradition of prayer, Christians learned to pray by recounting the *magnalia Dei*, that is, the great marvels worked by God both in the creation of the world and humanity, and in the history of Israel and the Church. This form of prayer drawn from Scripture does not exclude certain freer expressions, which will continue not only to characterize personal prayer, but also to enrich liturgical prayer itself, for example, with hymns and troparia. But the Book of Psalms remains the ideal source of Christian prayer and will continue to inspire the Church in the new millennium.

The spirit prays through us in the Psalms

1. Before beginning the commentary on the individual Psalms and Songs of Praise, let us complete today the introductory reflection which we began in the last catechesis. We will do so by starting with one aspect that is prized by our spiritual tradition: in singing the Psalms, the Christian feels a sort of harmony between the Spirit present in the Scriptures and the Spirit who dwells within him through the grace of Baptism. More than praying in his own words, he echoes those "sighs too deep for words" mentioned by St Paul (cf. *Rom* 8,26), with which the Lord's Spirit urges believers to join in Jesus' characteristic invocation: *"Abba! Father!"* (*Rom* 8,15; *Gal* 4,6).

The ancient monks were so sure of this truth that they did not bother to sing the Psalms in their mother tongue. It was enough for them to know that they were in a way "organs" of the Holy Spirit.

They were convinced that their faith would enable the verses of the Psalms to release a special "energy" of the Holy Spirit. The same conviction was expressed in their typical use of the Psalms known as *"ejaculatory prayer"* - from the Latin word *"iaculum"*, that is "a dart" - to indicate concise phrases from the Psalms which they could "let fly" almost like flaming arrows, for example, against temptations. John Cassian, a writer who lived between the fourth and fifth centuries, recalls that monks discovered the extraordinary efficacy of the short *incipit* of Psalm 69: "God, come to my assistance; Lord, make haste to help me," which from that time on became as it were the gate of entry to the *Liturgy of the Hours* (cf. *Conlationes*, 10, 10: *CPL* 512, 298ff).

2. In addition to the presence of the Holy Spirit, another important dimension is that of the priestly action which Christ carries out in this prayer, associating with himself the Church, his Bride. In this regard, referring to the *Liturgy of the Hours*, the Second Vatican Council teaches: "Jesus Christ, High Priest of the New and Eternal Covenant ... attaches to himself the entire community of mankind and has them join him in singing his divine song of praise. For he continues his priestly work through his Church. The Church, by celebrating the Eucharist and by other means, especially the celebration of the Divine Office, is ceaselessly engaged in praising the Lord and interceding for the salvation of the entire world" (*Sacrosanctum Concilium*, n. 83).

So then the *Liturgy of the Hours* has the character of a public prayer in which the Church is specifically involved. It is enlightening to rediscover how she gradually came to shape her specific commitment of prayer to coincide with the various phases of day. To do so we must go back to the apostolic community in the days when there was still a close connection between Christian prayer and the so-called "legal prayers", that is, those prescribed by Mosaic Law - which were prayed at specific hours of the day in the temple of Jerusalem. From the book of Acts, we know that the Apostles were in the habit of "attending the temple together" (*Acts* 2,46), and "going up to the temple at the hour of prayer, the ninth hour" (3,1). Moreover, we also know that the "legal prayers *par excellence*" were those of the morning and the evening.

3. Jesus' disciples gradually identified certain Psalms as particularly appropriate for specific moments of the day, week or year, finding in them a deep sense of the Christian mystery. An authoritative witness of this process is St Cyprian, who writes in the first half of the third century: "We must also pray at the beginning of the day that the Resurrection of the Lord may be celebrated by morning prayer. The Holy Spirit once set this forth, when he said in the Psalms: "O my king and my God. For to you will I pray: O Lord, in the morning you shall hear my voice. In the morning I will stand before you, and will see you' (*Ps* 5,3-4).... For since Christ is the true Sun and the true Day, as the sun and the day of the world recede, when we pray and petition that the light come upon us again, we pray for the coming of Christ to provide us with the grace of eternal light" (*De oratione dominica*, 35: PL 39: 655).

4. The Christian tradition is not limited to perpetuating Jewish practice but made certain innovations which end by giving a different character to the entire prayer experience lived by Jesus' disciples. In fact, in addition to reciting the *Our Father* in the morning and evening, the Christians freely chose the Psalms with which to celebrate their daily prayer. Down through history, this process suggested the use of specific Psalms for certain particularly significant moments of faith. Among these, pride of place was held by *the prayer of vigils*, which were a preparation for the Lord's Day, Sunday, on which the Resurrection was celebrated.

Later, a typically Christian characteristic was the addition at the end of each Psalm and Canticle of the Trinitarian doxology, "Glory be to the Father and to the Son and to the Holy Spirit". Thus every Psalm and Canticle is illumined by God's fullness.

5. Christian prayer is born, nourished and develops around the event of faith *par excellence*: Christ's paschal mystery. Thus Easter, the Lord's passing from death to life, is commemorated in the morning, in the evening, at sunrise and at sunset. The symbol of Christ, "Light of the world", can be seen in the lamp light during the prayer of Vespers, which is consequently also called *"lucernarium"*. The *hours of the day*, in turn, recall the events of the Lord's Passion, and the third hour, the descent of the Holy Spirit at Pentecost as well. Lastly, *prayer during the night* has an eschatological character, recalling the watching recommended by Jesus in expectation of his second coming (cf. *Mk* 13,35-37).

Giving their prayer this rhythm, Christians responded to the Lord's command "to pray always" (cf. *Lk* 18,1; 21,36; *1 Thes* 5,17; *Eph* 6,18), but without forgetting that their whole life must, in a certain way, become a prayer. In this regard, Origen writes: "One who prays ceaselessly is one who combines prayer with work and work with prayer" (*On Prayer*, XII, 2: *PG* 11, 452C).

The whole panorama constitutes the natural habitat of the recitation of the Psalms. If heard and lived in this way, the *Trinitarian doxology* that crowns every Psalm becomes for the believer in Christ a continual immersion in the waters of the Spirit and in communion with the People of God, in the ocean of life and of peace in which that people was immersed through Baptism, that is, in the mystery of the Father, of the Son and of the Holy Spirit.

The First Week

Sunday

---- ✠ ----

Of the First Week

Psalm 62

vv. 2-9

O God, you are my God, for you I long;
for you my soul is thirsting.
My body pines for you
like a dry, weary land without water.
So I gaze on you in the sanctuary
to see your strength and your glory.

For your love is better than life,
my lips will speak your praise.
So I will bless you all my life,
in your name I will lift up my hands.
My soul shall be filled as with a banquet,
my mouth shall praise you with joy.

On my bed I remember you.
On you I muse through the night
for you have been my help;
in the shadow of your wings I rejoice.
My soul clings to you;
your right hand holds me fast.

My soul is thirsting for you, O Lord

1. Psalm 62 on which we are reflecting today is the Psalm of mystical love, which celebrates total adherence to God based on an almost physical yearning and reaching its fullness in a close and everlasting embrace. Prayer becomes longing, thirst and hunger, because it involves the soul and the body.

As St Teresa of Avila wrote: *"Thirst, I think, means the desire for something very necessary for us so necessary that if we have none of it we shall die."* (*The Way of Perfection*, chap. XIX). The liturgy presents to us the first two verses of the Psalm which are indeed focused on the symbols of thirst and hunger, while the third verse evokes a dark

horizon, that of the divine judgment of evil, in contrast to the
brightness and confident longing of the rest of the Psalm.

Believers long to be filled with God, the source of living water

2. Let us begin our meditation with the first *song*, that of the thirst for
God (cf. vv. 2-4). It is dawn, the sun is rising in the clear blue sky of
the Holy Land, and the person praying begins his day by going to the
temple to seek God's light. He has an almost instinctive, one might
say "physical" need for that encounter with the Lord. Just as the dried-
out earth is dead until it is watered by the rain and the earth's gaping
cracks suggest the image of its parched and thirsty mouth, so the
believer yearns for God, to be filled with him and thus to live in
communion with him.

The Prophet Jeremiah had already proclaimed: the Lord is the
"source of living waters", and had reproached the people for building
"broken cisterns, that can hold no water" (2,13). Jesus himself would
exclaim aloud: "If anyone thirsts, let him come to me; let him drink
who believes in me" (*Jn* 7,37-38). At high noon on a quiet, sunny day,
he promises the Samaritan woman: "whoever drinks of the water that
I shall give will never thirst; the water that I shall give will become in
him a spring of water welling up to eternal life" (*Jn* 4,14).

3. The prayer of Psalm 62 is interwoven with the song of the
wonderful Psalm 42: "as the deer longs for flowing streams, so my
soul longs for you, O God.... When shall I come and behold the face
of God?" (vv. 2-3). Now in Old Testament language the Hebrew
"soul" is indicated by the term *nefesh*, which in some texts means
"throat" and whose meaning in many others is broadened to
encompass the whole of the person. Taken in these dimensions, the
word helps us to realize how essential and profound our need for
God is; without him we lack breath and even life itself. For this
reason the Psalmist comes to the point of putting physical existence
itself on the second level, if union with God should be lacking: "for
your steadfast love is better than life" (*Ps* 62,3). In Psalm 73 he will
also repeat to the Lord: "There is nothing upon earth that I desire
besides you. My flesh and my heart may fail, but God is the strength
of my heart and my portion for ever.... for me it is good to be near
God" (*Ps* 73,25-28).

4. After the song about thirst, the Psalmist sings a song about hunger (cf. *Ps* 62,5-8). With the images of "the soul feasting as with marrow and fat" and of being filled, the person praying is probably referring to one of the sacrifices that were celebrated in the temple of Zion: the so-called sacrifice "of communion", that is, a sacred banquet at which the faithful ate the flesh of the sacrifice. Another fundamental need of life is used here as a symbol of communion with God: hunger is appeased when people hear the divine Word and encounter the Lord. Indeed "man does not live by bread alone, but ... by everything that proceeds out of the mouth of the Lord" (*Dt* 8,3; cf. *Mt* 4,4). And here flashes across the Christian's mind the thought of the banquet that Christ prepared on the last evening of his earthly life, whose deep value he had explained in his discourse at Capernaum: "For my flesh is food indeed, and my blood is drink indeed. He who eats my flesh and drinks my blood abides in me, and I in him" (*Jn* 6,55-56).

5. Through the mystical food of communion with God, "the soul clings to him" as the Psalmist says. Once again the word "soul" suggests the whole human being. Here one rightly finds the mention of an embrace, an almost physical clinging; henceforth God and man are in full communion and on the lips of his creature only joyful and grateful praise can bloom. Even during the dark night we feel protected by God's wings, just as the ark of the Covenant is covered by the wings of the cherubim. And then the ecstatic expression of jubilation blossoms: "In the shadow of your wings I sing for joy". Fear is dispelled, the embrace does not cling to emptiness but to God himself, our souls are upheld by the power of his right hand (cf. *Ps* 62,7-8).

6. In reading the Psalm in the light of the Easter mystery, our hunger and thirst which impel us towards God find their fulfillment in the crucified and risen Christ, from whom we receive the gift of the Spirit and the sacraments which give us new life and the nourishment that sustains it.

St John Chrysostom reminds us in commenting on the Johannine phrase: from his side "flowed blood and water" (cf. *Jn* 19,34), he says "that baptism and the mysteries [that is, the Eucharist] were symbolized in that blood and water". And he concludes: "Have you seen how Christ has united his bride to himself? Have you seen with what kind of food he feeds us all? By the same food we are formed and are fed. As a woman feeds her child with her own blood and milk, so too Christ himself continually feeds those whom he has begotten with his own blood" (*Homily III address to catechumens*, 16-19 *passim*: SC 50 *bis*, 160-162).

Canticle   Dan 3,57-88.56

O all you works of the Lord, O bless the Lord.
To him be highest glory and praise for ever.
And you, angels of the Lord, O bless the Lord.
To him be highest glory and praise for ever.

And you, the heavens of the Lord, O bless the Lord.
And you, clouds of the sky, O bless the Lord.
And you, all armies of the Lord, O bless the Lord.
To him be highest glory and praise for ever.

And you, sun and moon, O bless the Lord.
And you, the stars of the heav'ns, O bless the Lord.
And you, showers and rain, O bless the Lord.
To him be highest glory and praise for ever.

And you, all you breezes and winds, O bless the Lord.
And you, fire and heat, O bless the Lord.
And you, cold and heat, O bless the Lord.
To him be highest glory and praise for ever.

And you, showers and dew, O bless the Lord.
And you, frosts and cold, O bless the Lord.
And you, frost and snow, O bless the Lord.
To him be highest glory and praise for ever.

And you, night-time and day, O bless the Lord.
And you, darkness and light, O bless the Lord.
And you, lightning and clouds, O bless the Lord.
To him be highest glory and praise for ever.

O let the earth bless the Lord.
To him be highest glory and praise for ever.

And you, mountains and hills, O bless the Lord.
And you, all plants of the earth, O bless the Lord.
And you, fountains and springs, O bless the Lord.
To him be highest glory and praise for ever.

And you, rivers and seas, O bless the Lord.
And you, creatures of the sea, O bless the Lord.
And you, every bird in the sky, O bless the Lord.
And you, wild beasts and tame, O bless the Lord.
To him be highest glory and praise for ever.

And you, children of men, O bless the Lord.
To him be highest glory and praise for ever.

O Israel, bless the Lord. O bless the Lord.
And you, priests of the Lord, O bless the Lord.
And you, servants of the Lord, O bless the Lord.
To him be highest glory and praise for ever.

And you, spirits and souls of the just, O bless the Lord.
And you, holy and humble of heart, O bless the Lord.
Ananias, Azarias, Mizael, O bless the Lord.
To him be highest glory and praise for ever.

Let us praise the Father, the Son, and Holy Spirit:
To you be highest glory and praise for ever.
May you be blessed, O Lord, in the heavens.
To you be highest glory and praise for ever.

Let every creature bless the Lord

1. "Bless the Lord, all works of the Lord" (*Dn* 3,57). A cosmic dimension imbues this Canticle taken from the Book of Daniel, which the *Liturgy of the Hours* proposes for Sunday Lauds in the first and third weeks. This marvellous litany-like prayer is well-suited to the *Dies Domini*, the Day of the Lord, that lets us contemplate in the risen Christ the culmination of God's plan for the cosmos and for history. Indeed, in him, the Alpha and the Omega, the beginning and the end of history (cf. *Rv* 22,13), creation itself acquires its full meaning since, as John recalls in the Prologue to his Gospel, "all things were made through him" (*Jn* 1,3). The history of salvation culminates in the resurrection of

Christ, opening human life to the gift of the Spirit and adoption as sons and daughters, while awaiting the return of the divine Spouse who will hand the world back to God the Father (cf. *1 Cor* 15,24).

2. In this text, in the form of a litany, it is as if our gaze passes all things in review. Our gaze focuses on the sun, the moon and the stars; it settles upon the immense expanse of the waters, rises to the mountains, lingers over the most varied elements of the weather; it passes from hot to cold, from light to darkness; considers the mineral and vegetable worlds, dwells on the various types of animals. Then the call becomes universal: it refers to God's angels, reaches all the "sons of men", but most particularly involves the People of God, Israel, the priests and the holy ones. It is an immense choir, a symphony in which the varied voices are raised in praise to God, Creator of the universe and Lord of history. Prayed in the light of Christian revelation, it is addressed to the Trinitarian God, as we are invited to do by the liturgy which adds a Trinitarian formula to the Canticle: "Let us praise the Father, the Son, and the Holy Spirit".

3. Reflected in the Canticle, in a certain sense, is the universal religious soul, which perceives God's imprint in the world and is lifted up to contemplate the Creator. However, in the context of the Book of Daniel, the hymn is presented as the thanksgiving of three young Israelites - Hananiah, Azariah, Mishael - who were condemned to die burnt in a furnace for refusing to adore the golden idol of Nebuchadnezzar, but were miraculously preserved from the flames. Against the background of this event is that special history of salvation in which God chooses Israel as his people and makes a covenant with them. It is the same covenant to which the three young Israelites want to stay faithful, even at the cost of martyrdom in the fiery furnace. Their fidelity meets with the fidelity of God who sends an angel to drive the flames away from them (cf. *Dn* 3,49).

In this way the Canticle is patterned on the Old Testament songs of praise for danger averted. Among them is the famous song of victory, cited in chapter 15 of Exodus, in which the ancient Hebrews express their gratitude to the Lord for that night in which they would inevitably have been overcome by Pharaoh's army, had the Lord not opened a passage for them, dividing the waters and hurling "the horse and his rider ... into the sea" (*Ex* 15,1).

4. It is not by chance, in the solemn Easter Vigil, that every year the liturgy makes us repeat the hymn sung by the Israelites in Exodus. That path which was opened for them, prophetically announced the new way that the risen Christ inaugurated for humanity on the holy night of his resurrection from the dead. Our symbolic passing through the waters of Baptism enables us to relive a similar experience of passing from death to life, thanks to the victory over death won by Jesus, for the benefit of us all.

By repeating the Canticle of the three young Israelites in the Sunday liturgy of Lauds, we disciples of Christ want to be swept up in the same wave of gratitude for the great works wrought by God, in creation and, above all, in the mystery of Christ's death and resurrection.

In fact, the Christian discerns a relationship between the release of the three young men, mentioned in the Canticle, and the resurrection of Jesus. In the latter, the Acts of the Apostles see granted the prayer of the believer who, like the Psalmist, confidently sings: "you will not abandon my soul to Hades, nor let your Holy One see corruption" (*Acts* 2,27; *Ps* 15,10).

It is traditional to associate the Canticle with the Resurrection. Some ancient records show the existence of the hymn in the prayer of the Lord's Day, the weekly Easter of Christians. Moreover, iconographical depictions which show three young men praying unharmed amidst the flames have been found in the Roman catacombs, thereby witnessing to the effectiveness of prayer and the certainty that the Lord will intervene.

5. "Blessed are you in the firmament of heaven praiseworthy and glorious forever" (*Dn* 3,56). In singing the hymn on Sunday, the Christian feels gratitude not only for the gift of creation but also because we are the recipients of the fatherly care of God, who in Christ has raised us to the dignity of being his sons and daughters.

God's fatherly care makes us see creation in a new way and its astounding beauty offers an elegant sign in which we can catch a glimpse of his love. With these sentiments Francis of Assisi contemplated creation and lifted his praise to God, the ultimate source of all beauty. It comes naturally to imagine that the prayers of the Biblical text were echoed in his soul when at San Damiano, after touching the peaks of physical and spiritual suffering, he composed the "Canticle of Brother Sun" (cf. *Fonti Francescane*, 263).

Psalm 149

Sing a new song to the Lord,
his praise in the assembly of the faithful.
Let Israel rejoice in its Maker,
let Sion's sons exult in their king.
Let them praise his name with dancing
and make music with timbrel and harp.

For the Lord takes delight in his people.
He crowns the poor with salvation.
Let the faithful rejoice in their glory,
shout for joy and take their rest.
Let the praise of God be on their lips
and a two-edged sword in their hand,

to deal out vengeance to the nations
and punishment on all the peoples;
to bind their kings in chains
and their nobles in fetters of iron;
to carry out the sentence pre-ordained:
this honour is for all his faithful.

Song of praise and joy sung by festive chorus and instruments

1. *"Let the faithful exult in glory, let them rise joyfully from their couches"*. The order which you have just heard in Psalm 149, points to a dawn which is breaking and finds the faithful ready to chant their morning praise. With a suggestive phrase, their song of praise is defined as "a new song" (v. 1), a solemn and perfect hymn, perfect for the final days, in which the Lord will gather together the just in a renewed world. A festive atmosphere pervades the entire Psalm; it begins with the initial *Alleluia* and then continues with chant, praise, joy, dance, the sound of drums and of harps. The Psalm inspires a prayer of thanksgiving from a heart filled with religious exultation.

2. The protagonists of the Psalm in the original Hebrew text are given two terms that are taken from the spirituality of the Old Testament.

Three times they are defined as the *hasidim* (vv. 1,5,9), "the pious, the faithful ones", who respond with fidelity and love (*hesed*) to the fatherly love of the Lord.

The second part of the Psalm provokes surprise because it is full of warlike sentiments. It is strange that in the same verse, the Psalm brings together "the praises of God on the lips" and "the two-edged sword in their hands" (v. 6). Upon reflection, we can understand why the Psalm was composed for the use of the "faithful" who were involved in a struggle for liberation; they were fighting to free an oppressed people and to give them the possibility of serving God. During the Maccabean era, in the 2nd century B.C., those fighting for freedom and faith, who underwent a severe repression from the Hellenistic power, were defined as the *hasidim*, the ones faithful to the Word of God and the tradition of the fathers.

3. In the present perspective of our prayer, the warlike symbolism becomes an image of the dedication of the believer who sings the praises of God in the morning and then goes into the ways of the world, in the midst of evil and injustice. Unfortunately powerful forces are arrayed against the Kingdom of God: the Psalmist speaks of "peoples, nations, leaders and nobles". Yet he is confident because he knows that he has at his side the Lord, who is the master of history (v. 2). His victory over evil is certain and so will be the triumph of love. All the *hasidim* participate in the battle, they are the faithful and just who with the power of the Spirit bring to fulfilment the wonderful work that is called the Kingdom of God.

4. St Augustine, starting with the reference of the Psalm to the "choir" and to the "drums and harps", commented: "What does the choir represent?... The choir is a group of singers who sing together. If we sing in a choir, we must sing in harmony. When one sings in a choir, one off-key voice strikes the listener and creates confusion in the choir" (*Enarr. in Ps* 149; *CCL* 40,7,1-4).

Referring to the instruments mentioned in the Psalm he asks: "Why does the Psalmist take in hand the drum and the harp?". He answers, "Because we praise the Lord not just with the voice, but also with our works. When we take up the drum and the harp, the hands have to be in accord with the voice. The same goes for you. When you sing the Alleluia, you must give bread to the poor, give clothes to the naked, give shelter to the traveler. If you do it, not only does your voice sing, but your hands are in accord with your voice because the works agree with the words" (*ibid.*, 8,1-4).

5. There is a second term which we use to define those who pray in the Psalm: they are the *anawim*, "the poor and lowly ones" (v. 4). The expression turns up often in the Psalter. It indicates not just the oppressed, the miserable, the persecuted for justice, but also those who, with fidelity to the moral teaching of the Alliance with God, are marginalized by those who prefer to use violence, riches and power. In this light one understands that the category of the "poor" is not just a social category but a spiritual choice. It is what the famous first Beatitude means: "Blessed are the poor in spirit, for theirs is the Kingdom of heaven" (*Mt* 5,3). The Prophet Zephaniah spoke to the *anawim* as special persons: "Seek the Lord, all you humble of the land, who do his commands; seek righteousness, seek humility; perhaps you may be hidden on the day of wrath of the Lord" (*Zep* 2,3).

6. The "day of the Lord's wrath" is really the day described in the second part of the Psalm when the "poor" are lined up on the side of God to fight against evil. By themselves they do not have sufficient strength or the arms or the necessary strategies to oppose the onslaught of evil. Yet the Psalmist does not admit hesitation: "The Lord loves his people, he adorns the lowly (*anawim*) with victory" (v. 4). What St Paul says to the Corinthians completes the picture: "God chose what is low and despised in the world, even things that are not, to bring to nothing things that are" (*1 Cor* 1,28).

With such confidence the "sons of Zion" (v. 2), the *hasidim* and *anawim*, the faithful and the poor, go on to live their witness in the world and in history. Mary's Canticle in the Gospel of Luke, the *Magnificat*, is the echo of the best sentiments of the "sons of Zion": glorious praise of God her Saviour, thanksgiving for the great things done by the Mighty One, the battle against the forces of evil, solidarity with the poor and fidelity to the God of the Covenant (cf. *Lk* 1,46-55).

Monday

———— ✠ ————

Of the First Week

Psalm 5
vv. 2-10.12-13

To my words give ear, O Lord,
give heed to my groaning.
Attend to the sound of my cries,
my King and my God.

It is you whom I invoke, O Lord.
In the morning you hear me;
in the morning I offer you my prayer,
watching and waiting.

You are no God who loves evil;
no sinner is your guest.
The boastful shall not stand their ground
before your face.

You hate all who do evil:
you destroy all who lie.
The deceitful and bloodthirsty man
the Lord detests.

But I through the greatness of your love
have access to your house.
I bow down before your holy temple,
filled with awe.

Lead me, Lord, in your justice,
because of those who lie in wait;
make clear your way before me.

No truth can be found in their mouths,
their heart is all mischief,
their throat a wide-open grave,
all honey their speech.

All those you protect shall be glad
and ring out their joy.

You shelter them; in you they rejoice,
those who love your name.

It is you who bless the just man, Lord:
you surround him with favour as with a shield.

Morning prayer for help

1. *"In the morning you hear me; in the morning I offer you my prayer watching and waiting"* (v. 4). These words make Psalm 5 a morning prayer, well suited for use at Lauds, the believer's prayer at the start of the day. Tension and anxiety over the dangers and bitterness which the believer has to face shape the background tone of the prayer. But confidence in God is never weakened because he is always ready to sustain the faithful person so that he will not stumble on the path of life.

"No one except the Church possesses such confidence" (*Jerome, 59th Treatise on the Psalms,* 5,27: *PL* 26,829). St Augustine, calling our attention to the title given the Psalm, which reads in the Latin version: *For her who receives the inheritance,* says: "It refers to the Church who receives the inheritance of eternal life through our Lord Jesus Christ, so that she possesses God himself, adheres to him, and finds her happiness in him, in keeping with what is written: "Blessed are the meek for they shall inherit the earth' (*Mt* 5,5)", (*Enarr. in ps.* 5: *CCL* 38,1,2-3).

2. As often happens in the Psalms of "supplication" addressed to the Lord to be freed from evil, three persons come into the picture in the Psalm. Above all, *God* appears (vv. 2-7), he is the real "You" to whom the person praying turns with confidence. A certainty emerges in the face of the worries of a tiring and perhaps dangerous day. The Lord is a God who is consistent, just in the face of injustice, far removed from any compromise with evil: "You are not a God who delights in wickedness" (v. 5).

A long list of evil persons the boastful, the foolish, evildoers, the liar, the bloodthirsty, the deceitful pass before the Lord's gaze. He is the holy and just God and he is on the side of the one who follows his way of truth and love, opposing the one who "chooses the paths which lead to the kingdom of shadows" (cf. *Prv* 2,18). The faithful person will not feel alone and abandoned when he will confront the city, taking his part in society and in the tangled web of daily affairs.

3. In verses 8-9 of our morning prayer the second person, the person who prays, presents himself as an "I" revealing that his whole person is dedicated to God and to his "great mercy". He is certain that the gates of the temple, the place of communion and of divine intimacy, locked for the unjust, are wide open for him. He enters them to enjoy the security of divine protection, while outside, evil flourishes and celebrates apparent and temporary victories.

From his morning prayer in the temple, the faithful one receives the interior energy to face an often hostile world. The Lord himself will take him by the hand and lead him through the streets of the city, even more, he "will make straight his way" before him, as the Psalmist says with a simple but provocative image. In the orginal Hebrew text such serene confidence is based on two terms (*hésed* and *sedaqáh*): "mercy or fidelity" on the one hand, and "justice or salvation" on the other. They are the typical words to celebrate the covenant that unites the Lord with his people and with each believer.

4. Finally, we see outlined on the horizon the dark figure of the third character of the daily drama: they are the *enemies*, the *evil ones*, who were already in the background in the preceding verses. After the "You" of God and the "I" of the person who prays, there is now a "They" that indicates a hostile group, symbol of the evil of *the world* (vv. 10-11). Their physiognomy is sketched on the basis of the word, the fundamental element in social communication. Four elements mouth, heart, throat and tongue express the radical nature of the inner malice of their choices. Their mouth is full of falsehood, their heart constantly plots perfidy, their throat is like an open tomb, quick to wish only death, their seductive tongue is "full of deadly poison" (*Jas* 3,8).

5. After such a bitter and realistic picture of the perverse person who attacks the just one, the Psalmist invokes the divine condemnation in a verse (v. 11) which the Christian use of the Psalm omits, since the Church wants to be conformed to the New Testament revelation of merciful love, which offers to the evil one the possibility of conversion.

The prayer of the Psalmist at this point comes to an end full of light and peace (vv. 12-13) after the dark profile of the sinner just drawn. A wave of serenity and joy wraps the one who is faithful to the Lord. The day which now begins, opens up before the believer. Even though it may be marked by effort and anxieties, it will always have over it the sun of divine blessing. The Psalmist, who knows the heart and style of God profoundly, has no doubt: "Lord, you bless the just; you cover him with benevolence as with a shield" (v. 13).

Canticle   1 Chron 29,10-13

Blessed are you, O Lord,
the God of Israel our father,
for ever and ever.

Yours, O Lord, is the greatness, and the power,
and the glory, and the victory, and the majesty;
for all that is in the heavens and in the earth is yours;

Yours is the kingdom, O Lord,
and you are exalted as head above all.

Both riches and honour come from you,
and you rule over all.
In your hand are power and might;
and in your hand it is to make great and to give strength to all.

And now we thank you, our God,
and praise your glorious name.

To God alone be honour and glory

1. "Blessed are you, O Lord, the God of Israel our father" (*1 Chr* 29,10). The Canticle of intense praise that the First Book of Chronicles puts on the lips of David makes us relive the outburst of joy with which the community of the first covenant greeted the great preparations made for the building of the temple, fruit of a common effort of the king and of so many who contributed generously with him. They had virtually competed in generosity, because this was called for by a dwelling that was not "destined for a man, but for the Lord God" (*1 Chr* 29,1).

Rereading that event centuries later, the chronicler intuits the sentiments of David and those of the whole people, their joy and their admiration for all those who made their contribution: "The people rejoiced because these had given willingly, for with a whole heart they had offered freely to the Lord; king David rejoiced greatly" (*1 Chr* 29,9).

2. Such is the context in which the Canticle is born. It does not dwell, except briefly, on human satisfaction but centres attention immediately on the glory of God: "Yours, O Lord, is the greatness ... yours is the kingdom ...". The great temptation that is always lurking, when one accomplishes works for the Lord, is that of putting oneself at the centre as if God were indebted to us. David, instead, attributes everything to the Lord. It is not the human being with his intelligence and strength who is the first architect of all that is done, but God himself.

In this way, David expresses the profound truth that all is grace. In a certain sense, all that has been put aside for the temple, is only the restitution, in a very meagre way at that, of all that Israel received in the invaluable gift of the covenant established by God with their Fathers. In the same way David credits the Lord with everything that constituted his fortune, in the military, the political and the economic field. All comes from him.

3. Herein lies the contemplative thrust of these verses. It seems that the author of the Canticle does not have enough words to confess the greatness and power of God. He considers him as "our father", first of all, in his special paternity shown to Israel. This is the first title which elicits our praise "now and forever".

In the Christian use of the prayer we cannot forget that God's fatherhood is fully revealed in the Incarnation of the Son of God. It is he, and only he, who can speak to God calling him properly and affectionately, "Abba" (*Mk* 14,36). At the same time, through the gift of the Spirit, we share in his sonship, and become "sons in the Son". God the Father's blessing of ancient Israel takes on for us the greater intensity that Jesus showed to us teaching us to call God "our Father".

4. The view of the biblical author extends from the history of salvation to the whole cosmos in order to contemplate the greatness of God the Creator: "All in heaven and on earth is yours". And again, "Yours is the sovereignty; you are exalted as head over all". As in Psalm 8, the one who prays the Canticle lifts his head towards the immense expanse of the heavens, then he looks in wonder at the immensity of the earth, and sees everything under the dominion of the Creator. How can he express the glory of God? The words pile up, in a kind of mystical pursuit: greatness, power, glory, majesty and splendour;

and then even force and power. All that man experiences as beautiful
and great must be referred to him who is at the origin of everything
and governs them. The human creature knows that everything he
possesses is the gift of God, as David emphasizes further on in the
Canticle: "Who am I and what is my people, that we should be able
thus to offer you this willingly? For all things come from you, and of
your own have we given you" (*1 Chr* 29,14).

5. The background of reality as the gift of God helps us to combine
the Canticle's sentiments of praise and thanksgiving with an authentic
spirituality of "offering" that the Christian liturgy makes us live, above
all, in the celebration of the Eucharist. It is what emerges from the two
prayers which the priest uses to offer the bread and wine destined to
become the Body and Blood of Christ: "Through your goodness we
have received this bread, fruit of the earth and of human work; we
present it to you so that it may become for us the bread of eternal life"
(*N.B.* literal translation of offertory prayer). The prayer is repeated for
the wine. We find similar sentiments in the Byzantine *Divine Liturgy*
and in the ancient *Roman Canon* when in the Eucharistic anamnesis
we express the intention of offering as a gift to God the things that
we have received from him.

6. A final application of this vision of God is realized in the Canticle
by looking at the human experience of riches and power. Both of
these dimensions emerged while David prepared all that was
necessary to build the temple. What is a universal temptation could
have been a temptation for him: to act as if he were the absolute ruler
of what he possessed, to make it the source of pride and the abuse of
others. The prayer articulated in the Canticle refers the human being
to his state as "poor person" who receives everything from God.

The kings of this earth are no more than images of divine kingship:
"Yours is the kingdom, O Lord". The rich cannot forget the origin of
their good things: "riches and honour come from you". The powerful
should know how to recognize God, the source of "all greatness and
power". The Christian is called to use such expressions in prayer,
contemplating with exultation the Risen Lord, glorified by God "above
all rule and authority, power and dominion" (*Eph* 1,21). Christ is the
true king of the universe.

Psalm 28

O give the Lord you sons of God,
give the Lord glory and power;
give the Lord the glory of his name.
Adore the Lord in his holy court.

The Lord's voice resounding on the waters,
the Lord on the immensity of waters;
the voice of the Lord, full of power,
the voice of the Lord, full of splendour.

The Lord's voice shattering the cedars,
the Lord shatters the cedars of Lebanon;
he makes Lebanon leap like a calf
and Sirion like a young wild-ox.

The Lord's voice flashes flames of fire.

The Lord's voice shaking the wilderness,
the Lord shakes the wilderness of Kadesh;
the Lord's voice rending the oak tree
and stripping the forest bare.

The God of glory thunders.
In his temple they all cry: "Glory!"
The Lord sat enthroned over the flood;
the Lord sits as king for ever.

The Lord will give strength to his people,
the Lord will bless his people with peace.

The Lord solemnly proclaims his word

1. Some experts consider Psalm 28 that we have just heard as one of the most ancient texts of the Psalter. A powerful image unifies it in its poetic and prayerful unfolding: in fact, we face the progressive unleashing of a storm. The Hebrew term *qol*, which signifies both "voice" and" thunder", repeated at the beginning of key verses creates the mounting tension of the Psalm. For this reason commentators call our Psalm the "Psalm of seven thunders", for the number of times in which the word resounds. In fact, one can say that the Psalmist thinks of thunder as a symbol of the divine voice, with its transcendent and unattainable mystery, that breaks into created reality in order to disturb and terrify it, but which in its innermost meaning is a word of peace and harmony. One thinks of chapter 12 of the Fourth Gospel, where the voice that responds to Jesus from heaven is perceived by the crowd as thunder (cf. *Jn* 12,28-29).

In proposing Psalm 28 for the prayer of Lauds, the *Liturgy of the Hours* invites us to assume an attitude of profound and trusting adoration of the divine Majesty.

2. The Biblical cantor takes us to two moments and two places. At the centre (vv. 3-9) we have the account of the storm which is unleashed from the "immensity of the waters" of the Mediterranean. In the eyes of Biblical man, the sea waters incarnate the chaos which attacks the beauty and splendour of creation, to corrode, destroy and demolish it. So, in observing the storm that rages, one discovers the immense power of God. The one who prays sees the hurricane move north and hammer the mainland. The tall cedars of Lebanon and of Mount Sirion, sometimes called Hermon, are struck by the flashing lightning and seem to jump under the thunderbolts like frightened animals. The crashes draw closer, crossing the entire Holy Land, and move south, to the desert steppes of Kadesh.

3. After this picture of strong movement and tension, by contrast, we are invited to contemplate another scene, portrayed at the beginning and the end of the Psalm (vv. 1-2 and 9b-11). Distress and fear are now countered by the adoring glorification of God in the temple of Zion.

There is almost a channel of communication that links the sanctuary of Jerusalem and the heavenly sanctuary: in both these sacred places, there is peace and praise is given to the divine glory. The deafening sound of the thunder gives way to the harmony of liturgical singing, terror gives way to the certainty of divine protection. God now appears, "enthroned over the flood" as "King for ever" (v. 10), that is as Lord and supreme Sovereign of all creation.

4. Before these two antithetical scenes, the praying person is invited to have a twofold experience.

First of all he must discover that God's mystery, expressed in the symbol of the storm, cannot be grasped or dominated by man. As the Prophet Isaiah sings, the Lord, like lightning or a storm, bursts into history sowing panic among the perverse and oppressors. With the coming of his judgment, his proud adversaries are uprooted like trees struck by a hurricane or like the cedars shattered by the divine thunderbolts (cf. *Is* 14,7-8).

What becomes evident in this light is what a modern thinker (Rudolph Otto) has described as the *tremendum* of God: his ineffable transcendence and presence as a just judge in the history of humanity. The latter is vainly deluded in opposing his sovereign power. In the *Magnificat* Mary was also to exalt this aspect of God's action: "He has shown strength with his arm, he has scattered the proud in the imagination of their hearts; he has put down the mighty from their thrones" (*Lk* 1,51-52a).

5. However, the Psalm gives us another aspect of God's face, the one that is discovered in the intimacy of prayer and in the celebration of the liturgy. According to the above-mentioned thinker, it is the *fascinosum* of God, that is the fascination that emanates from his grace, the mystery of love that is poured out upon the faithful, the serene certainty of the blessing reserved for the just. Even facing the chaos of evil, the storms of history, and the wrath of divine justice itself, the one who prays feels at peace, enfolded in the mantle of protection which Providence offers those who praise God and follow his ways. Through prayer, we learn that the Lord's true desire is to give peace.

In the temple, our anxiety is soothed and our terror wiped out; we participate in the heavenly liturgy with all "the children of God", angels and saints. And following the storm, image of the destruction of human malice like the deluge, there now arches in the heavens the rainbow of divine blessing, reminiscent of "the everlasting covenant between God and every living creature of all flesh that is upon the earth" (*Gn* 9,16).

The Father's exalted voice resounds at the Son's Baptism blessing the waters of the earth

This message stands out above all in the "Christian" rereading of the Psalm. If the seven "thunders" of our Psalm represent God's voice in the cosmos, the loftiest expression of this voice is the one in which the Father, in the theophany of Jesus' Baptism, revealed his deepest identity as the "beloved Son" (*Mk* 1,11 and paragraph). St Basil wrote: "Perhaps, and more mystically, 'the voice of the Lord on the waters' resounded when a voice came from on high at the baptism of Jesus and said: This is my beloved Son. Indeed the Lord then breathed upon many waters, sanctifying them with baptism. The God of glory thundered from on high with the strong voice of his testimony.... Then you can also understand by 'thunder' that change which, after Baptism, takes place through the great 'voice' of the Gospel" (*Homily on the Psalms: PG* 30,359).

Tuesday

———— ✠ ————

Of the First Week

Psalm 23

The Lord's is the earth and its fullness,
the world and all its peoples.
It is he who set it on the seas;
on the waters he made it firm.

Who shall climb the mountain of the Lord?
Who shall stand in his holy place?
The man with clean hands and pure heart,
who desires not worthless things,
who has not sworn so as to deceive his neighbour.

He shall receive blessings from the Lord
and reward from the God who saves him.
Such are the men who seek him,
seek the face of the God of Jacob.

O gates, lift high your heads;
grow higher, ancient doors.
Let him enter, the king of glory!

Who is the king of glory?
The Lord, the mighty, the valiant,
the Lord, the valiant in war.

O gates, lift high your heads;
grow higher, ancient doors.
Let him enter, the king of glory!

Who is he, the king of glory?
He, the Lord of armies,
he is the king of glory.

The Lord enters his temple!

1. The ancient chant of the People of God that we just heard, resounded in the temple of Jerusalem. To be able to grasp the main thrust of the prayer, we have to keep in mind three basic affirmations.

The first is the truth of creation: God has created the world and is its Lord. The second is the judgment to which he submits his creatures: we must appear before him and be questioned about what we have done. The third is the mystery of God's coming: he comes into the universe and into history and desires to be free to establish a relationship of intimate communion with human beings. A modern commentator said: "These are the three elementary forms of the experience of God and of our relationship with God; we live by the work of God, we live before God and we can live with God" (G. Ebeling, *On the Psalms*, [see in the Italian text *Sui Salmi*, Brescia, 1973, p. 97]).

2. The three parts of Psalm 23 correspond to these three basic premises that we will now examine, considering them as three successive scenes of a poetic triptych for our prayer. The first is a brief acclamation of the Creator, to whom belong the earth and all who dwell in it (vv. 1-2). It is a profession of faith in the Lord of the cosmos and of history. In the ancient vision of creation, the earth is conceived as an architectural work: God lays the foundations of the earth on the sea, the symbol of the chaotic and destructive waters, in turn the sign of creaturely limitation, conditioned by nothingness and evil. Creation is suspended over the watery abyss and God's creative and providential hand keeps it in being and in life.

3. From the cosmic horizon the Psalmist's perspective narrows down to the microcosm of Zion, "the mountain of the Lord". We are now in the second picture of the Psalm (vv. 3-6). We stand before the temple of Jerusalem. The procession of the faithful asks the guardians of the holy door an entrance question: "Who shall climb the mountain of the Lord, who shall stand in his holy place?".

The priests as happens in some other biblical texts called by the experts "liturgy of entrance" (cf. *Ps* 14; *Is* 33,14-16; *Mi* 6,6-8) respond by listing the conditions that enable one to enter into communion with the Lord in worship. They are not merely ritual or external norms to be observed, but moral and existential requisites to be lived. It is an examination of conscience or penitential act that precedes the liturgical celebration.

4. The priests lay down three requisites. Above all, one must have "clean hands and a pure heart". "Hands" and "heart" refer to both action and intention, the whole of the human being who should basically turn toward God and his law. The second requisite calls for one "not to tell lies", in biblical language it entails sincerity, but even more, the struggle against idolatry, for idols are false gods, that is "lies". The precept confirms the first commandment of the Decalogue, the purity of religion and of worship. The third and last requisite deals with relations with our neighbour: "Do not swear so as to deceive your neighbour". In an oral culture like that of ancient Israel, the word was the symbol of social relationships based on justice and uprightness and should not be used to deceive.

5. So we reach the third scene of our triptych which describes indirectly the joyful entry of the faithful into the temple to meet the Lord (vv. 7-10). With a thought-provoking exchange of appeals, questions and answers, God reveals himself progressively with three of his solemn titles: "the King of Glory, the Lord Mighty and Valiant, the Lord of Armies". The gates of the temple of Zion are personified and invited to lift up their lintels to welcome the Lord who takes possession of his home.

The triumphal scene, described by the Psalm in the third poetic picture, has been applied by the Christian liturgy of the East and of the West to the victorious Descent of Christ to the Limbo of the fathers, spoken of in the First Letter of Peter (cf. *1 Pet* 3,19), and to the Risen Lord's Ascension into heaven (cf. *Acts* 1,9-10). Even today, in the Byzantine Liturgy, the Psalm is sung by alternating choirs on Holy Saturday night at the Easter Vigil, and in the Roman Liturgy it is used on the second Sunday of the Passion at the end of the procession of palms. The Solemn Liturgy of the opening of the Holy Door at the beginning of the Jubilee Year allowed us to relive with great interior emotion the same sentiments the Psalmist felt as he crossed the threshold of the ancient temple of Zion.

6. The last title, "Lord of Armies", is not really a military title as may appear at first sight even if it does not exclude a reference to Israel's ranks. Instead, it has a cosmic value: the Lord, who now comes to meet humanity within the restricted space of the sanctuary of Zion, is the Creator who has all the stars of heaven as his army, that is, the creatures of the universe who obey him. In the book of the Prophet Baruch we read: "Before whom the stars at their posts shine and rejoice; when he calls them, they answer, 'Here we are!' shining with joy for their Creator" (*Bar* 3,34-35). The infinite, almighty and eternal God adapts himself to the human creature, draws near to meet, listen and enter into communion with him. The liturgy is the expression of this coming together in faith, dialogue and love.

———— ✖ ————

Canticle   Tob 13,1-5b.7-8

Blessed is God who lives for ever,
and blessed is his kingdom.
For he afflicts, and he shows mercy;
he leads down to Hades, and brings up again,
and there is no one who can escape his hand.

Acknowledge him before the nations, O sons of Israel;
for he has scattered us among them.
Make his greatness known there,
and exalt him in the presence of all the living;
because he is our Lord and God,
he is our Father for ever.

He will afflict us for our iniquities;
and again he will show mercy,
But see what he will do with you;
give thanks to him with your full voice.
Praise the Lord of righteousness,
and exalt the King of the ages.

I give him thanks in the land of my captivity,
and I show his power and majesty to a nation of sinners.
Turn back, you sinners, and do right before him;
who knows if he will accept you and have mercy on you?

I exalt my God;
my soul exalts the King of heaven,
and will rejoice in his majesty.
Let all men speak,
and give him thanks in Jerusalem.

1. "I exalt my God and my spirit rejoices in the King of heaven" (*Tb* 13,7). The one who speaks these words in the Canticle just recited, is the elderly Tobit of whom the Old Testament gives a brief and edifying story, in the book that is named (in the Latin Vulgate) after his son Tobias (Tobit in the Revised Standard Version and New American Bible). In order to understand fully the meaning of this hymn, we must keep in mind the pages of the story that precede it. The story is set among the exiled Israelites of Niniveh. The sacred author, writing centuries later, looks to them as an example of brothers and sisters in the faith dispersed among a foreign people and tempted to abandon the traditions of their fathers. The portrait of Tobit and of his family is offered as a programme of life. Here is the man who, despite everything that happens to him, remains faithful to the norms of the law, and in particular, to the practice of giving alms. He is stricken by misfortune with the onset of poverty and blindness, but his faith never fails.

God's response was not slow in coming, through the Archangel Raphael, who leads the young Tobias on a risky journey, guiding him into a happy marriage and, in the end, healing his father Tobit from his blindness.

The message is clear: Those who do good, above all, by opening their hearts to the needs of their neighbours, are pleasing to the Lord, even if they are tried; in the end, they will experience his goodness.

2. With this premise, the words of our hymn can make a strong point. They invite us to lift up our eyes on high to "God who lives forever", to his kingdom which "lasts for all ages". From this contemplation of God, the sacred author can offer a short sketch of a theology of history in which he tries to respond to the question which the dispersed and tried People of God are raising: why does God treat us like this? The response turns both to divine justice and mercy: "He chastises you for your injustices, but he will show mercy towards all of you" (v. 5). The chastisement appears thus to be a kind of divine pedagogy, in which the last word is reserved to mercy: "He scourges and then shows mercy, casts down to the depths of the nether world, and he brings up from the great abyss" (v. 2).

Suffering, even the Cross, has a positive meaning if lived in accord with God's plan.

One can have absolute confidence in God who never abandons his creature. Moreover, the words of the hymn lead to another perspective, which attributes a salvific meaning to the situation of suffering, turning the exile into an occasion to praise the works of God: "Praise him, you Israelites, before the Gentiles for though he has scattered you among them, he has shown his greatness even there" (vv. 3-4).

3. From this invitation to read the exile in a providential way, our meditation can be extended to consider the mysteriously positive meaning which suffering assumes when it is lived in abandonment to God's plan. Already in the Old Testament several passages delineate such a theme. Think of the story of Joseph in the *Book of Genesis* (cf. *Gn* 37,2-36) who was sold by his brothers and destined to be their future saviour. How can we forget the book of Job? Here the innocent man suffers, and doesn't know how to explain his drama in any way except by surrendering to the greatness and wisdom of God (cf. *Jb* 42,1-16).

For us who read these Old Testament passages from a Christian perspective, the point of reference can only be the Cross of Christ which offers a profound response to the mystery of suffering in the world.

4. To sinners who are chastised for their injustices (cf. v. 5), Tobit's hymn directs a call for conversion that opens the wonderful prospect of a "reciprocal" conversion of God and man: "When you turn back to him with all your heart, to do what is right before him, then he will turn back to you, and no longer hide his face from you" (v. 6). The use of the word "conversion" for the creature and for God speaks volumes, even though it is with different meanings.

If the author of the Canticle thinks of the benefits which accompany the "return" of God, his renewed favour towards his people, in the light of the mystery of Christ, we must think above all of the gift which consists of God himself. The human person has need of him more than of all of his gifts. Sin is a tragedy not just because it draws God's punishments upon us, but because it banishes Him from our hearts.

5. The Canticle raises our eyes to the face of God as Father, inviting us to bless and praise him: "He is the Lord, our God, our Father". One feels the sense of being special children which Israel experienced with the gift of the covenant and which prepared for the mystery of the Incarnation of the Son of God. Then, in Jesus, the face of the Father will shine forth and his mercy without limits will be revealed.

Here we can think of the parable of the merciful Father as told by the Evangelist Luke. Not only does the Father respond to the conversion of the prodigal son with pardon, but with an embrace of infinite tenderness, coupled with joy and feasting. "When he was still a long way off, the father saw him and was filled with compassion. He ran to his son, embraced him and kissed him" (*Lk* 15,20).

The expressions of our Canticle are in line with the touching image of the Gospel. The need to praise and thank God springs forth: "So now consider what he has done for you and praise him with full voice. Bless the Lord of justice and exalt the King of the ages" (v. 7).

Psalm 32

Ring out your joy to the Lord, O you just;
for praise is fitting for loyal hearts.

Give thanks to the Lord upon the lyre,
with a ten-stringed harp sing him songs.
O sing him a song that is new,
play loudly, with all your skill.

For the word of the Lord is faithful
and all his works to be trusted.
The Lord loves justice and right
and fills the earth with his love.

By his word the heavens were made,
by the breath of his mouth all the stars.
He collects the waves of the ocean;
he stores up the depths of the sea.

Let all the earth fear the Lord,
all who live in the world revere him.
He spoke; and it came to be.
He commanded; it sprang into being.

He frustrates the designs of the nations,
he defeats the plans of the peoples.
His own designs shall stand for ever,
the plans of his heart from age to age.

They are happy, whose God is the Lord,
the people he has chosen as his own.
From the heavens the Lord looks forth,
he sees all the children of men.

From the place where he dwells he gazes
on all the dwellers on the earth,
he who shapes the hearts of them all
and considers all their deeds.

A king is not saved by his army,
nor a warrior preserved by his strength.
A vain hope for safety is the horse;
despite its power it cannot save.

The Lord looks on those who revere him,
on those who hope in his love,
to rescue their souls from death,
to keep them alive in famine.

Our soul is waiting for the Lord.
The Lord is our help and our shield.
In him do our hearts find joy.
We trust in his holy name.

May your love be upon us, O Lord,
as we place all our hope in you.

Hymn of joy and acclamation to God's providence

1. Psalm 32 [33], which has 22 verses, the same number as the letters of the Hebrew alphabet, is a hymn of praise to the Lord of the universe and of history. A quiver of joy runs through it from the very first lines: *"Rejoice, in the Lord, you just! Praise from the upright is fitting. Praise the Lord with the lyre, make melody to him with the harp of ten strings! Sing to the Lord a new song, play skilfully on the strings, with loud shouts"* (vv. 1-3). This acclamation (*tern'ah*) is accompanied by music and expresses an interior voice of faith and hope, of joy and trust. The hymn is "new," not only because it renews the certainty of the divine presence within creation and human events, but also because it anticipates the perfect praise that will be intoned on the final day of salvation, when the Kingdom of God will have attained its glorious realization.

St Basil looks longingly toward this final fulfilment in Christ when he explains this passage: "In general, 'new' means something unusual or which has only recently come into existence. If you think of the astounding, unimaginable way of the Incarnation of the Lord, you would have to sing a new and unheard of song. And if you review the regeneration and renewal of all humanity, surrendered of old to sin, and proclaim the mysteries of the Resurrection, then you too would sing a new and unusual Canticle" (*Homily on Psalm 32,2; PG* 29, 327). In short, according to St Basil, the Psalmist's invitation: "Sing to God a new song" means for believers in Christ: "Do not honour God ccording to the ancient custom of the 'letter', but in the newness of the 'spirit'. Indeed, he who does not understand the Law externally but recognizes the 'spirit' in it sings a 'new song' (*ibid.*).

2. In its central part, the hymn is articulated in three parts that form a trilogy of praise. In the first (cf. vv. 6-9), the creative word of God is celebrated. The wonderful architecture of the universe, like a cosmic temple, did not arise or develop from a struggle among gods, as some cosmogonies of the ancient Near East suggested, but from the basis of effective divine word. Just as the first page of Genesis teaches (cf. *Gn* 1): "God said ... and it was so". In fact the Psalmist repeats: "For he spoke, and it came to be, commanded, and it stood forth" (*Ps* 32,9).

The man of prayer gives special importance to control of the sea waters, since in the Bible they are the sign of chaos and evil. Despite its limits, the world is preserved in being by the Creator who, as mentioned in the Book of Job, commands the sea to halt at the seashore: "Thus far shall you come, and no farther, and here shall your proud waves be stayed" (*Jb* 38,11).

3. The Lord is also the sovereign of human history, as stated in the second part of Psalm 32 [33], in verses 10-15. With vigorous antithesis, the plans of terrestrial powers are opposed to the wonderful design that God is tracing in history. Human programmes, intended as alternatives, introduce injustice, evil and violence, rising up against the divine plan of justice and salvation. And, despite short-lived and apparent successes, they are reduced to mere machinations, destined to dissolution and failure. It is summed up in the biblical Book of Proverbs: "Many are the plans in a man's heart, but it is the purpose of the Lord that will be established" (*Prv* 19,21). Similarly, the Psalmist reminds us that, from heaven, his transcendent dwelling, God follows all humanity's ways, even the foolish and the absurd, and intuits all the secrets of the human heart.

"Wherever you go, whatever you do, whether in darkness, or in the light of day, God's eye sees you," St Basil comments (*Homily on Psalm 32,8 PG* 29, 343). Happy will be the people who, accepting the divine revelation, observes its instructions for life, following its paths through history. In the end, only one thing endures: "The plan of the Lord stands for ever, the thoughts of his heart to all generations" (*Ps* 32,11).

4. The third and last part of the Psalm (cf. vv. 16-22) takes up again, from two new angles, the topic of the unique lordship of God over human affairs. On the one hand, he invites the powerful not to be deluded by the military force of armies and cavalry. Then he invites the faithful, often oppressed, starving and on the brink of death to hope in the Lord who will not let them fall into the abyss of destruction. In this way, the "catechetical" function of the Psalm is also revealed. It is transformed into a call to faith in a God who is not indifferent to the arrogance of the powerful and is close to the weakness of humanity, raising it and sustaining it if it is confident, if it entrusts itself to him, if it raises its prayer and praise to him.

"The humility of those who serve God" - St Basil further explains - "shows that they hope in his mercy. Indeed, anyone who does not trust his own great enterprises or expect to be justified by his own works, sees in God's mercy his only hope for salvation" (*Homily on Psalm 32,10; PG* 29,347).

5. The Psalm ends with an antiphon that has become part of the well-known *Te Deum* hymn: "May your kindness always be upon us Lord, for we have hoped in you" (v. 22). Divine grace and human hope meet and embrace. Indeed, God's loving faithfulness (according to the meaning of the original Hebrew word used here, *hésed*), envelops, warms and protects us like a mantle, offering serenity and giving our faith and hope a sound foundation.

Wednesday

———— ✠ ————

Of the First Week

Psalm 35

Sin speaks to the sinner
in the depths of his heart.
There is no fear of God
before his eyes.

He so flatters himself in his mind
that he knows not his guilt.
In his mouth are mischief and deceit.
All wisdom is gone.

He plots the defeat of goodness
as he lies on his bed.
He has set his foot on evil ways,
he clings to what is evil.

Your love, Lord, reaches to heaven;
your truth to the skies.
Your justice is like God's mountain,
your judgments like the deep.

To both man and beast you give protection.
O Lord, how precious is your love.
My God, the sons of men
find refuge in the shelter of your wings.

They feast on the riches of your house;
they drink from the stream of your delight.
In you is the source of life
and in your light we see light.

Keep on loving those who know you,
doing justice for upright hearts.
Let the foot of the proud not crush me
nor the hand of the wicked cast me out.

See how the evil-doers have fallen!
Flung down, they shall never arise.

The malice of the sinner versus the goodness of the Lord

1. There are two fundamental attitudes that every man can adopt every time that a new day of work and human relations begins: we can choose good or give way to evil. Psalm 35 (36), which we have just heard, draws up the two opposing views. On the one hand, there is the person who plots iniquity on the "bed" he is about to rise from; on the other hand, instead, is the upright person who seeks the light of God, "source of all life" (see v. 10). The abyss of the goodness of God, a living fountain that quenches our thirst and a light that enlightens our hearts, is opposed to the abyss of malice of the wicked person.

There are two types of men described in the prayer of the Psalm just recited, which the *Liturgy of the Hours* prescribes for Lauds of Wednesday of the First Week.

2. The first portrait presented by the Psalmist is that of the sinner (cf. vv. 2-5). As the original Hebrew says, "transgression speaks to the wicked deep in his heart" for in his heart there is "the oracle of sin" (v. 2). This expression is forceful. It makes us think that a Satanic word, as opposed to a divine word, resounds in the heart and words of the wicked.

Evil seems to be innate to him, to the point that it flows out in word and deed (cf. vv. 3-4). He spends his days choosing "evil ways", from early morning when he is still "on his bed" (v. 5), until evening when he is ready to fall asleep. The sinner's constant choice derives from an option that involves his whole life and generates death.

3. However the Psalmist tends completely toward the other portrait in which he desires to be reflected: that of the man who seeks the face of God (cf. vv. 6-13). He raises a true and proper chant to divine love (cf. vv. 6-11), which he follows in the end, with a humble prayer to be delivered from the dark fascination of evil and to be enlightened forever with the light of grace.

The prayer articulates a true and proper litany of terms, which express in images the God of love: grace, faithfulness, justice, judgment, salvation, protective shadow, abundance, delight, and life. In particular, it underlines four of the divine traits; they are expressed with Hebrew terms which have a more intense value than can be appreciated in the terms we use in modern languages.

4. There is above all the term, *hésed*, "grace", which is at once faithfulness, love, loyalty and tenderness. It is one of the basic ways to express the covenant between the Lord and his people. It is important to note that it can be found 127 times in the Psalter, more than half of all the times it occurs in the rest of the Old Testament. Then there is the term *'emunáh*, coming from the root of *amen*, the word of faith, and meaning stability, security, unconditional fidelity. *Sedeqáh* follows, "justice", which has a salvific meaning: it is the holy and provident attitude of God, who through his interventions in history, frees the faithful from evil and from injustice. Last of all, we find *mishpát*, the "judgment" with which God governs his creatures, caring for the poor and the oppressed and humbling the arrogant and the overbearing.

Four theological terms, which the person who prays repeats in his profession of faith, while he steps out on the paths of the world, with the certainty of having with him a loving, faithful, just and saving God.

5. To the various titles with which we exalt God, the Psalmist adds two powerful images. On the one hand, the abundance of food: it makes us think above all of the sacred banquet, which was celebrated in the temple of Zion with the flesh of sacrificial victims. There are also the images of the fountain and the torrent, whose waters quench not just the parched throat, but also the soul (cf. vv. 9-10; *Ps* 41,2-3; 62,2-6). The Lord refreshes and satisfies the person who prays, making him share in his fullness of immortal life.

The symbol of light provides another image: "in your light we see the light" (v. 10). It is a brightness that radiates almost as "a cascade" and is a sign of God's unveiling his glory to the faithful. This is what happened to Moses on Sinai (cf. *Ex* 34,29-30) and it takes place for the Christian to the degree that "with unveiled face reflecting the glory of the Lord, [we] are being transformed in the same likeness" (*2 Cor* 3,18).

In the language of the Psalms, "to see the light of the face of God" means concretely to meet the Lord in the temple, whenever the liturgical prayer is celebrated and the word of God is proclaimed. The Christian also shares the same experience when he celebrates the praise of the Lord at the beginning of the day, before he goes out to face the challenges of daily life that are not always straightforward.

———— ✖ ————

Canticle   Jud 16,2-3a.13-15

Begin a song to my God with tambourines,
sing to my Lord with cymbals.
Raise to him a new Psalm;
exalt him, and call upon his name.
For God is the Lord who crushes wars;

I will sing to my God a new song:
O Lord, you are great and glorious,
wonderful in strength, invincible.

Let all your creatures serve you,
for you spoke, and they were made.
You sent forth your Spirit, and it formed them;
there is none that can resist your voice.

For the mountains shall be shaken to their foundations
    with the waters;
at your presence the rocks shall melt like wax,
but to those who fear you
you will continue to show mercy.

The Lord, creator of the world, protects his people

1. The Canticle of praise we have just recited (*Jdt* 16,1-7) is attributed
to Judith, a heroine who became the pride of all the women of Israel,
because it was her mission to demonstrate the liberating power of
God at a dark moment in the life of his people. The *Liturgy of Lauds*
gives us only a few verses to recite. They invite us to celebrate, to sing
with a full voice, play drums and cymbals, to praise the Lord "who
crushes wars" (v. 2).

The last expression, which defines the true countenance of God,
who loves peace, introduces us into the world of ideas in which the
hymn was conceived. It was about a victory which the Israelites won
in a totally amazing way, a work of God who intervened to rescue
them from the prospect of an impending and total defeat.

2. The sacred author reconstructs the event several centuries later to
offer his brothers and sisters in the faith, tempted to discouragement
by a difficult situation, an example that can encourage them.

So he refers to what happened to Israel, when Nebuchadnezzar,
irritated by this people's failure to cooperate with his expansionist
plans and idolatrous claims, sent the general Holofernes with the
specific order to subdue and annihilate them. No one would dare to
resist him who claimed the honours of a god. His general, who shared
his presumption, derided the warning he was given not to attack
Israel, because it would amount to attacking God himself.

In reality, the sacred author wants to emphasize this principle, to
confirm believers of his time in faithfulness to the God of the
covenant: one must have confidence in God. The true enemy that
Israel must fear, are not the powerful ones of the earth, but infidelity
to the Lord. This is what deprives them of God's protection and makes
them vulnerable. Otherwise, when they are faithful, the people can
count on the power of God "wonderful in his power and
unsurpassable" (v. 13).

3. The whole story of Judith splendidly illustrates this principle. The
scene is that of the land of Israel now invaded by her enemies. From
the Canticle emerges the drama of the moment: "The Assyrian came
down from the mountains of the north; he came with myriads of
warriors; their multitude blocked up the valleys, their cavalry covered

the hills" (v. 3). The Canticle highlights with sarcasm the fleeting arrogance of the enemy: "He boasted that he would burn up my territory, and kill my young men with the sword, and dash my infants to the ground and seize my children as prey, and take my virgins as booty" (v. 4).

The situation described in the words of Judith is like others lived by Israel, in which salvation arrived when there seemed to be no way out. Was not the salvation of Exodus with its miraculous passage through the Red Sea also like this? Now too the siege by a powerful and numerous army removed all hope. But all this does but manifest the power of God, who is revealed as the invincible protector of his people.

4. The work of God appears even more gloriously since he did not rely on a warrior or an army. As happened before, in the time of Deborah, he eliminated Sisera through Jael, a woman (*Jgs* 4,17-21), now he makes use of an unarmed woman to come to the aid of his people in trouble. Strong in faith, Judith enters the enemy camp, charms the commander with her beauty and kills him in a humiliating way. The Canticle strongly underlines this fact: "The Lord Almighty has foiled them by the hand of a woman. For their mighty one did not fall by the hands of young men, nor did the sons of Titans smite him, nor did the tall giants set upon him: but Judith the daughter of Merari undid him with the beauty of her countenance" (*Jdt* 15,5-6).

Judith is example of woman's mission and prefiguration of Mary's cooperation in redemption

The person of Judith will become the archetype that would permit not just the Jewish tradition, but even the Christian tradition to emphasize God's preference for what is fragile and weak, but precisely, for this reason, chosen to manifest divine power. She is also an exemplary figure who showed the vocation and mission of the woman, called to be man's equal, and to play a significant role in the plan of God. Some of the expressions of the book of Judith will pass, more or less integrally into Christian tradition which sees in the Jewish heroine a prefiguration of Mary. Do we not hear an echo of the words of Judith, when Mary sings in the Magnificat: "He has put down the mighty from their thrones and has raised up the humble" (*Lk* 1,52). One can understand why the liturgical tradition common to Christians of the East and of the West loves to ascribe to Mary the Mother of

Jesus, the praise given to Judith: "you are the exaltation of Jerusalem, you are the great glory of Israel, you are the great pride of our nation" (*Jdt* 15,9).

5. From the experience of the victory, the Canticle of Judith ends with an invitation to raise a new song to God, acknowledging him as "great and glorious". At the same time, all creatures are admonished to remain subject to Him who with his word made everything and with his spirit fashioned it all. Who can resist the voice of God? Judith recalls it very forcefully: before the Creator and Lord of history, the mountains shall be shaken to their foundations and the rocks melt like wax (cf. *Jdt* 16,15). They are effective metaphors to recall that everything is "nothing" before the power of God. However the Canticle of victory does not want to terrify, but to comfort. In fact, God puts his invincible power at the support of those who are faithful to him: "to those who fear you, you will continue to show mercy" (*Jdt* 16,15).

Psalm 46

All peoples, clap your hands,
cry to God with shouts of joy!
For the Lord, the Most High, we must fear,
great king over all the earth.

He subdues peoples under us
and nations under our feet.
Our inheritance, our glory, is from him.
given to Jacob out of love.

God goes up with shouts of joy;
the Lord ascends with trumpet blast.
Sing praise for God, sing praise,
sing praise to our king, sing praise.

God is king of all the earth.
Sing praise with all your skill.
God is king over the nations;
God reigns on his holy throne.

The princes of the peoples are assembled
with the people of Abraham's God.
The rulers of the earth belong to God,
to God who reigns over all.

Praise the Lord, king of all the earth

1. *"The Lord, the most high, is a great King over all the earth!"*. This
initial acclamation is repeated in different tones in Psalm 46 (47),
which we just prayed. It is designed as a hymn to the sovereign Lord
of the universe and of history: *"God is king over all the earth ... God
rules over all nations"* (vv. 8-9).

Like other similar compositions in the Psalter (cf. *Ps* 92; 95-98), this
hymn to the Lord, the king of the world and of mankind presumes an
atmosphere of liturgical celebration. For that reason, we are at the
heart of the spiritual praise of Israel, which rises to heaven from the
Temple, the place where the infinite and eternal God reveals himself
and meets his people.

2. We will follow this Canticle of joyful praise in its fundamental
moments like two waves of the sea coming toward the shore. They
differ in the way they consider the relationship between Israel and
the nations. In the first part of the Psalm, the relationship is one of
domination: God "has subdued the peoples under us, he has put
the nations under our feet" (v. 4); in the second part, instead, the
relationship is one of association: "the princes of the peoples are
gathered with the people of the God of Abraham" (v. 10). One can
notice great progress.

In the first part (cf. vv. 2-6) it says, "All you peoples clap your hands,
shout to God with joyful cries!" (v. 2). The centre of this festive applause
is the grandiose figure of the supreme Lord, to whom the Psalm
attributes three glorious titles: "most high, great and terrible" (v. 3).
They exalt the divine transcendence, the absolute primacy of being,
omnipotence. The Risen Christ will also exclaim: "All power in heaven
and on earth has been given to me" (*Mt* 28,18).

3. In the universal lordship of God over all the peoples of the earth
(cf. v. 4) the Psalmist stresses his particular presence in Israel, the
people of divine election, "the favourite", the most precious and dear

inheritance (cf. v. 5). Israel is the object of a particular love of God which is manifested with the victory over hostile nations. During the battle, the presence of the Ark of the Covenant with the troops of Israel assured them of God's help; after the victory, the Ark was returned to Mount Zion (cf. *Ps* 67,19) and all proclaimed, "God mounts his throne amid shouts of joy, the Lord amid trumpet blasts" (*Ps* 46,6).

4. The second part of the Psalm (cf. vv. 7-10) opens with another wave of praise and festive chant: "Sing praise to God, sing praise; sing praise to our king, sing praises ... sing hymns of praise!" (vv. 7-8). Even now one sings to the Lord seated on his throne in the fullness of his sovereignty (cf. v. 9). The royal seat is defined as "holy", because it is unapproachable by the finite and sinful human being. But the Ark of the Covenant present in the most sacred part of the Temple of Zion is also a heavenly throne. In this way the distant and transcendent God, holy and infinite, draws near to his creatures, adapting himself to space and time (cf. *1 Kgs* 8,27.30).

5. The Psalm finishes on a surprising note of universalist openness: "the princes of the peoples are gathered with the people of the God of Abraham" (v. 10). One goes back to Abraham the patriarch who is at the root, not only of Israel but also of other nations. To the chosen people who are his descendents, is entrusted the mission of making converge towards the Lord all nations and all cultures, because he is the God of all mankind. From East to West they will gather on Zion to meet the king of peace and love, of unity and brotherhood (cf. *Mt* 8,11). As the Prophet Isaiah hoped, the peoples who are hostile to one another, will receive the invitation to lay down their arms and to live together under the divine sovereignty, under a government of justice and peace (*Is* 2,2-5). The eyes of all are fixed on the new Jerusalem where the Lord "*ascends*" to be revealed in the glory of his divinity. It will be "*an immense multitude, which no one can count, from every nation, race, people and tongue ... they (all) cried out with a loud voice: Salvation belongs to our God who is seated on his throne and to the Lamb*" (*Apoc* 7,9.10).

6. The *Letter to the Ephesians* sees the realization of this prophecy in the mystery of Christ the Redeemer when it affirms, addressing Christians who did not come from Judaism: "Remember, that one time you pagans by birth,... were without Christ, excluded from the citizenship of Israel, extraneous to the covenant of the promise, without hope and without God in this world. Now instead, in Christ Jesus, you who were once far off have been brought near thanks to the blood of Christ. In fact, he is our peace, he who made of the two one people, destroying the dividing wall of enmity" (*Eph* 2,1-14).

In Christ then, the kingship of God, sung by our Psalm, is realized on earth in the meeting of all people. This is the way an anonymous 8th century homily commented on this mystery: "Until the coming of the Messiah, hope of the nations, the Gentiles did not adore God and did not know who he is. Until the Messiah redeemed them, God did not reign over the nations through their obedience and their worship. Now instead, with his Word and his Spirit, God reigns over them because he saved them from deception and made them his friends" (Anonymous Palestinian, *Arab-Christian Homily of the Eighth Century*, Rome 1994, p. 100).

Thursday

Of the First Week

Psalm 56

Have mercy on me, God, have mercy
for in you my soul has taken refuge.
In the shadow of your wings I take refuge
till the storms of destruction pass by.

I call to God the Most High,
to God who has always been my help.
May he send from heaven and save me
and shame those who assail me.

May God send his truth and his love.

My soul lies down among lions,
who would devour the sons of men.
Their teeth are spears and arrows,
their tongue a sharpened sword.

O God, arise above the heavens;
may your glory shine on earth!

They laid a snare for my steps,
my soul was bowed down.
They dug a pit in my path
but fell in it themselves.

My heart is ready, O God,
my heart is ready.
I will sing, I will sing your praise.

Awake my soul,
awake lyre and harp,
I will awake the dawn.

I will thank you Lord among the peoples,
among the nations I will praise you
for your love reaches to the heavens
and your truth to the skies.

O God, arise above the heavens;
may your glory shine on earth!

1. It is a dark night; devouring wild beasts are perceived in the surroundings. The one who prays is waiting for the coming of dawn so that the light will dispel the darkness and fear. This is the background of Psalm 56 (57) on which we reflect today. It is a night prayer made by the one who prays at the break of day, anxiously awaited, in order to be able to praise the Lord with joy (cf. vv. 9-12). In fact, the Psalm passes from dramatic lament addressed to God to serene hope and joyful thanksgiving, the latter using words that resound again in another Psalm (cf. *Ps* 107,2-6).

In reality, one witnesses the passage from fear to joy, from night to day, from nightmare to serenity, from supplication to praise. It is an experience that is often described in the Psalter: "You changed my mourning into dancing, you took off my sackcloth and clothed me with gladness. With my whole being I sing endless praise to you. Lord, my God, forever I will give you thanks" (*Ps* 29,12-13).

2. Psalm 56 (57) that we are meditating on has two parts. The first part is the experience of fear before the assault of the evil which tries to strike the just one (cf. vv. 2-7). At the centre of the scene there are lions poised to attack. In no time this image is transformed into a picture of war, complete with spears, arrows, and swords. The one who prays feels assailed by a kind of death squadron. Around him there is a band of hunters, setting traps and digging pits to capture their prey. But this tense atmosphere is suddenly dissolved. In fact, already at the beginning (cf. v. 2), the protective symbol of the divine wings appears which refer, specifically, to the Ark of the Covenant with the winged cherubim, sign of the presence of God among the faithful in the holy temple on Mount Zion.

3. The one who prays asks God insistently to send from heaven his messengers to whom he assigns the symbolic names of "Faithfulness" and "Grace" (v. 4), the qualities proper to the saving love of God. For that reason, even if he shudders at the terrible roaring of the wild beasts and the perfidy of his persecutors, the faithful one remains serene and confident within, like Daniel in the lions' den (cf. *Dn* 6,17-25).

The presence of the Lord does not delay in showing its efficacy by means of the self inflicted punishment of his adversaries: they tumble into the pit which they had dug for the just one (cf. v. 7). Such confidence in divine justice, which is always expressed in the Psalter, wards off discouragement and surrender to the power of evil. Sooner or later, God sides with the faithful one upsetting the manoeuvres of the wicked, tripping them up in their own evil plots.

4. Now we reach the second part of the Psalm, that of thanksgiving (cf. vv. 8-12). There is a passage which shines because of its intensity and beauty: "My heart is steadfast, O God, my heart is steadfast. I will sing and make melody. Awake my soul. Awake O harp and lyre. I will awake the dawn" (vv. 8-9). Now the darkness has been dispelled: the dawn of salvation has coloured the song of the one who prays.

Applying this image to himself, the Psalmist seems to translate into terms that belong to the religious imagery of the Bible, which is rigorously monotheistic, the custom of the Egyptian or Phoenician priests who were in charge of "awakening the dawn", of making the sun reappear, since it was considered a beneficent god. He also alludes to the use of hanging up musical instruments and covering them in a time of mourning and trial (cf. *Ps* 136,2), and of "reawakening" them to a festive sound in times of liberation and joy. Hope blossoms from the liturgy: one turns to God asking him to draw near to his people again and to hear their prayer. In the Psalter, dawn is often the moment when God grants a favour after a night of prayer.

5. The Psalm closes with a hymn of praise to the Lord, who works with his two great saving qualities, that already appear with different names in the first part of the supplication (cf. v. 4). Now virtually personified, divine Goodness and Faithfulness enter the scene. They flood the heavens with their presence and are like light that shines in the darkness of trials and persecutions (cf. v. 11). For this reason the Christian tradition has used Psalm 56 [57] as a Canticle of awakening to Easter light and joy, which shines out to the faithful removing the fear of death and opening the horizon of heavenly glory.

6. Gregory of Nyssa discovers in the words of the Psalm a kind of typical description of what happens in every human experience open to the recognition of the wisdom of God. "Indeed, He saved me - he exclaims - by shading me with the cloud of the Spirit, and those who trampled me underfoot were humiliated" (From the Italian translation of *On the Titles of the Psalms*, Rome, 1994, p. 183).

Later, quoting the expressions at the end of the Psalm, where it says, "Be exalted, O God, above the heavens. Let your glory be above the earth", he concludes, "To the degree that the glory of God is extended on earth, increased by the faith of those who are saved, the heavenly powers extol God, exulting for our salvation" (*ibid.* p. 184).

———— ✠ ————

Canticle   Jer 31,10-14

O Nations, hear the word of the Lord,
proclaim it to the far-off coasts:
Say: "He who scattered Israel will gather him
and guard him as a shepherd guards his flock."
For the Lord has ransomed Jacob,
has saved him from an overpowering hand.

They will come and shout for joy on Mount Sion,
they will stream to the blessings of the Lord,
to the corn, the new wine and the oil,
to the flocks of sheep and the herds.
Their life will be like a watered garden.
They will never be weary again.

Then the young girls will rejoice and will dance,
the men, young and old, will be glad.
I will turn their mourning into joy,
I will console them, give gladness for grief.
Their priests I will again feed with plenty,
and my people shall be filled with my blessings.

1. "Hear the word of the Lord, O nations, proclaim it on the distant coasts" (*Jer* 31, 10). What is the good news that is to be announced with the solemn words of Jeremiah in the Canticle which we have just heard? It is consoling news, and it is no accident that the chapters that contain it (cf. 30-31) are called the "Book of Consolation". The announcement refers directly to ancient Israel, but in some way it foreshadows the message of the Gospel.

Here is the heart of this announcement: "The Lord will redeem Jacob, he shall redeem him from the hand of his conqueror" (*Jer* 31,11). The historical background of these words is found in a moment of hope experienced by the People of God, about a century after the Assyrians in 722 occupied the Northern part of the Holy Land. In the days of the Prophet Jeremiah, the religious reform of King Josiah brought about a return of the people to the covenant with God and fostered the hope that the time of punishment was over. It fostered the further hope that the North might regain its freedom and that Israel and Judah might be reunited. All, even "the distant coasts" should be witnesses of this wonderful event: God the Shepherd of Israel is about to intervene. He who allowed his people to be scattered, now comes to gather them together.

2. The invitation to rejoice is constructed with the aid of the profoundly moving images. It is an oracle which makes one dream! It delineates a future in which the exiles "will come and sing", and will find not only the Temple of the Lord, but also every good thing: wine, wheat, oil, the young of flocks and herds. The Bible does not know of an abstract spirituality. The promised joy does not just affect man's inner being because the Lord takes care of human life in all its dimensions. Jesus himself highlights this, when he invites his disciples to trust in Providence even for their material needs (cf. *Mt* 6,25-34). Our Canticle insists on this point of view: God wants to make the whole man happy. To convey how all embracing is the happiness, the Prophet uses the image of the "watered garden" (*Jer* 31,12), images of freshness and fruitfulness. Mourning is turned into feasting, being satiated with choice portions (cf. v. 14) and abundant goods, so that it will come naturally for them to dance and sing. It will be an unlimited joy, the joy of the people.

3. We know from history that this dream has not yet come true. Certainly not because God has failed to keep his promise: because of their infidelity. the people were to blame for this delusion.

The Book of Jeremiah undertakes to demonstrate it with the unfolding of the prophecy which becomes suffering and hardship, and gradually leads to some of the saddest phases of the history of Israel. Not only do the exiles of the North not return, but Judah itself will be occupied by Nebuchadnezzar in 587 BC. Bitter days now begin when, on the shore of Babylon, the lyres were hung from the willows (cf. *Ps* 136,2). There was no desire to sing for the satisfaction of the jailers; no one can rejoice when he is uprooted by force from his own country, the land where God made his dwelling.

4. The Canticle's invitation to rejoice does not lose its meaning. Indeed, the final reason for rejoicing on which it leans remains firm, and we find it in some very intense verses that precede the verses we use in the *Liturgy of the Hours*. One must keep the verses in mind while reading the expressions of joy in our Canticle. The verses describe in vibrant terms the love of God for his people. They indicate an irrevocable covenant: "I have loved you with an everlasting love" (*Jer* 31,3). They sing the fatherly outburst of the God who calls Ephraim his first born and covers him with his tenderness: "They shall go forth with weeping, I will lead them back with consolations; I will make them walk by brooks of water, in a straight path in which they shall not stumble; because I am a father to Israel" (*Jer* 31,9). Although the promise could not then be fulfilled because of the children's lack of correspondence, the Father's love retains all its touching tenderness.

5. This love is the golden thread that brings together into unity the ups and downs of the history of Israel, its joys and sorrows, successes and failures. God's love does not fail, and punishment is an expression of his love since it intends to teach and to save.

On the solid rock of this love, the invitation to joy of our Canticle evokes a future plan of God which, though delayed, will come sooner or later, despite all of human frailty. The future comes to fulfilment in the new covenant with the death and resurrection of Christ and the gift of the Spirit.

However, it will be totally fulfilled with the final return of the Lord at the end of time. Interpreted by the light of such certainty, the "dream" of Jeremiah continues to be a real historical opportunity, conditioned by the faithfulness of human beings, and, above all, it refers to a final goal, guaranteed by the faithfulness of God and already begun by his love in Christ.

In reading the oracle of Jeremiah, we should let the Gospel resound in our hearts, the wonderful news proclaimed by Christ in the synagogue of Nazareth (cf. *Lk* 4,16-21). Christian life is called to be a true "Jubilation", which only our sin can threaten. By making us pray these words of Jeremiah, the *Liturgy of the Hours* invites us to keep our life attached to Christ our Redeemer (cf. *Jer* 31,11) and in our personal and communal life to find in him the secret of true joy.

———— ✠ ————

Psalm 47

The Lord is great and worthy to be praised
in the city of our God.
His holy mountain rises in beauty,
the joy of all the earth.

Mount Sion, true pole of the earth,
the Great King's city!
God, in the midst of its citadels,
has shown himself its stronghold.

For the kings assembled together,
together they advanced.
They saw; at once they were astounded;
dismayed, they fled in fear.

A trembling seized them there,
like the pangs of birth,
By the east wind you have destroyed
the ships of Tarshish.

As we have heard, so we have seen
in the city of our God,
in the city of the Lord of hosts
which God upholds for ever.

O God, we ponder your love
within your temple.
Your praise, O God, like your name
reaches to the ends of the earth.

With justice your right hand is filled.
Mount Sion rejoices;
the people of Judah rejoice
at the sight of your judgments.

Walk through Sion, walk all round it;
count the number of its towers.
Review all its ramparts,
examine its castles,

that you may tell the next generation
that such is our God,
our God for ever and always.
It is he who leads us.

O God we ponder your love within your temple

1. The Psalm just proclaimed is a Canticle in honour of Zion, "the city of the great King" (*Ps* 47,3), at the time, the seat of the temple of the Lord and the place of his presence in the midst of humanity. Christian faith now applies it to "Jerusalem above" which is "our mother" (*Gal* 4,26).

The liturgical tone of this hymn, which evokes a festive procession (cf. vv. 13-14), the peaceful vision of Jerusalem that reflects divine salvation, renders Psalm 47 [48] a prayer that we can use to begin the day, offering a Canticle of praise, even if clouds form on the horizon.

To appreciate the meaning of the Psalm, three helpful acclamations are placed at the beginning, the middle and the end, almost as though offering the spiritual key of the composition and introducing us to its interior atmosphere. The three invocations are: "The Lord is great and worthy to be praised in the city of our God" (v. 2); "O God we ponder your love within your temple" (v. 10); "Such is our God, our God forever and always, it is he who leads us" (v. 15).

2. These three acclamations, which exalt the Lord but also "the city of our God" (v. 2), frame two great parts of the Psalm. The first is a joyful celebration of the holy city, Zion, victorious against the assaults of her enemies, serene under the mantle of divine protection (cf. vv. 3-8). There is a virtual litany of definitions of this city: it is a wonderful height that is set up as a beacon of light, a source of joy for the peoples of the earth, the only true "Olympus" where heaven and earth meet. It is - to use the expression of the Prophet Ezekiel - the Emmanuel-city because "the Lord is there", present in it (cf. *Ez* 48,35). But besieging troops are massed around Jerusalem for an assault, it is a symbol of the evil that attacks the splendour of the city of God. The clash has an immediate and foreseen outcome.

3. Indeed, the powerful of the earth, by assaulting the holy city, also provoked its king, the Lord. The Psalmist shows the dissolution of the pride of a powerful army with the thought-provoking image of the pains of childbirth: "A trembling seized them there like the pangs of birth" (v. 7). Arrogance is transformed into feebleness and weakness, power into collapse and rout.

Another image expresses the same idea: the routed army is compared to an invincible naval fleet, on which a typhoon is unleashed caused by a violent East wind (cf. v. 8). What remains is an unshaken certainty for the one who stands within the shadow of divine protection: the last word is not in the hands of evil, but of good; God triumphs over hostile powers, even when they seem great and invincible.

4. The faithful one celebrates his thanksgiving to God the deliverer in the temple itself. His is a hymn to the merciful love of the Lord, expressed with the Hebrew word *bésed*, typical of the theology of the covenant. We come now to the second part of the Psalm (cf. vv. 10-14).

After the great Canticle of praise to the faithful, just and saving God (cf. vv. 10-12), there is a sort of procession around the temple and the holy city (cf. vv. 13-14). The towers of the sure protection of God are counted, the ramparts are observed, expressions of the stability offered to Zion by its Founder. The walls of Jerusalem speak and its stones recall the deeds which must be transmitted "to the next generation" (v. 14) through the stories that fathers will tell their children (cf. Ps 77,3-7).

Zion is the place of an uninterrupted chain of saving actions of the Lord, that are announced in the catechesis and celebrated in the liturgy, so that believers will continue to hope in God who intervenes to set them free.

5. In the concluding antiphon there is one of the most beautiful definitions of the Lord as shepherd of his people: "It is he who leads us" (v. 15). The God of Zion is the God of the Exodus, of freedom, of closeness to the people enslaved in Egypt and pilgrims in the desert. Now that Israel is settled in the promised land, she knows that the Lord will not abandon her: Jerusalem is the sign of his closeness and the temple is the place of his presence.

As he rereads these expressions, the Christian moves to the contemplation of Christ, the new and living temple of God (cf. Jn 2,21), and he turns to the heavenly Jerusalem, which no longer needs a temple or an external light, because "its temple is the Lord God Almighty and the Lamb... the glory of God is its light and its lamp is the Lamb" (Apoc 21,2-23). St Augustine invites us to this "spiritual" rereading because he was convinced that in the Books of the Bible "there is nothing that only concerns the earthly city, because all that is said about it refers to her, or what is realized by her, symbolizes something that by allegory can also be referred to the heavenly Jerusalem" (City of God, XVII, 3,2). St Paulinus of Nola echoes him, because commenting on the words of the Psalm he exhorts us to pray so that "we can be found to be living stones in the walls of the heavenly and free Jerusalem" (Letter 28,2 to Severus). Contemplating the solidity and compactness of this city, the same Father of the Church continues: "In fact, he who dwells in this city, is revealed to be One in three persons.... Christ is not only the foundation of the city but also its tower and door.... If the house of our soul is founded on Him and a construction rises on Him worthy of such a great foundation, then the door of admission into the city will be precisely him who will lead us forever and will take us to the place of his pasture" (ibid.).

Friday

Of the First Week

Psalm 50

Have mercy on me, God, in your kindness.
In your compassion blot out my offence.
O wash me more and more from my guilt
and cleanse me from my sin.

My offences truly I know them;
my sin is always before me.
Against you, you alone, have I sinned;
what is evil in your sight I have done.

That you may be justified when you give sentence
and be without reproach when you judge,
O see, in guilt I was born,
a sinner was I conceived.

Indeed you love truth in the heart;
then in the secret of my heart teach me wisdom.
O purify me, then I shall be clean;
O wash me, I shall be whiter than snow.

Make me hear rejoicing and gladness,
that the bones you have crushed may revive.
From my sins turn away your face
and blot out all my guilt.

A pure heart create for me, O God,
put a steadfast spirit within me.
Do not cast me away from your presence,
nor deprive me of your holy spirit.

Give me again the joy of your help;
with a spirit of fervour sustain me,
that I may teach transgressors your ways
and sinners may return to you.

O rescue me, God, my helper,
and my tongue shall ring out your goodness.
O Lord, open my lips
and my mouth shall declare your praise.

For in sacrifice you take no delight,
burnt offering from me you would refuse,
my sacrifice, a contrite spirit.
A humbled, contrite heart you will not spurn.

In your goodness, show favour to Sion:
rebuild the walls of Jerusalem.
Then you will be pleased with lawful sacrifice,
holocausts offered on your altar.

Miserere - **Against you alone have I sinned**

1. We have just heard the *Miserere*, one of the most famous prayers of the Psalter, the most intense and commonly used penitential Psalm, the hymn of sin and pardon, a profound meditation on guilt and grace. The *Liturgy of the Hours* makes us pray it at *Lauds* every Friday. For centuries the prayer has risen to heaven from the hearts of many faithful Jews and Christians as a sigh of repentance and hope poured out to a merciful God.

The Jewish tradition placed the Psalm on the lips of David, who was called to repentance by the severe words of the Prophet Nathan (cf. vv. 1-2; 2 *Sam* 11-12), who rebuked him for his adultery with Bathsheba and for having had her husband Uriah killed. The Psalm, however, was enriched in later centuries, by the prayer of so many other sinners, who recovered the themes of the "new heart" and of the "Spirit" of God placed within the redeemed human person, according to the teaching of the Prophets Jeremiah and Ezekiel (cf. v. 12; *Jer* 31,31-34; *Ez* 11,19. 36,24-28).

2. Psalm 50 [51] outlines two horizons. First, there is the dark region of sin (cf. vv. 3-11) in which man is placed from the beginning of his existence: "Behold in guilt I was born, a sinner was I conceived" (v. 7). Even if this declaration cannot be taken as an explicit formulation of the doctrine of original sin as it was defined by Christian theology, undoubtedly it corresponds to it: indeed, it expresses the profound dimension of the innate moral weakness of the human person. The first part of the Psalm appears to be an analysis of sin, taking place before God. Three Hebrew terms are used to define this sad reality, which comes from the evil use of human freedom.

3. The first term, *hattá*, literally means "falling short of the target": sin is an aberration which leads us far from God, the fundamental goal of our relations, and, consequently, also from our neighbour.

The second Hebrew term is "*awôn*, which takes us back to the image of "twisting" or of "curving".

Sin is a tortuous deviation from the straight path; it is an inversion, a distortion, deformation of good and of evil; in the sense declared by Isaiah: "Woe to those who call good evil and evil good, who change darkness into light and light into darkness" (*Is* 5,20). Certainly, for this reason in the Bible conversion is indicated as a "return" (in Hebrew *shûb*) to the right way, correcting one's course.

The third term the Psalmist uses to speak of sin is *peshá*. It expresses the rebellion of the subject toward his sovereign and therefore an open challenge addressed to God and to his plan for human history.

4. If, however, man confesses his sin, the saving justice of God is ready to purify him radically. Thus we come to the second spiritual part of the Psalm, the luminous realm of grace (cf. vv. 12-19). By the confession of sins, for the person who prays there opens an horizon of light where God is at work. The Lord does not just act negatively, eliminating sin, but recreates sinful humanity by means of his life-giving Spirit: he places in the human person a new and pure "heart", namely, a renewed conscience, and opens to him the possibility of a limpid faith and worship pleasing to God.

Origen spoke of a divine therapy, which the Lord carries out by his word and by the healing work of Christ: "As God prepares remedies for the body from therapeutic herbs wisely mixed together, so he also prepared for the soul medicines with the words he infused, scattering them in the divine Scriptures.... God gave yet another medical aid of which the Lord is the Archetype who says of himself: "*It is not the healthy who have need of a physician but the sick'. He is the excellent physician able to heal every weakness, and illness*" (Origen, *Homilies on the Psalms*, From the Italian edition, *Omelie sui Salmi*, Florence, 1991, pp. 247-249).

5. The richness of Psalm 50 [51] merits a careful exegesis of every line. It is what we will do when we will meet it again at *Lauds* on successive Fridays. (See pp. 136, 205 and 265 below) The overall view, which we have taken of this great Biblical supplication, reveals several fundamental components of a spirituality which should permeate the daily life of the faithful. There is above all a lively sense of sin, seen as a free choice, with a negative connotation on the moral and theological level: "Against you, you alone, have I sinned, I have done what is evil in your sight" (v. 6).

There is also in the Psalm a lively sense of the possibility of conversion: the sinner, sincerely repentant, (cf. v 5), comes before God in his misery and nakedness, begging him not to cast him out from his presence (v. 13).

Finally, in the *Miserere*, a rooted conviction of divine pardon "cancels, washes, cleanses" the sinner (cf. vv. 3-4) and is able to transform him into a new creature who has a transfigured spirit, tongue, lips and heart (cf. 4-19). "Even if our sins were as black as the night, divine mercy is greater than our misery. Only one thing is needed: the sinner has to leave the door to his heart ajar.... God can do the rest.... Everything begins and ends with his mercy", so writes St Faustina Kowalska (M. Winowska, *The Ikon of Divine Mercy, the Message of Sister Faustina*, from the Italian version, *L'Icona dell'Amore Misericordioso. Il messaggio di Suor Faustina*, Rome, 1981, p. 271).

———— ❈ ————

Canticle   Is 45,15-26

Truly, God of Israel, the Saviour,
you are a God who lies hidden.
They will be put to shame and disgraced,
all who resist you.
They will take themselves off in dismay,
the makers of idols.

But Israel is saved by the Lord,
saved for evermore.
You will never be ashamed or disgraced
through endless ages.

For this is the word of the Lord,
the creator of heaven,

the God who made earth and shaped it,
he who made it firm.
He did not create it in vain,
he made it to be lived in.

I am the Lord, there is no other.
I have not spoken in secret, in some dark place,
I have not said to Jacob's sons
"Search for me in vain."

I am the Lord, I speak the truth,
I proclaim what is right.
Assemble, all of you, draw near
you who have escaped from the nations.

They know nothing, who carry around
their idols made of wood
and keep on praying to a god
that cannot save them.

State your case and bring your proofs,
consult among yourselves.
Who proclaimed this beforehand,
who foretold it long ago?

Was it not I, the Lord ?
There is no god but me,
a God of justice, a saviour
There is none but me.

Turn to me and be saved,
all the ends of the earth!
For I am God, there is no other;
by myself I swear it.

It is truth that goes forth from my mouth,
a word beyond recall.
To me every knee shall bow,
every tongue shall swear.

They will say: "In the Lord alone
are victory and power.

And to him will come in dismay
all who have resisted.
Through the Lord will come victory and glory
for all Israel's Sons.'"

On the mystery and providence of God

1. "Truly, you are a hidden God" (*Is* 45,15). The verse which
introduces the Canticle prayed at Lauds on Friday of the first week of
the Psalter, is taken from a meditation of the Deutero-Isaiah on the
greatness of God manifested in creation and in history: a God who
reveals himself, though he remains hidden in the impenetrability of
his mystery. He is by definition *"the hidden God"*. No thought can
encompass him. Man can only contemplate his presence in the
universe, discern his imprint and bow down in adoration and praise.

The meditation arises from the historical event of the amazing
liberation that God wrought for his people at the time of the
Babylonian exile. Who would ever have thought that the exiles of
Israel would be able to return to their country? Considering the power
of Babylon, they could easily have despaired. Yet there came the great
announcement, the surprise of God, which vibrates in the words of
the Prophet: as at the time of the Exodus, God will intervene. If then
he broke the resistance of Pharaoh with tremendous punishments,
now he chooses a king, Cyrus of Persia, to defeat the power of
Babylon and restore freedom to Israel.

2. "You are a God who hides yourself, God of Israel, the Saviour" (*Is*
45,15). With these words the Prophet invites us to recognize that God
intervenes in history, even if it is not immediately apparent. We could
say that he acts "behind the scenes". He is the mysterious and invisible
director, who respects the freedom of his creatures, but at the same
time, holds in his hand the thread of world events. The certainty of
the Providential action of God is a source of hope for the believer,
who knows he can count on the constant presence of Him, "who has
formed the earth and made it, he established it" (*Is* 45,18).

Indeed, the creative act is not an episode that is lost in the night
of time, so that the world, after that beginning, must be considered
as abandoned to itself. God continually brings into being the
creation that came from his hands. To acknowledge him is to confess

his uniqueness: "Was it not I, the Lord? Outside of me there is no other God" (*Is* 45,21). God is by definition the only God. Nothing can be compared with him. Everything is subject to him. From here follows the repudiation of idolatry, for which the Prophet pronounces harsh words: "They have no knowledge who carry about their wooden idols, and keep praying to a god that cannot save" (*Is* 45,20). How can we bow down in adoration before a human product?

3. For our present day sensitivity this polemic might seem exaggerated, as if it were criticising the images themselves, without realizing that they might have a symbolic value, which is compatible with the spiritual adoration of the one God. Certainly, what comes into play is the wise divine pedagogy which, by the rigid discipline of the exclusion of images, historically protected Israel from polytheistic contamination. The Church, basing herself on the face of God manifested in the Incarnation of Christ, recognised in the Second Council of Nicea (787) the possibility of using sacred images, provided they are understood in their essentially relational value.

The prophetic admonition retains its importance in view of all the forms of idolatry, not consisting in the improper use of images, but rather often hidden in the attitudes with which men and things are considered as absolute values that are substituted for God himself.

4. On the side of creation, the hymn places us within history, where Israel often did experience the beneficent and merciful power of God, his fidelity and his providence. Particularly, the love of God for his people appears again in such an open and striking way in setting them free from exile that the Prophet calls to witness it the "survivors of the nations". He invites them to debate, if they can: "Assemble yourselves and come, draw near together you survivors of the nations" (*Is* 45,20). The Prophet concludes that the intervention of the God of Israel is indisputable.

Then a magnificent universalist perspective emerges. God proclaims: "Turn to me and be saved, all the ends of the earth, because I am God and there is no other" (*Is* 45,22). So it becomes clear that the predilection which God has shown Israel as his people is not an act of exclusion, but rather an act of love from which all of humanity is destined to benefit.

Hence, we find outlined in the Old Testament the "sacramental" concept of the history of salvation, which, does not see in the special election of the sons of Abraham and later of the disciples of Christ in the Church, a privilege which does not mean to "close" or "exclude", but the sign and instrument of a universal love.

5. The invitation to adore and the offer of salvation is directed to all peoples: "To me every knee shall bow, every tongue shall swear" (*Is* 45,23). To read these words from a Christian perspective means to go in thought to the full revelation of the New Testament, which points out in Christ "the Name which is above every other name" (*Phil* 2,9), so that "at the name of Jesus, every knee must bend, in heaven, on earth and under the earth, and every tongue proclaim that Jesus Christ is Lord, to the glory of God the Father" (*Phil* 2,10-11).

Through this hymn, our morning praise acquires a universal dimension and speaks in the name of those who have not yet had the grace to know Christ. It is a praise which becomes "missionary", forcing us to travel to every corner of the globe, announcing that God has revealed himself in Jesus as Saviour of the world.

Psalm 99

Cry out with joy to the Lord, all the earth.
Serve the Lord with gladness.
Come before him, singing for joy.

Know that he, the Lord, is God.
He made us, we belong to him,
we are his people, the sheep of his flock.

Go within his gates, giving thanks.
Enter his courts with songs of praise.
Give thanks to him and bless his name.

Indeed, how good is the Lord,
eternal his merciful love.
He is faithful from age to age.

The joy of those who enter the temple of the Lord

1. The tradition of Israel gave the title *"Psalm for the todâh"* to the hymn of praise we just heard, that is thanksgiving in liturgical chant. That is why it is appropriately intoned in the morning Lauds. We can identify three noteworthy elements in the four verses of the joyful hymn, that make its use spiritually fruitful for the Christian community at prayer.

2. First of all, there is an urgent call to prayer, clearly described in a liturgical dimension. Suffice it to list the imperative verbs coupled with indications of liturgical usage that are articulated in the Psalm: "Cry out..., serve the Lord with gladness, come before him singing for joy. Know that the Lord is God... Enter his gates with thanksgiving, his courts with praise, give thanks to him and bless his name". It is series of invitations not just to enter the sacred area of the temple through the gates and courts (cf. *Ps* 14,1;23,3.7-10), but also to praise God joyfully.

It is like a constant unbroken thread of praise taking the form of a continuous profession of faith and love. Praise that rises from the earth to God, and at the same time nourishes the spirit of the believer.

3. I would like to highlight a secondary detail at the beginning of the hymn, where the Psalmist calls all the earth to acclaim the Lord (cf. v.1). Certainly, the Psalm will then focus attention on the chosen people, but the perspective of the praise is universal, as usual in the Psalter with the "hymns to the Lord the king" (cf. *Ps* 95-98, [96-99]). The world and history are not at the mercy of chance, chaos, or blind necessity. Instead, a mysterious God governs them, who desires that humanity live in stability according to just and authentic relations. He "is King. The world is established, it shall never be moved;he will judge the peoples with equity... He will judge the world with righteousness and the peoples with his truth" (*Ps* 95,10.13).

4. We are in the hands of God, Lord and King, Father and Creator, and we celebrate it, confident that he will not let us fall from his hands. In this light we can appreciate better the third central element of the Psalm. At the centre of the praise that the Psalmist places on our lips, there is, in fact, a profession of faith, expressed through a series of attributes that define the profound reality of God. The essential creed contains the following affirmations: "The Lord is God, our maker to whom we belong, whose people we are. ... Good indeed is the Lord, his steadfast love endures forever, his faithfulness lasts through every age" (cf. vv. 3-5).

5. In the first place, there is a renewed profession of faith in the one God, as required by the first commandment of the Decalogue: "I am the Lord, your God ...You shall not have other gods before me" (*Ex* 20,2.3). As is often repeated in the Bible: "Know then today and keep well in your heart that the Lord is God in the heavens above, in the earth below and there is no other" (*Dt* 4,39). Then faith in God the creator is proclaimed, source of being and of life. Then expressed through a "covenant formula", comes the affirmation of the certainty that Israel has of her divine election: "We are his, his people and the sheep of his pasture" (v. 3). It is a certainty that the faithful of the new People of God make their own, in the awareness of being the flock that the supreme Shepherd of souls leads to the eternal pastures of heaven (cf. *1 Pt* 2,25).

6. After the proclamation of the one God, creator and source of the covenant, the portrait of the Lord sung by our Psalm continues with the meditation on three divine qualities that the Psalter often exalts: God's goodness, merciful love (*hésed*), faithfulness. They are the three virtues that belong to the covenant of God with his people; they express a bond which will never be broken, through generations, despite the muddy stream of sins, rebellions and human infidelity. With serene confidence in divine love that will never diminish, the people of God journey through history with their daily temptations and weaknesses.

This confidence becomes a hymn, for which sometimes words fail, as St Augustine comments: "the more charity increases, the more aware you will become of what you said and did not say. In fact, before savouring certain things, you thought you could use words to speak about God; when you began to enjoy the taste, you realized that you were not able to explain adequately what you tasted.

If you realize you did not know how to express in words what you tasted, should you for this reason be silent and not praise?...

Absolutely not. You will not be so ungrateful. To him are owed honour, respect and the greatest praise ... Listen to the Psalm: "All the earth, cry out with joy to the Lord'. Then you will understand the joy of all the earth if you rejoice before the Lord" (From the *Exposition on the Psalms*, Italian version, *Esposizioni sui Salmi* III/1, Rome 1993, p. 459).

Saturday

───── ✖ ─────

Of the First Week

Psalm 118   vv. 145-152 XIX (Koph)

I call with all my heart; Lord, hear me,
I will keep your commands.
I call upon you, save me
and I will do your will.

I rise before dawn and cry for help,
I hope in your word.
My eyes watch through the night
to ponder your promise.

In your love hear my voice, O Lord;
give me life by your decrees.
Those who harm me unjustly draw near:
they are far from your law.

But you, O Lord, are close:
your commands are truth.
Long have I known that your will
is established for ever.

Praise God for the gift of his law

1. What the *Liturgy of Lauds* for Saturday of the first week offers us is a single *strophe* of Psalm 118, (the verses 145-152), in the monumental prayer of 22 strophes or stanzas, that correspond to the letters of the Hebrew alphabet. Each strophe begins with a different letter of the Hebrew alphabet and the order of the

strophes follows that of the alphabet. The one we have
proclaimed is the 19th strophe (verses 145-152) corresponding to
the letter *qoph*.

This introductory preface is a great help for understanding the
meaning of this hymn in honour of the divine law. It is similar to
Eastern music, whose sonorous waves seem never ending, ascending
to heaven in a repetition which involves the mind and senses, the
spirit and body of the one who prays.

2. In a sequence that goes from *"aleph* to *tav'*, from the first to the last
letter of the Hebrew alphabet, we would say from A to Z in our
alphabets, the one who prays pours out his thanks for the Law of
God, that he adopts as a lamp for his steps in the often dark path of
life (cf. v. 105).

It is said that the great philosopher and scientist Blaise Pascal recited
this fullest of all the Psalms every day, while the theologian Dietrich
Bonhoeffer, assassinated by the Nazis in 1945, made it become a living
and timely prayer when he wrote: "Undoubtedly, Psalm 118 [119] is
tedious on account of its length and monotony, but we must proceed
very slowly and patiently word by word, phrase by phrase. Then we
will discover that the apparent repetitions in reality are new aspects
of one and the same reality: love for the Word of God. Since this love
is never ending, so are the words that profess it. They can accompany
us all our life, and in their simplicity they become the prayer of the
youth, the mature man and the venerable old man" (*Pray the Psalms
with Christ*, English translation of the Italian title, *Pregare i Salmi con
Cristo*, Brescia, 1978, 3a edizione, p. 48).

3. The fact of repetition, in addition to helping the memory in the
choral chant, is also a good way to foster inner attachment and
confident abandonment into the arms of God, who is invoked and
loved. Among the repetitions of the Psalm 118 [119], I want to point
out an important one. Each of the 176 verses which make up this
praise of the *Torah*, of the divine Law and Word, contains at least one
of the eight words used to define the *Torah* itself: law, word, witness,
judgment, saying, decree, precept, and order. We celebrate divine
revelation this way because it is the revelation of the mystery of God
and the moral guide of the life of the faithful.

In this way God and man are united in a dialogue composed of words and deeds, teaching and listening, truth and life.

4. Now we come to our strophe (cf. vv. 145-152) that is well suited to the spirit of morning Lauds. In fact the scene at the centre of this set of 8 verses is nocturnal, but open to the new day. After a long night of waiting and of prayerful vigil in the Temple, when the dawn appears on the horizon and the liturgy begins, the believer is certain that the Lord will hear the one who spent the night in prayer, hoping and meditating on the divine Word. Fortified by this awareness and facing the day that unfolds before him, he will no longer fear dangers. He knows that he will not be overcome by his persecutors who besiege him with treachery (cf. v. 150) because the Lord is with him.

5. The strophe expresses an intense prayer: "I call with all my heart, Lord; answer me.... I rise before the dawn and cry for help; I hope in your word ..." (vv.145.147). In the Book of Lamentations, we read this invitation: "Arise, cry out in the night, at the beginning of the watches; pour out your heart like water in the presence of the Lord! Lift your hands toward him" (*Lam* 2,19). St Ambrose repeated: "O man, know you not that every day you should offer God the first fruits of your heart and voice? Make haste at dawn to carry to the Church the first fruits of your devotion" (*Exp. in ps. CXVIII*; PL 15, 1476 A).

At the same time our *strophe* is also the exaltation of a certainty: we are not alone because God listens and intervenes. The one who prays, says: "Lord, you are near" (v. 151). The other Psalms confirm it: "Draw near to me, redeem me, set me free because of my enemies!" (*Ps* 68,19); "The Lord is near to the broken-hearted, and saves the crushed in spirit" (*Ps* 33,19). (See also pp. 214-216 below)

———— ※ ————

Canticle   Ex 15,1-4a.8-13.17-18

I will sing to the Lord, glorious his triumph!
Horse and rider he has thrown into the sea!
The Lord is my strength, my song, my salvation.
This is my God and I extol him.
my father's God and I give him praise.
The Lord is a warrior! The Lord is his name.

The chariots of Pharaoh he hurled into the sea.
At the breath of your anger the waters piled high;
The moving waters stood up like a dam.
The deeps turned solid in the midst of the sea.

The enemy said "I will pursue and overtake them,
I will divide the plunder, I shall have my will.
I will draw my sword, my hand shall destroy them."

You blew with your breath, the sea closed over them.
They went down like lead into the mighty waters.
Who is like you among the gods, O Lord,
who is like you, so glorious in holiness,
spreading fear through your deeds, you who do marvels?

You stretched forth your hand,
the earth engulfed them;
Your love has guided the people you redeemed;
your power has led them to your holy dwelling-place.

You will lead them and plant them on your mountain,
The place, O Lord, where you have made your home,
The sanctuary, Lord, which your hands have made.
The Lord will reign for ever and ever.

Sing to the Lord for he is triumphant

1. This hymn of victory (cf. *Ex* 15,1-18), used at Lauds on Saturday of the first week, transports us to the key moment in the history of salvation: the event of the Exodus, when God saved Israel from a humanly desperate situation. The facts are well known: following the long time of slavery in Egypt, the Hebrews were on their way to the promised land when the army of Pharoah overtook them and nothing would have saved them from annihilation if the Lord had not intervened with his powerful hand. The hymn delights in describing the arrogance of the plans of the armed enemy: "I will pursue, I will overtake, I will divide the spoils" (*Ex* 15,9).

What can the greatest army do against divine omnipotence? God commands the sea to make a passage for the assailed people and then to close the passage to the aggressors: "When your wind blew: the sea covered them, they sank like lead in the mighty waters" (*Ex* 15,10).

These are vigorous images that attempt to describe the greatness of God, while expressing the wonder of a people who can scarcely believe their eyes, and break out with one voice in a glorious hymn of praise: "The Lord is my strength and my song, and he has become my salvation. This is my God and I will praise him, the God of my father and I will exalt him" (*Ex* 15,2).

2. The Canticle does not just sing of the liberation obtained; it also indicates the positive objective, none other than entry into the dwelling place of God to live in communion with him: "You have led in your steadfast love the people whom you redeemed, you guided them by your strength to your holy abode" (*Ex* 15,13). So understood, the event was not only at the base of the covenant between God and his people, but became the "symbol" of the whole history of salvation. On many other occasions, Israel will survive similar situations, and the Exodus will be repeated regularly. In a special way that event prefigures the great redemption that Christ will bring about with his death and resurrection.

For this reason our Canticle resounds in a special way in the liturgy of the Easter Vigil to demonstrate with its intense imagery what has taken place in Christ. In Christ we have been saved not from a human oppressor, but from the slavery to Satan and sin, that has weighed on human destiny from the beginning. With Christ humanity takes up the road again on the path that leads us to the house of the Father.

3. This liberation, already achieved in mystery and present in Baptism as the seed of life destined to grow, will attain its fullness at the end of time, when Christ will return in glory and "hand over the Kingdom to God the Father" (*1 Cor* 15,24). It is this final, eschatological horizon that the *Liturgy of the Hours* certainly invites us to look for when it introduces our Canticle with a quote from the Apocalypse: "They have conquered the beast ... [They] were singing the Canticle of Moses, the servant of God" (*Apoc* 15,2.3).

At the end of time what the Exodus event prefigured and what Easter accomplished in a definitive way that is still open to the future will be fully realized for all the saved. Indeed, our salvation is real and entire, but it lies between the "already" and the "not yet" of our earthly condition, as the Apostle Paul recalls: "It is in hope that we are saved" (*Rom* 8,24).

4. "I will sing to the Lord for he is gloriously triumphant" (*Ex* 15,1). Putting on our lips the words of the ancient hymn, the liturgy of lauds invites us to see our day in the great horizon of the history of salvation. This is the Christian way of perceiving the passage of time. In the accumulation of passing days, there is no fatality that oppresses us, but a plan that goes on unfolding and that we must learn to read with discernment in the events of our time.

The Fathers of the Church were particularly attuned to this perspective. Indeed, originating from the history of salvation meant they loved to read the salient facts of the Old Testament - from the deluge at the time of Noah to the calling of Abraham, from the liberation of the Exodus to the return of the Hebrews after the Babylonian exile - as "prefigurations" of future events, seeing in those facts an "archetypal" value: in them were pre-announced the fundamental characteristics that would be repeated in some way throughout the course of human history.

5. As for the Prophets, they had already reread the events of the history of salvation, showing how they influenced present reality and pointing to the full realization in the future. Thus, meditating on the mystery of the covenant that God established with Israel, they even began to speak of a "new covenant" (*Jer* 31,31; cf. *Ez* 36,26-27), in which the law of God would be written in the heart of the human person. It is easy to see in the prophecy the new covenant sealed in the blood of Christ and realized through the gift of the Spirit. By reciting this hymn of victory on the ancient Exodus, now, with the full light of the Easter exodus, the faithful can live joyously as a pilgrim Church that moves in time towards the heavenly Jerusalem.

6. We can contemplate with increased wonder what God has wrought for his people: "You will bring them in, and plant them on your own mountain, the place, O Lord, which your hands have established" (*Ex* 15,17). The hymn of victory sings the triumph of God, not of man. It is a Canticle, not of war, but of love.

Allowing our days to be permeated by the ancient Hebrews' thrill of praise, we will walk on the roads of the world, full of threats, risk, and suffering, but with the certainty of being encompassed by the merciful gaze of God. Nothing can resist the power of his love.

Psalm 116

O praise the Lord, all you nations,
acclaim him all you peoples!

Strong is his love for us;
he is faithful for ever.

All peoples praise God's faithful love

1. This is the shortest of the Psalms. In Hebrew it has only 17 words, and nine of them are noteworthy. It is a short doxology, namely, an essential hymn of praise, that ideally functions as the conclusion of longer Psalms. This happened sometimes in the liturgy, as it happens now with our *Glory be to the Father,* that we use to end the recitation of every Psalm.

Indeed, these few words of prayer are found to be deeply meaningful for acclaiming the covenant of the Lord with his people from a universal point of view. In this light, the Apostle Paul uses the first verse of the Psalm to invite the peoples of the world to glorify God. In fact, he writes to the Christians of Rome: That the Gentiles might glorify God for his mercy as it is written: "Praise the Lord, all you nations; all you peoples exalt him'" (*Rom* 15,9.11).

2. As often happens with this kind of Psalm, the brief hymn that we are meditating on opens with an invitation to praise that is directed not only to Israel, but to all the peoples of the earth. An *Alleluia* should burst forth from the hearts of all the just who seek and love God with a sincere heart. Once again, the Psalter reflects a vision of vast perspective, nourished by Israel's experience during the Babylonian exile in the 6th century before Christ. At the time the Hebrew people met other nations and cultures and felt the need to announce their own faith to those among whom they lived. The Psalter portrays the concept that good flourishes in many places and can be directed toward the one Lord and Creator.

Hence, we can speak of an "ecumenism" of prayer that now holds in one embrace peoples who are different by origin, history and culture. We are in line with the great "vision" of Isaiah who describes "at the end of days" the procession of all the nations towards "the mountain of the house of the Lord". Then the swords and spears will fall from their hands; they will beat their swords into plowshares and their spears into pruning hooks, so that humanity can live in peace, singing its song of praise to the one Lord of all, listening to his word and observing his law (cf. *Is* 2,1-5).

3. Within this universal horizon Israel, the Chosen People, has a mission to fulfill. They should proclaim two great divine virtues, that they had experienced living the covenant with the Lord (cf. v.2). The two virtues, that are the fundamental features of the face of God, the "good binomial" of God, as St Gregory of Nyssa said (cf. *On the Titles of the Psalms*, the Italian original is *Sui titoli dei Salmi*, Rome, 1994, p.183), are expressed with other Hebrew words which, in translation, do not convey the full richness of their meaning.

The first is *hésed*, a term repeatedly used in the Psalter, that I have commented on before. It points to the richness of the profound sentiments that pass between two persons, linked by an authentic and constant bond. It includes values such as love, fidelity, mercy, goodness, and tenderness.

Between God and us, there is a relationship which is not cold, as is the case between an emperor and his subject, but alive like that between two friends, two spouses, parents and their children.

4. The second term is *eméth* and is a synonym for the first. It is beloved of the Psalter, where it appears half of all the times that it is used in the rest of the Old Testament.

The term itself expresses "truth", namely, the genuineness of a relationship, its authenticity and loyalty, that remain despite obstacles and trials; it is pure and joyful fidelity that knows no betrayal. It is no accident that the Psalmist declares that it "is faithful forever" (v.2). The faithful love of God will never fail and will not abandon us to ourselves or to the darkness of nihilism, or to a blind destiny, or to the void or to death.

God loves us with an unconditional, tireless, never ending love. It is the message of our Psalm, brief as a sigh of prayer from the heart, but intense as a great Canticle.

5. The words that it suggests are like an echo of the song that resounds in the heavenly Jerusalem, where a great multitude of every tongue, people and nation, sings the divine glory before the throne of God and the Lamb (cf. *Apoc* 7,9). The pilgrim Church joins in this Canticle with infinite expressions of praise, often accompanied by poetic genius and musical art. We think, for example, of the *Te Deum*, which generations of Christians throughout the centuries have used to praise and to thank: "We praise you O God, we confess you O Lord, all the earth venerates you, eternal Father". For its part, the short Psalm that we are meditating on today, is an effective synthesis of the perennial liturgy of praise with which the Church raises her voice in the world uniting herself to the perfect praise that Christ himself addresses to his Father.

Let us praise the Lord! Let us praise him unceasingly. But our lives must express our praise, more than our words. We will hardly be credible if with our Psalm we invite the peoples to give glory to the Lord, and we did not take seriously the Lord's admonition: "So let your light shine before men that they may see your good works and give glory to your Father who is in heaven" (*Mt* 5,16). In singing Psalm 116 [117], as in all the Psalms praising the Lord, the Church, People of God, strives to become herself a hymn of praise. (See also pp. 219-220 below)

The Second Week

Sunday

—— ✄ ——

Of the Second Week

Psalm 117

Give thanks to the Lord for he is good,
for his love endures for ever.

Let the sons of Israel say:
'His love endures for ever.'
Let the sons of Aaron say:
'His love endures for ever.'
Let those who fear the Lord say:
'His love endures for ever.'

I called to the Lord in my distress;
he answered and freed me.
The Lord is at my side; I do not fear.
What can man do against me?
The Lord is at my side as my helper:
I shall look down on my foes.

It is better to take refuge in the Lord
than to trust in men:
it is better to take refuge in the Lord
than to trust in princes.

The nations all encompassed me;
in the Lord's name I crushed them.
They compassed me, compassed me about;
in the Lord's name I crushed them.
They compassed me about like bees;
they blazed like a fire among thorns.
In the Lord's name I crushed them.

I was hard-pressed and was falling
but the Lord came to my help.
The Lord is my strength and my song;
he is my saviour.

There are shouts of joy and victory
in the tents of the just.

The Lord's right hand has triumphed;
his right hand raised me up.
The Lord's right hand has triumphed;
I shall not die, I shall live
and recount his deeds.
I was punished, I was punished by the Lord
but not doomed to die.

Open to me the gates of holiness:
I will enter and give thanks.
This is the Lord's own gate
where the just may enter.
I will thank you for you have answered
and you are my saviour.

The stone which the builders rejected
has become the corner stone.
This is the work of the Lord,
a marvel in our eyes.
This day was made by the Lord;
we rejoice and are glad.

O Lord, grant us salvation;
O Lord, grant success.
Blessed in the name of the Lord
is he who comes.
We bless you from the house of the Lord;
the Lord God is our light.

Go forward in procession with branches
even to the altar.
You are my God, I thank you.
My God, I praise you.
Give thanks to the Lord for he is good;
for his love endures for ever.

The stone rejected ... has become cornerstone

1. When a Christian, in unison with the voice of prayer in Israel, sings Psalm 117 [118], that we just heard, he feels within him a special thrill. In fact, he finds in this liturgical hymn two phrases that echo with a new meaning in the New Testament. The first is verse 22, "The stone rejected by the builders has become the corner-stone". The phrase is quoted by Jesus, who applies it to his mission of death and glory, after having told the parable of the murderous vinedressers (cf. *Mt* 21,42). The phrase is also recalled by Peter in the Acts of the Apostles: *"This Jesus is the stone, rejected by you the builders, which has become the cornerstone. There is no salvation in anyone else nor is there any other name given to men under heaven by which we are to be saved"* (*Acts* 4,11-12). St Cyril of Jerusalem comments: *"We say the Lord Jesus Christ is only one because his sonship is one; only one we say so that you do not think that there is another ... In fact he called stone,* not inanimate stone nor cut by human hands, *but the cornerstone,* because he who believes in him will not remain disappointed" (*The Catecheses*, English title of the Italian version of St Cyril's Catecheses, *Le Catechesi*, Rome, 1993, p. 312-313).

The second phrase that the New Testament takes from Psalm 117 [118] is proclaimed by the crowd at the solemn Messianic entrance of Christ into Jersualem: "Blessed is he who comes in the name of the Lord!" (*Mt* 21,9; cf. *Ps* 117,26). The acclamation is framed by a *Hosanna* that takes up the Hebrew petition *hoshiac na'*, "please, save us!"

2. The splendid Biblical hymn is placed at the heart of the small collection of Psalms, 112 [113] to 117 [118], called the Passover *Hallel*, namely, the Psalms of praise used in Hebrew worship for the Passover and the major solemnities of the liturgical year. The processional rite can be taken as the theme of Psalm 117 [118] articulated with the chants by the soloist or choir, with the Holy City and its Temple as the background. A beautiful antiphon begins and ends the Psalm: "Praise the Lord for he is good, his mercy endures forever" (vv. 1 and 29).

The word "mercy" translates the Hebrew word *hesed*, that designates the generous fidelity of God towards the covenanted and friendly people. Three categories of people are told to praise this fidelity: all of Israel, the "house of Aaron", namely the priests, and those "who fear the Lord", a way of speaking that includes the faithful and the proselytes, namely, the members of other nations who desire to follow the law of the Lord (cf. vv. 2-4).

3. The procession makes its way through the streets of Jerusalem, because the Psalm speaks of the "tents of the righteous" (cf. v. 15). There is, however, a hymn of thanksgiving (cf. vv. 5-18) whose basic message is: Even when we are in anguish, we must keep high the torch of confidence, because the powerful hand of the Lord leads his faithful people to victory over evil and to salvation.

The sacred poet uses strong and vivid images; he compares the cruel adversaries to a swarm of bees or to a column of flames that advances turning everything to ashes (cf. v.12). There is the vehement reaction of the just person, sustained by the Lord. He repeats three times "In the name of the Lord I cut them off" where the Hebrew verb refers to an intervention that destroys evil (cf. vv. 10,11,12). Behind all of it, indeed, there is the powerful right hand of God, namely, his effective intervention, and certainly not the weak and uncertain hand of man. For this reason the joy of the victory over evil leads to a vibrant profession of faith: "The Lord is my strength and my song, he has become my salvation" (v. 14).

4. The procession then arrives at the temple, at the "gates of justice" (v. 19), at the Holy Door of Zion. Here a second song of thanksgiving is sung, that begins with a dialogue between the congregation and the priests to be admitted to worship. "Open to me the gates of justice: I will enter to give thanks to the Lord", the soloist says in the name of the congregation in procession: "This is the gate of the Lord, the righteous shall enter through it" (v. 20), and others reply, probably the priests.

Once they enter, they begin the hymn of thanksgiving to the Lord, who in the Temple offers himself as the stable and secure "corner stone" on which to build the house of life (cf. *Mt* 7,24-25). A priestly blessing descends upon the faithful who have come into the temple to express their faith, to raise their prayer and to celebrate their worship.

5. The last scene that opens before our eyes is constituted by the joyful rite of sacred dances, accompanied by the festive waving of branches: "Bind the festal procession with branches, up to the horns of the altar" (v. 27). The liturgy is a joyful, festive celebration, expression of the entire life that praises the Lord. The rite of the branches brings to mind the Jewish Feast of Booths [Tabernacles], observed in memory of the pilgrimage of Israel through the desert, a solemnity in which there was a procession with palm, myrtle and willow branches.

This rite evoked by the Psalm is proposed to the Christian in Jesus' entry into Jerusalem, celebrated in the liturgy of Palm Sunday. Christ is acclaimed as the "Son of David" (cf. *Mt* 21,9) by the crowd, who, "having come for the feast ... took branches of palms and went out to greet him shouting: *Hosanna! Blessed is he who comes in the name of the Lord, the king of Israel*" (*Jn* 12,12-13). At that festive celebration that is, however, the prelude to the hour of the Passion and Death of Jesus, the symbol of the cornerstone, proposed at the beginning, takes its full meaning, a glorious Easter meaning.

Psalm 117 [118] encourages Christians to recognize in the Easter event of Jesus "the day that the Lord has made", on which "the stone rejected by the builders has become the cornerstone". With the Psalm they can then sing with great thanksgiving: " The Lord is my strength and my song; he has become my salvation" (v. 14); "This is the day the Lord has made, let us rejoice and exult in it" (v. 24). (See p. 223 below)

Canticle   Dan 3,52-57

You are blest, Lord God of our fathers.
To you glory and praise for evermore.

Blest your glorious holy name.
To you glory and praise for evermore.

You are blest in the temple of your glory.
To you glory and praise for evermore.

You are blest who gaze into the depths.
To you glory and praise for evermore.

You are blest in the firmament of heaven.
To you glory and praise for evermore.

You who walk on the wings of the wind:
To you glory and praise for evermore.

May they bless you, the saints and the angels.
To you glory and praise for evermore.

From the heavens, the earth and the sea,
To you glory and praise for evermore.

You are blest, Lord God of our fathers.
To you glory and praise for evermore.

Canticle uses language of Love

1. The Canticle we have just heard is the first part of a long and beautiful hymn that is found in the Greek version of the Book of Daniel. It is sung by three young Hebrew men who were thrown into the furnace for refusing to worship the statue of the Babylonian King Nebuchadnezzar. Another part of the same hymn is found in the *Liturgy of the Hours* for Sunday Lauds in the first and third weeks of the liturgical psalter. (See pp. 18 and 162)

As is known, the Book of Daniel reflects the ferments, hopes and apocalyptic expectations of the Chosen People, who in the era of the Maccabeans (2nd century B.C.) were struggling to live according to the Law given by God.

From the furnace, the three young men, miraculously preserved from the flames, sing a hymn of praise addressed to God. The hymn is like a litany, at once repetitive in the form of the verses and new with each verse: the invocations rise to God like billowing incense that glides through the air in similar but unique clouds. Prayer does not eschew repetition, just as the lover, who wants to express his love repeats his love over and over again. To emphasize the same things conveys the intensity and multiple nuances of one's interior feelings and affections.

2. We heard the beginning of the cosmic hymn of the third chapter of Daniel, in verses 52-57. It is the introduction that precedes the grandiose parade of the creatures engaged in the work of praise. An overall view of the entire Canticle, as an extended litany, makes us discover a succession of components that make up the theme of the hymn. It begins with six invocations spoken directly to God; they contain a universal appeal to "all you works of the Lord" to open their lips so ideal for praising God (cf. v. 57).

This is the part that we consider today and that the Liturgy proposes for Lauds of Sunday of the second week. Later on, the Canticle will be prolonged by summoning all the creatures of heaven and earth to praise and magnify their Lord.

3. Our initial passage will be taken up again by the Liturgy at Lauds of the Sunday of the fourth week. We will now choose only a few elements for our reflection. The first is the invitation to blessing: "Blessed are you..." that at the end will become "Bless the Lord...!".

In the Bible there are two forms of blessing, which are intertwined. There is, first of all, the blessing that comes down from God: the Lord blesses his people (cf. *Nm* 6,24-27). It is an effective blessing, source of fruitfulness, happiness and prosperity. Then there is the blessing that earth lifts towards heaven. The human person who receives so many blessings from the divine generosity, blesses God, praising, thanking and exalting him: "Bless the Lord, my soul!" (*Ps* 102 [103],1;103 [104],1).

Priests often mediate the divine blessing (cf. *Num* 6,22-23.27; *Sir* 50,20-21) through the imposition of hands; human blessing is expressed in the liturgical hymn that rises to the Lord from the congregation of the faithful.

4. The antiphon is another element we should consider in the passage that we are reflecting on. We can imagine the soloist, in the crowded temple, intoning the blessing: "Blessed are you, Lord...", recounting God's wonderful deeds while the congregation of the faithful continuously repeats the formula: "praiseworthy and glorious above all forever". It is what happened with Psalm 135 [136], the *"great Hallel"*, the great praise, where the people repeat "His mercy endures forever", while a soloist enumerated the various acts of salvation that the Lord wrought in favour of his people.

In our Psalm, the object of praise is above all the "glorious and holy" name of God, whose proclamation resounds in the temple, which is also "holy and glorious". When they contemplate in faith God who is seated on "the throne of his kingdom" the priests and the people are conscious of being the object of his gaze which "penetrates the abysses" and this awareness calls forth from their hearts the praise: "Blessed ... blessed ...". God, who "sits upon the cherubim" and has for his dwelling the "firmament of the heavens", is also close to his people who, for this reason, feel protected and safe.

5. When proposing this Canticle afresh for use on Sunday morning, the weekly Easter of Christians, the Church is inviting us to open our eyes to the new creation which has its beginning with the resurrection of Jesus. Gregory of Nyssa, a fourth century Greek Father of the Church, explains that with the Passover [Easter] of the Lord a "new heavens and new earth are created ... a different, renewed man comes into being in the image of his Creator by means of the birth from on high" (cf. *Jn* 3,3-7). And he continues: "As the one who looks toward the sensible world deduces from visible things the invisible beauty ... so the one who looks toward this new world of the ecclesial creation sees in it him who became everything in everyone, leading the mind by the hand, by means of the things that are understandable for our rational nature, toward that which goes beyond human comprehension" (Langerbeck H., *Gregorii Nysseni Opera*, VI, 1-22 *passim*, p. 385).

Thus in singing this Canticle, the Christian believer is invited to contemplate the world of the first creation, intuiting the outline of the second, inaugurated with the death and resurrection of the Lord Jesus. And this contemplation leads all by the hand to enter into the one Church of Christ almost dancing with joy. (See also p. 225 below)

Psalm 150

Praise God in his holy place,
praise him in his mighty heavens.
Praise him for his powerful deeds,
praise his surpassing greatness.

O praise him with sound of trumpet,
praise him with lute and harp.
Praise him with timbrel and dance,
praise him with strings and pipes.

O praise him with resounding cymbals,
praise him with clashing of cymbals.
Let everything that lives and that breathes
give praise to the Lord.

Let every living being praise the Lord

1. The hymn which just served as a support of our prayer is Psalm 150, the last Canticle in the Psalter. The last word that rings out in Israel's book of prayers is *alleluia*, namely, the pure praise of God, and this is why the Psalm is presented twice in the *Liturgy of Lauds*, on the second and fourth Sundays. (See p. 227 below)

The brief text is punctuated with a set of 10 imperatives repeating the same word, "*hallelû*", "praise!". As if they were eternal music and song, they never seem to end, rather like what happens with the famous *Alleluia* chorus of Handel's *Messiah*. Praise of God becomes like the continuous breath of the soul. As has been written, "this is one of the rewards for being human: quiet exaltation and the capacity for celebration; it is summed up well in a phrase that *Rabbi Akiba* offered his disciples: A song every day, / a song for every day" (A.J. Heschel, *Chi è l'uomo?*, Milan 1971, p. 178, the English title is *Who is Man?*).

2. Psalm 150 seems to unfold in three moments. At the beginning, in the first two verses (vv. 1-2) we fix our gaze on "the Lord" in "his sanctuary", on "his power", "his wonderful works", his "greatness". Then, in the second moment, as in a genuine musical movement, the orchestra of the temple of Zion is involved in praising the Lord (vv. 3-5b) that accompanies the sacred dances and songs. Finally, in the last verse of the Psalm (cf. v. 5c) the universe appears, represented by "every living thing" or, if one wishes to follow the original Hebrew, by "everything that breathes". Life itself becomes praise, praise that rises to the Creator from the beings he created.

3. In our first encounter with Psalm 150, it will be enough to reflect on the first and last parts of the hymn. They frame the second part, the heart of the composition, that we shall examine in the future, the next time the Psalm is proposed by the *Liturgy of Lauds*.

The "sanctuary" is the first place where the musical and the prayerful theme unfolds (cf. v. 1). The original Hebrew speaks of the pure, transcendent "sacred" area in which God dwells. It is then a reference to the horizon of heaven and paradise where, as the *Book of the Apocalypse* will explain, the eternal, perfect liturgy of the Lamb is celebrated (cf. for example, *Apoc* 5,6-14). The mystery of God, in which the saints are welcomed for full communion, is a place of light and joy, of revelation and love. We can understand why the Septuagint translation and the Latin Vulgate use the word "saints" instead of "sanctuary": "Praise the Lord in his saints!"

4. From heaven our thought moves to earth, with an emphasis on the "mighty deeds" wrought by God that manifest "his great majesty" (v. 2). These mighty deeds are described in Psalm 104 [105], that invites the Israelites to "meditate on all his wonderful works" (v. 2), to remember "the wonderful works that he has done, his prodigies, and the judgements he uttered" (v. 5). The Psalmist then recalls "the covenant which he [the Lord] made with Abraham" (v. 9), the extraordinary story of Joseph, the miracles of the liberation from Egypt and the journey through the desert, and lastly, the gift of the land. Another Psalm speaks of the troubles from which the Lord delivers those who "cry" to him; those he sets free are asked repeatedly to "Let them thank the Lord for his mercy, for his wonderful works for the sons of men!" (*Ps* 106 [107],8,15,21,31).

Thus in our Psalm we can understand the reference to "mighty deeds" as the original Hebrew says, that is, the powerful "prodigies" (cf. v. 2) that God disseminates in the history of salvation. Praise becomes a profession of faith in God the Creator and Redeemer, a festive celebration of divine love that is revealed by creating and saving, by giving life and by delivering.

5. Thus we come to the last verse of Psalm 150 (cf. v. 5c [6]). The Hebrew word used for the "living" who praise God refers to "breathing", as I said earlier, but also to something intimate and profound that is inherent in man.

Although one might think that all created life should be a hymn of praise to the Creator, it is more correct to maintain that the human creature has the primary role in this chorus of praise. Through the human person, spokesman for all creation, all living things praise the Lord. Our breath of life that also presupposes self-knowledge, awareness and freedom (cf. *Prv* 20,27) becomes the song and prayer of the whole of life that vibrates in the universe.

That is why all of us should address one another "with Psalms and hymns and spiritual songs, singing and making melody to the Lord" with all our hearts (*Eph* 5,19).

6. In transcribing the verses of Psalm 150, the authors of the Hebrew manuscripts often portray the *Menorah*, the famous seven-branched candlestick set in the Holy of Holies of the temple of Jerusalem. In this way they suggest a beautiful interpretation of the Psalm, a true and proper *Amen* to the prayer that our "elder brothers" have always prayed: the whole man with all the instruments and musical forms that his genius has invented trumpet, harp, zither, drums, dance, strings, flutes, sounding cymbals, clashing cymbals, as the Psalm says as well as "everything that breathes", is invited to burn like the *Menorah* before the Holy of Holies, in a constant prayer of praise and thanksgiving.

In union with the Son, perfect voice of the whole universe that he created, let us too become a constant prayer before God's throne.

Monday

———— ✠ ————

Of the Second Week

Psalm 41

Like the deer that yearns
for running streams,
so my soul is yearning
for you, my God.

My soul is thirsting for God,
the God of my life;
when can I enter and see
the face of God?

My tears have become my bread,
by night, by day,
as I hear it said all the day long:
"Where is your God?"

These things will I remember
as I pour out my soul:
how I would lead the rejoicing crowd
into the house of God,

amid cries of gladness and thanksgiving,
the throng wild with joy.

Why are you cast down, my soul,
why groan within me?
Hope in God; I will praise him still,
my saviour and my God.

My soul is cast down within me
as I think of you,
from the country of Jordan and Mount Hermon,
from the Hill of Mizar.

Deep is calling on deep,
in the roar of waters:
your torrents and all your waves
swept over me.

By day the Lord will send
his loving kindness;
by night I will sing to him,
praise the God of my life.

I will say to God, my rock:
"Why have you forgotten me?
Why do I go mourning
oppressed by the foe?"

With cries that pierce me to the heart,
my enemies revile me,
saying to me all the day long:
"Where is your God?"

Why are you cast down, my soul,
why groan within me?
Hope in God; I will praise him still,
my saviour and my God.

The thirsting deer longs for streams of living water

1. A deer with a parched throat cries out its lament in an arid desert longing for the fresh waters of a flowing stream. Psalm 41 [42] that has just been sung opens with this famous image. We can see in it the symbol of the deep spirituality of this composition, a real pearl of faith and poetry.

Indeed, according to experts in the Psalter, our Psalm is closely linked with the one following, Psalm 42 [43], from which it was separated when the Psalms were put in order to form the prayer book of the People of God. In fact, in addition to being united by their topic and development, both Psalms are dramatically interrupted by the same antiphon: "Why are you cast down, O my soul, and why are you disquieted within me? Hope in God; for I shall again praise him, my help and my God" (*Ps* 41 [42],6,12; 42 [43],5). This appeal, repeated twice in our Psalm and a third time in the one that follows, is an invitation the person praying addresses to himself, with a view to banishing melancholy by trusting in God who will certainly manifest himself again as Saviour.

2. But let us return to the image at the beginning of the Psalm; it would be pleasant to meditate upon it with the musical background of Gregorian chant or with the polyphonic masterpiece of Palestrina, *Sicut cervus*. In fact, the thirsting deer is the symbol of the praying person who tends with his whole being, body and soul, towards the Lord, who seems distant and yet very much needed: "My soul thirsts for God, for the living God" (*Ps* 41 [42],3). In Hebrew a single word, *nefesh*, means both "soul" and "throat". Therefore we can say that the body and soul of the person praying are absorbed by the primary, spontaneous and substantial desire for God (cf. *Ps* 61 [62],2). It is no accident that a long tradition describes prayer as a type of "breathing": it is as primeval, necessary and basic as life-giving breathing.

Origen, the great Christian author of the third century, explained that the human search for God is a never-ending venture because progress is ever possible and necessary. In one of his homilies on the *Book of Numbers* he writes: "Those who make their journey on the road to seek God's wisdom do not build permanent homes but mobile tents, for they are in constant movement covering new ground, and the further they go, the more the road that lies ahead of them opens up, presenting a horizon lost in immensity" (*Homily XVII, In Numeros [on Numbers]* GCS VII, 159-160).

3. Let us now try to set out the basic design of this supplication. We can think of it as composed of three actions, two of them belong to our Psalm, while we find the third in the one that follows, Psalm 42 [43], to be considered later. (See p. 105-108 below) The first scene (cf. *Ps* 41 [42],2-6) expresses deep longing, kindled by the memory of a past made happy by beautiful liturgical celebrations to which the one praying no longer has access: "These things I remember, as I pour out my soul: how I went with the throng and led them in procession to the house of God, with glad shouts and songs of thanksgiving, a multitude keeping festival" (v. 5).

"The house of God" with its liturgy, is that temple of Jerusalem which the faithful person once frequented; it is also the centre of intimacy with God, "the fountain of living waters" as Jeremiah sings (2,13). Now his tears at the absence of the fountain of life are the only water that glistens in his eyes (Ps 41 [42],4). The festive prayer of former times, raised to the Lord during worship in the temple, is now replaced by weeping, lament and supplication.

4. Unfortunately, a sorrowful present is contrasted with the serene and joyful past. The Psalmist now finds himself far from Zion: the horizon all around him is that of Galilee, the northern region of the Holy Land, suggested by the reference to the sources of the Jordan, the summit of Hermon from which this river flows, and another mountain, unknown to us, Mount Mizar (cf. v. 7). Thus we are more or less in the region of the cataracts of the Jordan, the cascades that are the source of this river that flows through the entire Promised Land. However, these waters are not thirst-quenching as are those of Zion. Rather, in the eyes of the Psalmist, they are like the turbulent flood waters that devastate everything. He feels them falling upon him like a raging torrent that wipes out life: "All your waves and billows have gone over me" (v. 8). In the Bible, chaos, evil and divine judgement are portrayed by the deluge that generates destruction and death (Gn 6, 5-8; Ps 68 [69],2-3).

5. The symbolic value of this irruption is defined later on. It stands for the perverse, the adversaries of the person praying, perhaps even the pagans who dwell in this remote region to which the faithful one has been banished. They despise the righteous person and deride him for his faith, asking him ironically: "Where is your God?" (v. 11; cf. v. 14). And to God he raises his anguished question: "Why have you forgotten me?" (v. 10). The "why" addressed to the Lord, who seems absent on the day of trial, is typical of Biblical supplications.

Can God remain silent in the face of these parched lips that cry out, this tormented soul, this face that is about to be submerged in a sea of mud? Of course not! Hence once again, the person praying is encouraged to hope (cf. vv. 6, 12). The third act, found in the next Psalm 42 [43], will be a trusting invocation addressed to God (*Ps* 42 [43],1.2a.3a.4b) using words of joy and gratitude: "I will go to the altar of God, to God my joy, my delight".

―――― ✖ ――――

Canticle   Sir 36,1-7.13-16

Save us, God of all things,
strike all the nations with terror;
raise your hand against foreign nations
that they may see the greatness of your might.

Our sufferings proved your holiness to them;
let their downfall prove your glory to us.
Let them know, as we ourselves know,
that there is no other God but you.

Give us signs again, work further wonders,
clothe your hand, your right arm in glory.

Assemble all the tribes of Jacob,
as when they first received their inheritance.
Pity the poor people called by your name,
pity Israel, chosen as your first-born.

Have compassion on the holy city,
Jerusalem, the place of your rest.
Let Sion ring with your praises,
let your temple be filled with your glory.

Glimmers of hope during the exile

1. There is not just the official prayer book of the People of God in the Old Testament, namely, the Psalter. Many Biblical pages are embellished with Canticles, hymns, Psalms, supplications, prayers and invocations that rise to the Lord as a response to his Word. The Bible thus turns out to be a dialogue of God with humanity, an interaction placed under the seal of the word of God, word of grace and love.

This is the case of the supplication that we have just addressed to "the Lord God of the universe" (*Sir* 36,1). It is contained in the book of Sirach, a sage who gathered his reflections, counsels and hymns probably around 190-180 B.C. on the threshold of the epoch of liberation that Israel lived under the guidance of the Maccabees. In 138 B.C. a grandson of this sage translated into Greek, as he tells us in the prologue of the volume, the work of his grandfather in order to offer these teachings to a wider circle of readers and disciples.

The *Book of Sirach* is called "*Ecclesiasticus*" by the Christian tradition. Though it was not included in the Hebrew canon, this book, along with other "sapiential books", ended up setting forth the so-called "*Christian truth*" ("*veritas Christiana*"). Thus the values proposed by this sapiential work entered into Christian education in the Patristic age, above all, in the monastic world, becoming a manual of practical behaviour for the disciples of Christ.

2. The invocation of chapter 36 of *Sirach*, incorporated in a simplified form in the prayer of Lauds of the *Liturgy of the Hours* develops a few key themes.

Above all, we find the supplication to God to intervene in favour of Israel and against the foreign nations that oppress her. In the past God showed his holiness when he punished the sins of his people, by putting them in the hands of their enemies. Now the one praying asks God to show his greatness by undoing the power of his oppressors and establishing a new Messianic-like era.

Certainly, the request reflects the tradition of prayer in Israel, and in reality is full of Biblical references. In a certain sense, it can be considered a model of prayer to be used in time of persecution or oppression, as it was at the time the author lived, under the rather harsh and severe dominion of the foreign Syro-Hellenic sovereigns.

3. The first part of this prayer opens with an ardent appeal to the Lord that he may have mercy and pay attention to what is happening (cf. *Sir* 36,1). But immediately attention is directed to the divine action, that is exalted by a series of remarkable verbs: "Have mercy ... pay attention ... put in dread ... raise your hand ... show yourself great ... renew your signs ... work new wonders ... glorify your hand and your right arm...".

The God of the Bible is not indifferent in the face of evil. Even if his ways are not our ways, and his times and plans are different from ours (cf. *Is* 55,8-9), yet he takes sides with the victims and will be a severe judge of the violent, the oppressor, those who triumph without showing mercy.

His intervention does not seek destruction. By showing his power and the faithfulness of his love, he can generate even in the conscience of the evil one a shudder that can lead to his conversion. "They will know, as we know, that there is no God but you, O Lord" (*Sir* 36,4).

4. The second part of the hymn opens with a more positive perspective. In fact, while the first part asks for the intervention of God against one's enemies, the second part no longer speaks of enemies, but asks the favour of God for Israel, begs his mercy for the Chosen People and for the holy city, Jerusalem.

The dream of the return of those sent into exile, even those belonging to the Northern kingdom, became the goal of the prayer: "Gather all the tribes of Jacob, that they may inherit the land as of old" (v. 10). The prayer is for the rebirth of the entire Israel, as in the happy days of the occupation of the whole of the Promised Land.

In order to make the prayer more urgent, the one praying insists on the relation that binds God to Israel and Jerusalem. Israel is designated "the people called by *your* name", those "whom you *have* treated as your firstborn"; Jerusalem is "*your* holy city", "*your* dwelling place". It then expresses the desire that the relation become still closer and more glorious: "Fill Zion with your majesty, *your* people with your glory" (cf. v. 13). By filling with his majesty the temple of Jerusalem, that will attract all nations to itself (cf. *Is* 2,2-4; *Mi* 4,1-3), the Lord will fill his people with his glory.

5. In the Bible, the lament of those who suffer never ends in desperation, but is always open to hope. It is based on the certainty that the Lord does not abandon his children, he does not let those he made fall out of his hands.

The selection made by the liturgy has left out a very beautiful expression in the prayer. It asks God to "give evidence to the creatures that are yours from the beginning" (*Sir* 36,14). From all eternity God has a plan of love and salvation for all his creatures, called to become his people. It is a plan that St Paul recognized as "revealed to his holy apostles and Prophets by the Spirit ... the eternal purpose that he accomplished in Christ Jesus our Lord" (*Eph* 3,5-11).

Psalm 18

The heavens proclaim the glory of God
and the firmament shows forth the work of his hands.
Day unto day takes up the story
and night unto night makes known the message.

No speech, no word, no voice is heard
yet their span extends through all the earth,
their words to the utmost bounds of the world.

There he has placed a tent for the sun;
it comes forth like a bridegroom coming from his tent,
rejoices like a champion to run its course.

At the end of the sky is the rising of the sun;
to the furthest end of the sky is its course.
There is nothing concealed from its burning heat.

God the creator creates the brilliance of the sun

1. The sun, with its increasing brilliance in the heavens, the splendour of its light, the beneficial warmth of its rays, has captivated humanity from the outset. In many ways human beings have shown their gratitude for this source of life and well-being, with an enthusiasm that often reaches the peaks of true poetry. The wonderful Psalm, 18 [19], whose first part has just been proclaimed, is not only a prayerful hymn of extraordinary intensity; it is also a poetic song addessed to the sun and its radiance on the face of the earth. In this way the Psalmist joins the long series of bards of the ancient Near East, who exalted the day star that shines in the heavens, and which in their regions dominates with its burning heat. It reminds us of the famous hymn to Aton, composed by the Pharoah Akhnaton in the 14th century BC and dedicated to the solar disc regarded as a deity.

But, for the man of the Bible, there is a radical difference in regard to these hymns to the sun: the sun is not a god but a creature at the service of the one God and Creator. It is enough to think of the words of Genesis: "God said, 'Let there be lights in the firmament of the heavens to separate the day from the night; and let them be for signs and for seasons and for days and years....' God made the two great lights, the greater light to rule the day, and the lesser light to rule the night.... And God saw that it it was good" (*Gn* 1, 14,16,18).

2. Before examining the verses of the Psalm chosen by the liturgy, let us take a look at it as a whole. Psalm 18 [19] is like a diptych: in the first part (vv. 2-7) - that has today become our prayer - we find a hymn to the Creator, whose mysterious greatness is manifest in the sun and in the moon. In the second part of the Psalm (vv. 8-15), instead, we find a sapiential hymn to the *Torah*, the Law of God.

A common theme runs through both parts: God lights the world with the brilliance of the sun and illuminates humanity with the splendour of his word contained in biblical Revelation. It is almost like a double sun: the first is a cosmic epiphany of the Creator; the second is a free and historical manifestation of God our Saviour. It is not by chance that the Torah, the divine Word, is described with "solar" features: "The commandment of the Lord is pure, enlightening the eyes" (v. 9).

3. But let us now examine the first part of the Psalm. It begins with a wonderful personification of the heavens, that to the sacred author appear as eloquent witnesses to the creative work of God (vv. 2-5). Indeed, they "narrate", or "proclaim" the marvels of the divine work (cf. v. 2). Day and night are also portrayed as messengers that transmit the great news of creation. Their witness is a silent one, but makes itself forcefully felt, like a voice that resounds throughout the cosmos.

With the interior gaze of the soul, men and women can discover that the world is not dumb but speaks of the Creator when their interior spiritual vision, their religious intuition, is not taken up with superficiality. As the ancient sage says: "from the greatness and beauty of created things their original author is seen by analogy" (*Wis* 13,5). St Paul too, reminds the Romans that "ever since the creation of the world, his (God's) invisible perfections can be perceived with the intellect in the works that have been made by him" (*Rom* 1,20).

4. The hymn then yields place to the sun. The shining globe is depicted by the inspired poet as a warrior hero who emerges from the marital chamber where he spent the night, that is, he comes forth from the heart of darkness and begins his unwearying course through the heavens (vv. 6-7). The sun is compared to an athlete, who does not know rest or fatigue, while our entire planet is enveloped in its irresistible warmth.

So the sun is compared to a bridegroom, a hero, a champion, who, by divine command, must perform a daily task, a conquest and a race in the starry spaces. And here the Psalmist points to the sun, blazing in the open sky, while the whole earth is wrapped in its heat, the air is still, no point of the horizon can escape its light.

5. The solar imagery of the Psalm is taken up by the Christian liturgy of Easter to describe Christ's triumphant exodus from the dark tomb and his entry into the fullness of the new life of the Resurrection. At Matins for Holy Saturday, the Byzantine liturgy sings: "As the sun rises after the night in the dazzling brightness of renewed light, so you also, O Word, will shine with new brightness, when after death, you leave your nuptial bed". An Ode (the first) for Matins of Easter links the cosmic revelation with the Easter event of Christ: "Let the heavens rejoice and the earth exult with them because the whole universe, visible and invisible, takes part in the feast: Christ, our everlasting joy, is risen". And another Ode (the third) adds: "Today the whole universe, heaven, earth, and abyss, is full of light and the entire creation sings the resurrection of Christ our strength and our joy". Finally, another (the fourth), concludes: "Christ our Passover is risen from the tomb like a sun of justice shining upon all of us with the splendour of his charity".

The Roman liturgy is not as explicit as the Eastern in comparing Christ to the sun. Yet it describes the cosmic repercussions of his Resurrection, when it begins the chant of Lauds on Easter morning with the famous hymn: "*Aurora lucis rutilat, caelum resultat laudibus, mundus exultans iubilat, gemens infernus ululat*" - "The dawn has spread her crimson rays, And heaven rings with shouts of praise; The glad earth shouts her triumph high, And groaning hell makes wild reply".

6. The Christian interpretation of the Psalm, however, does not invalidate its basic message, that is an invitation to discover the divine word present in creation. Of course, as stated in the second half of the Psalm, there is another and more exalted Word, more precious than light itself, that of biblical Revelation.

Anyway, for those who have attentive ears and open eyes, creation is like a first revelation that has its own eloquent language: it is almost another sacred book whose letters are represented by the multitude of created things present in the universe. St John Chrysostom says: "The silence of the heavens is a voice that resounds louder than a trumpet blast: this voice cries out to our eyes and not to our ears, the greatness of Him who made them" (*PG* 49, 105). And St Athanasius says: "The firmament with its magnificence, its beauty, its order, is an admirable preacher of its Maker, whose eloquence fills the universe" (*PG* 27, 124).

Tuesday

Of the Second Week

Psalm 42

Defend me, O God, and plead my cause
against a godless nation.
From deceitful and cunning men
rescue me, O God.

Since you, O God, are my stronghold,
why have you rejected me?
Why do I go mourning
oppressed by the foe?

O send forth your light and your truth;
let these be my guide.
Let them bring me to your holy mountain
to the place where you dwell.

And I will come to the altar of God,
the God of my joy.

My redeemer, I will thank you on the harp,
O God, my God.

Why are you cast down, my soul,
why groan within me?
Hope in God; I will praise him still,
my saviour and my God.

With confidence on road toward the heavenly 'Zion'

1. In a General Audience sometime ago, commenting on the Psalm
that precedes the one we have just heard, we said that it was closely
related to the following one. (See p. 97 above) In fact, Psalms 41 [42]
and 42 [43] form one song, divided into three parts by the same
antiphon: "Why are you cast down, O my soul? Why do you groan
within me? Hope in God; for I shall praise him again, the saviour of
my countenace and my God" (*Ps* 41 [42],6.12; 42 [43],5).

These words, that have the form of a soliloquy, lay bare the
Psalmist's innermost sentiments. He was far from Zion, point of
reference of his existence, because it is the privileged place of the
divine presence and of the faithful's worship. Because of this he feels
the loneliness caused by misunderstanding and even by aggression on
the part of the impious, aggravated by his isolation and silence on the
part of God. However, the Psalmist reacts against sadness with an
appeal to confidence, that he directs to himself and with a beautiful
assertion of hope: he is confident that he will still praise God "the
salvation of my countenance".

In Psalm 42 [43], instead of speaking only to himself as in the
previous Psalm, the Psalmist turns to God and entreats him to defend
him against his adversaries. Taking up, almost literally, an invocation
announced in the other Psalm (cf. 41 [42],10), the praying person this
time effectively addresses his desolate cry to God "Why then do you
spurn me? Why must I go about in sadness, with the enemy
oppressing me?" (*Ps* 42 [43],2).

2. Yet he feels at this point that the the dark period of distance is
about to end, and expresses the certainty of his return to Zion to find
again the divine dwelling. The Holy City is no longer the lost
homeland as it was in the case of the lament of the previous Psalm

(cf. 41 [42],3-4), instead, it is the joyful goal toward which he is moving. The guide of his return to Zion will be the "truth" of God and his "light" (cf. *Ps* 42 [43],3). The Lord himself will be the final destination of the journey, he is invoked as judge and defender (cf.vv. 1-2). Three verbs mark his implored intervention: "Grant me justice", "defend my cause", "rescue me" (v. 1). They are like three stars of hope that burn in the dark skies of the trial, that point to the imminent dawn of salvation.

St Ambrose's reading of the Psalmist's experience is significant, applying it to Jesus praying at Gethsemane: "You should not be surprised that the Prophet says that his soul was shaken, for the Lord Jesus himself said: *'Now my soul is troubled'*. In fact, he has taken our weaknesses upon himself, even our sensibility, and this was why he was saddened even unto death, but not because of death. A voluntary death, on which the happiness of all mankind depended, could not have caused sadness.... So he was saddened unto death, while waiting for the grace to be carried to fulfilment. This is reflected in his own witness when he says of his death: *"I have a baptism to be baptized with; and how I am in anguish until it is accomplished!"* (*Le rimonstranze di Giobbe e di Davide*, Rome 1980, VII, 28, p. 233, *The Remonstrances of Job and David*).

3. Now, continuing with Psalm 42 [43], the solution he longs for is about to open before the eyes of the Psalmist: his return to the fountain of life and communion with God. "Truth", that is the loving fidelity of the Lord, and the "light", that is the revelation of his goodness, are represented as messengers that God himself will send from heaven to take the faithful one by the hand and lead him to the desired goal (cf. *Ps* 42 [43],3).

Very eloquent is the sequence of stages of his drawing closer to Zion and its spiritual centre. First appears the holy hill on which stand the temple and citadel of David. Then the "dwellings" appear on the scene, the sanctuary of Zion with all the different spaces and buildings that make it up. Then "the altar of God", the place of sacrifice and of the official worship of the whole people. The last and decisive goal is the God of joy; his embrace, the intimate encounter with him who at first was distant and silent.

4. At this point everything becomes song, joy and celebration (cf. v. 4). The original Hebrew speaks of "God who is the joy of my jubilation". This is a Semitic form of speech that expresses the superlative: the Psalmist wants to stress that the Lord is the source of all happiness, he is supreme joy, he is the fullness of peace. The Greek translation of the Septuagint had recourse, it seems, to an equivalent Aramaic term that means "youth", and translated it "to God the joy of my youth", thus introducing the idea of the freshness and intensity of joy that the Lord gives. Thus the Latin Psalter of the Vulgate, a translation made from the Greek, says: *"ad Deum qui laetificat juventutem meam"* (To God who gives joy to my youth). In this form the Psalm was recited at the foot of the altar, in the preceding Eucharistic liturgy, as an introductory invocation to the encounter with the Lord.

5. The initial lament of the antiphon of Psalms 41 [42]-42 [43] resounds for the last time at the end (cf. *Ps* 42 [43],5). The person praying has not yet reached the temple of God, he is still overwhelmed by the darkness of the trial; but now before his eyes shines the light of the future encounter, and his lips already experience the tone of the song of joy. At this point, the appeal is largely characterized by hope. In commenting on our Psalm St Augustine in fact observes: *"Hope in God*, he will respond to him whose soul disquiets him.... Meanwhile live in hope: for 'hope that is seen is not hope; but if we hope for that which we cannot see, it is thanks to patience that we wait for it' (cf. *Rom* 8,24-25)" (*Esposizioni sui Salmi, I*, Rome 1982, p. 1019 [*Expositions on the Psalms, I*]).

The Psalm then becomes the prayer of the one who is a pilgrim on earth and still finds himself in contact with evil and suffering, but has the certainty that the endpoint of history is not an abyss of death, but rather a saving encounter with God. This certainty is even stronger for Christians, to whom the Letter to the Hebrews proclaims: "You have come to Mount Zion and to the city of the living God, the heavenly Jerusalem, and to countless angels in festal gathering, and to the assembly of the first-born who are enrolled in heaven, and to God the judge of all, and to the spirits of the just made perfect, and to Jesus, the mediator of a new covenant, and to the sprinkled blood that speaks more eloquently than that of Abel" (*Heb* 12,22-24).

Canticle   Is 38,10-14.17-20

I said: In the noontide of my days I must depart;
I am consigned to the gates of Sheol
for the rest of my years.

I said, I shall not see the Lord
in the land of the living;
I shall look upon man no more
among the inhabitants of the world.

My dwelling is plucked up and removed from me
like a shepherd's tent;
like a weaver I have rolled up my life;
he cuts me off from the loom.

From day to night you bring me to an end;
I cry for help until morning;
like a lion he breaks all my bones;
from day to night you bring me to an end.

Like a swallow or a crane I clamour,
I moan like a dove.
My eyes are weary with looking upward.
O Lord, I am oppressed; be my security.

Lo, it was for my welfare
that I had great bitterness;
but you have held back my life
from the pit of destruction,
for you have cast all my sins
behind your back.

For Sheol cannot thank you,
death cannot praise you;
those who go down to the pit
cannot hope for your faithfulness.

The living, the living, he thanks you,
as I do this day;
the father makes known to the children your faithfulness.

The Lord will save me,
and we will sing to stringed instruments
all the days of our life,
at the house of the Lord.

Canticle of thanksgiving after nightmare of illness

1. In the various Canticles that it combines with the Psalms, the *Liturgy of the Hours* offers us a hymn of thanksgiving with the title: "The Canticle of Hezekiah, King of Judah, after he had been sick and recovered from his sickness" (*Is* 38,9). It is found in a section of the book of the Prophet Isaiah that is given to historical narratives (cf. *Is* 36-39), whose histories repeat, with few variants, those presented in the *Second Book of Kings* (cf. chapters 18-20).

Following the *Liturgy of Lauds*, today we have heard and used for our prayer two strophes of the Canticle that describe the two typical movements of the prayer of thanksgiving: first, one evokes the nightmare of suffering from which the Lord has freed his faithful one, and second, one joyfully sings in thanksgiving for the recovery of life and salvation.

King Hezekiah, a just ruler and friend of the Prophet Isaiah, was struck down by a serious illness, said by the Prophet Isaiah to be mortal (*Is* 38,1). "Then Hezekiah turned his face to the wall and prayed to the Lord, and said 'Remember Lord I beseech you, how I have walked before you in faithfulness and with a whole heart, and have done what is good in your sight'. Hezekiah wept bitterly. Then the word of the Lord came to Isaiah: 'Go and say to Hezekiah, Thus says the Lord, the God of David your father: I have heard your prayer and have seen your tears; behold I will add fifteen years to your life!'"(*Is* 38,2-5).

2. At this point the Canticle of thanksgiving bursts from the heart of the king. As I said earlier, he first looks to the past. According to the ancient conception of Israel, death introduced one into a subterranean existence, in Hebrew *Sheol*, where light was put out, life faded away and became almost ghostlike, time came to a halt, hope was extinguished, and above all there was no longer any possibility of calling upon God and meeting him in worship.

This is why Hezekiah recalled first of all the words full of bitterness that he spoke when his life was sliding towards the frontier of death: "I shall not see the Lord in the land of the living" (v. 11). The Psalmist also prayed this way on the day of his sickness: "No one among the dead remembers you, O Lord. Who sings your praises in Sheol?" (*Ps* 6,6). Instead, freed from the danger of death, Hezekiah could confirm forcefully and joyfully: "The living, the living, give you thanks as I do this day" (*Is* 38,19).

3. On this subject, the Canticle of Hezekiah takes a new tone, if read in the light of Easter. Already in the Old Testament, great flashes of light were reflected in the Psalms, when the one praying proclaimed his certainty that "you will not abandon me to Sheol, nor let your faithful one see corruption. You will show me the path of life, fullness of joy in your presence, at your right hand rejoicing without end" (Ps 15 [16], 10-11; cf. *Ps* 48 [49] and 72 [73]). For his part, the author of the *Book of Wisdom* no longer hesitates to affirm that the hope of the righteous is "full of immortality" (*Wis* 3,4), because he is convinced that the experience of communion with God lived during the earthly life will not be broken. We will remain always beyond death, sustained and protected by the eternal and infinite God, because the "souls of the just are in the hand of God, and no torment shall touch them" (*Wis* 3,1).

Above all, with the death and resurrection of Jesus Christ, the Son of God, a seed of eternity was planted and made grow in our mortal perishability, which is why we can repeat the words of the Apostle, based on the Old Testament: "And when that which is corruptible clothes itself with incorruptibility and that which is mortal clothes itself with immortality, then the word that is written shall come about: "Death is swallowed up in victory. Where, O death, is your victory? Where, O death, is your sting?' " (*1 Cor* 15,54-55; cf. *Is* 25,8; *Hos* 13,14).

4. However, the Canticle of King Hezekiah also invites us to reflect on the fragility of the creature. The images are thought-provoking. Human life is described with the nomadic symbol of the tent: we are always pilgrims and guests on earth. It also refers to images of cloth, that is woven and can remain incomplete when the thread is cut and the work is interrupted (cf. *Is* 38,12). The Psalmist feels the same sensation: "You have given my days a very short span; my life is as nothing before you. All mortals are but a breath. Mere shadows, we go our way; mere vapour our restless pursuits" (*Ps* 38 [39],6-7). We should recover an awareness of our limitations, knowing that "seventy is the sum of our years, or eighty, if we are strong; most of them are sorrow or toil; they pass quickly, we are all but gone", as the Psalmist says again (*Ps* 89 [90],10).

5. Therefore, in the day of sickness and suffering, it is right to raise one's lament to God, as Hezekiah teaches us; using poetic images, he describes his weeping as the chirping of a swallow and the moaning of a dove (cf. *Is* 38,124). And, even if he doesn't hesitate to admit that he feels that God is an adversary, almost like a lion that breaks all his bones (cf.v.13), he does not cease to invoke him: "O Lord, I am in straits; be my surety!" (v. 14).

The Lord is not indifferent to the tears of the one who suffers, and he responds, consoles and saves, although not always in ways that coincide with what we expect. It is what Hezekiah confesses at the end, encouraging all to hope, to pray, to have confidence, with the certainty that God will not abandon his creatures: "The Lord is our saviour; we shall sing to stringed instruments in the house of the Lord all the days of our life" (v.20).

6. The medieval Latin tradition conserves a spiritual commentary on the Canticle of King Hezekiah by one of the most important mystics of Western monasticism, St Bernard of Clairvaux. It is the third of his *Various Sermons*. In it, Bernard, applying to the life of each one the drama lived by the ruler of Judah, and internalizing his experience, writes: "*I will bless the Lord at all times*, namely from morning until evening, as I have learned to do, and not like those *who only praise you when you do good to them*, nor like those who *believe for a certain time, but in the hour of temptation give way*; but with the saints I will say: *If we received good things from the hand of God, should we not also accept evil things?* ... Thus both these moments of the day will be a time of service to God, because at night there will be weeping, and in the morning, joy. I will submerge myself in suffering at night so that I can then enjoy the happiness of the morning" (*Scriptorium Claravallense, Sermo III*, n. 6, Milan 2000, pp. 59-60).

Thus, St Bernard reads the prayer of the king as representing the prayerful song of the Christian that should have the same constancy and serenity in the darkness of the night and of trial, and in the light of day and of joy.

Psalm 64

To you our praise is due
in Sion, O God.
To you we pay our vows,
you who hear our prayer.

To you all flesh will come
with its burden of sin.
Too heavy for us, our offences,
but you wipe them away.

Blessed is he whom you choose and call
to dwell in your courts.
We are filled with the blessings of your house,
of your holy temple.

You keep your pledge with wonders,
O God our saviour,
the hope of all the earth
and of far distant isles.

You uphold the mountains with your strength,
you are girded with power.
You still the roaring of the seas,
the roaring of their waves
and the tumult of the peoples.

The ends of the earth stand in awe
at the sight of your wonders.
The lands of sunrise and sunset
you fill with your joy.

You care for the earth, give it water,
you fill it with riches.
Your river in heaven brims over
to provide its grain.

And thus you provide for the earth;
you drench its furrows,
you level it, soften it with showers,
you bless its growth.

You crown the year with your goodness.
Abundance flows in your steps,
in the pastures of the wilderness it flows.

The hills are girded with joy,
the meadows covered with flocks,
the valleys are decked with wheat.
They shout for joy, yes, they sing.

To you all flesh shall come with its burden of sin

1. Our journey through the *Psalms of the Liturgy of Lauds* leads us
now to a hymn that captivates us with the fascinating spring scene of
the last part (cf. *Ps* 64 [65],10-14), a scene full of freshness, ablaze with
colours and pervaded by joyful voices.

In fact Psalm 64 [65] has a broader structure, the result of the
interlacing of two different tones: first, the historical theme of the
forgiveness of sins and God's closeness emerges (cf. vv. 2-5), then
the cosmic subject of God's action in the confrontation of seas and
mountains (cf. vv. 6-9a); lastly, the description of spring is developed
(cf. vv. 9b-14): in the sun-baked, arid panorama of the Middle East,
the rain that brings fruitfulness expresses the Lord's fidelity toward
creation (cf. *Ps* 103 [104],13-16). For the Bible, creation is the home
of humanity and sin an attack on the order and perfection of the
world. Thus conversion and forgiveness restore integrity and
harmony to the cosmos.

2. In the first part of the Psalm we are inside the temple of Zion.
Burdened by the moral miseries they have accumulated, the people
flock there to pray for deliverance from evil (cf. *Ps* 64 [65],2-4a). Once
they have obtained absolution from their sins, the faithful feel
welcomed by God, close to him, ready to be led to his banquet, and
to take part in the feast of divine intimacy (cf. vv. 4b-5).

The Lord who rises in the temple is then represented with a
glorious, cosmic profile. Indeed, he is called "the hope of all the ends
of the earth, and of the farthest seas ... who by [his] strength has
established the mountains ... girded with might ... stills the roaring of
the seas, the roaring of their waves and the tumult of the peoples, so
that those who dwell at farthest bounds of the earth are afraid at [his]
signs", from east to west (vv. 6-9).

3. At the heart of this celebration of God the Creator, we would like to highlight one event: the Lord is also able to dominate and silence the tumult of the ocean waters, which in the Bible are the symbol of chaos, opposed to the order of creation (cf. *Jb* 38,8-11). This is a way of exalting the divine victory, not only over nothingness, but also over evil: this is why the "tumult of the peoples" (cf. *Ps* 64 [65],8), that is, the rebellion of the proud is also associated with the motif of the "roaring of the seas" and the "roaring of their waves".

St Augustine comments aptly: "The sea is the figure of this world, bitter with saltiness, troubled by storms, where men and women with their perverse and depraved appetites have become like fish devouring one another at will. Look at this tempestuous sea, the bitter sea with its cruel waves!... Let us not behave like this, brothers, for the Lord is *the hope of all the ends of the earth*" (*Esposizione sui Salmi [Exposition on the Psalms] II*, Rome 1990, p. 475).

The conclusion the Psalm suggests is an easy one: God, who imposes order on chaos and puts an end to the evil in the world and in history, can overcome and forgive the malice and sin that the praying person bears within and presents in the temple with the certainty of divine purification.

4. At this point, the other waters enter the scene: the waters of life and fruitfulness that in spring drench the earth and spiritually represent the new life of the faithful who have been pardoned. The last verses of the Psalm (cf. *Ps* 64 [65],10-14), as has been said, are of great beauty and meaning.

God quenches the thirst of the earth parched by drought and by the winter ice, by showering it with rain. The Lord is like a farmer (cf. *Jn* 15,1) who with his labour makes the wheat grow and the grass spring up. He prepares the ground, he irrigates the furrows, he breaks up the clods, and waters every part of his field.

The Psalmist uses 10 verbs to describe the loving action of the Creator for the earth, transformed into a kind of living creature. Indeed, all its parts "shout and sing together for joy" (*Ps* 64 [65],14).

The three verbs connected with the symbol of clothing are thought-provoking in this regard: "The hills gird themselves with joy, the meadows clothe themselves with flocks, the valleys deck themselves with grain" (vv. 13-14). The image is one of a meadow specked with the white of the sheep; perhaps the hills are girded with vines, a sign of their product, wine, "to gladden the heart of man" (*Ps* 103 [104],15); the valleys put on the golden mantle of the harvests. Verse 12 also recalls the crowns, perhaps reminiscent of the garlands set upon the heads of the guests at festive banquets (cf. *Is* 28,1.5).

5. As though in a sort of procession all the creatures together turn to their Creator and Sovereign, dancing and singing, praising and praying. Once again nature becomes an eloquent sign of divine action; it is a page, open to all, ready to express the message the Creator has written on it, so that "from the greatness and beauty of created things their original author by analogy is perceived" (*Wis* 13,5; cf. *Rom* 1,20). In this lyric, theological contemplation and poetic abandon blend to become adoration and praise.

However, the most intense meeting which the Psalmist looks forward to throughout his song is that which unites creation and redemption. Just as in springtime the earth revives once again through the action of the Creator, so man rises from his sin through the action of the Redeemer. Creation and history thus are under the provident, saving gaze of the Lord, who calms the tumultuous and destructive waters and gives water that purifies, fertilizes, and quenches thirst. The Lord, in fact, "heals the broken hearted and binds up their wounds", but also "covers the heavens with clouds, prepares rain for the earth, makes grass grow on the mountains" (*Ps* 146 [147],3.8).

Thus the Psalm becomes a hymn to divine grace. Once again, St Augustine in commenting on our Psalm recalls this transcendent, unique gift: "The Lord God is telling you in your heart: I am your treasure. Do not go after what the world promises, but after what the Creator of the world promises! Pay attention to what God promises you, if you observe justice; and despise what man promises, to lure you away from righteousness. Do not go after what the world promises you! Rather, consider what the Creator of the world promises" (*l.c.*, p. 481).

Wednesday

——— ✼ ———

Of the Second Week

Psalm 76

I cry aloud to God,
cry aloud to God that he may hear me.

In the day of my distress I sought the Lord.
My hands were raised at night without ceasing;
my soul refused to be consoled.
I remembered my God and I groaned.
I pondered and my spirit fainted.

You withheld sleep from my eyes.
I was troubled, I could not speak.
I thought of the days of long ago
and remembered the years long past.
At night I mused within my heart.
I pondered and my spirit questioned.

'Will the Lord reject us for ever?
Will he show us his favour no more?
Has his love vanished for ever?
Has his promise come to an end?
Does God forget his mercy
or in anger withhold his compassion?'

I said: 'This is what causes my grief;
that the way of the Most High has changed.'
I remember the deeds of the Lord,
I remember your wonders of old,
I muse on all your works
and ponder your mighty deeds.

Your ways, O God, are holy.
What god is great as our God?
You are the God who works wonders.
You showed your power among the peoples.
Your strong arm redeemed your people,
the sons of Jacob and Joseph.

The waters saw you, O God,
the waters saw you and trembled;
the depths were moved with terror.
The clouds poured down rain,
the skies sent forth their voice;
your arrows flashed to and fro.

Your thunder rolled round the sky,
your flashes lighted up the world.
The earth was moved and trembled
when your way led through the sea,
your path through the mighty waters
and no one saw your footprints.

You guided your people like a flock
by the hand of Moses and Aaron.

God renews the saving wonders of his love

1. By including Psalm 76 [77] that we have just proclaimed in the morning Lauds, the liturgy wants to remind us that the beginning of a new day is not always bright. Just as dark days dawn when the sky is covered with clouds threatening a storm, so our life knows days that are filled with sorrows and fears. This is why already at daybreak our prayer becomes a lament, a supplication, a plea for help.

Our Psalm is precisely a plea that rises to God with insistence, deeply motivated by trust, indeed, by the certainty that he will intervene. In fact, for the Psalmist the Lord is not an impassive emperor relegated to his shining heavens and indifferent to our affairs. From this impression that sometimes grips us arise questions so bitter that could bring about a crisis of faith: "Is God denying his love and his election? Has he forgotten the past when he sustained us and made us happy?". As we will see, such questions are swept away by renewed trust in God, our Redeemer and our Saviour.

2. So let us follow the way this prayer develops as it begins in a dramatic tone, in anguish, and then gradually opens to serenity and hope. First of all, we have before us the lamentation on the sad present and the silence of God (cf. vv. 2-11). A cry for help is raised to a seemingly mute heaven, imploring hands are lifted, the heart misses a beat through sorrow. In the sleepless night of tears and prayers, a song "returns to the heart", as is said in verse 7, a sorrowful refrain continually re-echoes in the depths of the soul.

When pain reaches its limit and one wishes that the cup of suffering be removed (cf. *Mt* 26,39), words explode and become an agonizing question, as we said earlier (cf. *Ps* 76 [77],8-11). This loud cry questions the mystery of God and of his silence.

3. The Psalmist wonders why the Lord is ever rejecting him, why he has changed his appearance and action, forgetting his love, his promise of salvation and his tender mercy. "The right hand of the Most High" that accomplished the saving wonders of the Exodus, now seems paralyzed (cf. v. 11). It is a real "torment" that brings into crisis the faith of the person praying.

Were this true, God would be unrecognizable, he would become a cruel being or a presence like that of idols that cannot save because they are incapable of it, indifferent and powerless. These verses of the first part of Psalm 76 [77] contain the whole drama of faith in the time of trial and of God's silence.

4. But there are reasons for hope. This is what emerges from the second part of the plea (cf. vv. 12-21), similar to a hymn that is intended to propose again the courageous confirmation of faith, even on the dark day of pain. The Psalmist sings of the salvation of the past, that had its epiphany of light in the creation and in the liberation from the slavery of Egypt. The bitter present is illuminated by the saving experience of the past, a seed sown in history: it is not dead but only buried, and will spring up again (cf. *Jn* 12,24).

The Psalmist then has recourse to an important biblical concept, that of the "memorial" which is not merely a vague, consoling memory, but the certainty of divine action that is unfailing: "I will call to mind the deeds of the Lord; yes, your wonders of old I will remember" (Ps 76 [77],12). To profess faith in the works of salvation of the past leads to faith in what the Lord is constantly doing, hence also in the present: "Your way, O God, is holy.... You are the God who works wonders" (vv. 14-15). Thus the present that seemed without a way out and without light, is illuminated by faith in God and open to hope.

5. To sustain this faith the Psalmist cites what is probably a more ancient hymn, perhaps chanted in the liturgy of the Temple of Zion (cf. vv. 17-20). It is a deafening theophany in which the Lord bursts into the scene of history, overwhelming nature and in particular, the waters, a symbol of chaos, evil and suffering. Very beautiful is the image of God's path on the waters, sign of his triumph over negative forces: "Your way was through the sea, your path through the great waters, yet your footprints were unseen" (v. 20). And we are reminded of Christ walking on the waters, an eloquent symbol of his victory over evil (cf. *Jn* 6,16-20).

Recalling at the end that God guided his people "like a flock by the hand of Moses and Aaron" (*Ps* 76 [77],21), the Psalm leads implicitly to a certainty: God will return to lead us to salvation. His powerful and invisible hand will be with us through the visible hand of the pastors and guides he has established. The Psalm, that begins with a cry of distress, ends by awakening sentiments of faith and hope in the great shepherd of our souls (cf. *Heb* 13,20; *1 Pt* 2,25).

———— ✖ ————

Canticle   1 Sam 2,1-10

My heart exults in the Lord,
I find my strength in my God;
my mouth laughs at my enemies
as I rejoice in your saving help.
There is none like the Lord,
there is none besides you.
There is no Rock like our God.

Bring your haughty words to an end,
let no boasts fall from your lips,
for the Lord is a God who knows all.
It is he who weighs men's deeds.

The bows of the mighty are broken,
but the weak are clothed with strength.
Those with plenty must labour for bread,
but the hungry need work no more.

The childless wife has children now
but the fruitful wife bears no more.

It is the Lord who gives life and death,
he brings men to the grave and back;
it is the Lord who gives poverty and riches.
He brings men low and raises them on high.

He lifts up the lowly from the dust,
from the ash heap he raises the poor
to set him in the company of princes,
to give him a glorious throne.

For the pillars of the earth are the Lord's,
on them he has set the world.
He guards the steps of his faithful,
but the wicked perish in darkness,
for no man's power gives him victory.
The enemies of the Lord shall be broken.

The Most High will thunder in the heavens,
the Lord will judge the ends of the earth.
He will give power to his king
and exalt the might of his anointed.

The humble hope in God and rejoice in him

1. The voice of a woman leads us today in the prayer of praise to the Lord of life. In fact, in the story of the *First Book of Samuel*, it is Anna who sings the hymn we have just proclaimed, after offering her child, the little Samuel to the Lord. He was to be a prophet in Israel and his action was to mark the transition of the Hebrew people to a new form of government, monarchy, in which the unfortunate King Saul and the glorious King David would play the lead. Anna had a history of suffering in her past, for, as the story says, the Lord "had closed her womb" (*1 Sam* 1,5).

In ancient Israel, a barren woman was considered as a withered branch, a dead presence, in part because she prevented her husband from having continuity in the memory of the generations to follow, an important factor in what was a hazy and uncertain vision of the hereafter.

2. But Anna had put her trust in the God of life and prayed: "O Lord of hosts, if you will indeed look on the affliction of your maidservant and remember me and not forget your maidservant, but will give your maidservant a son, then I will give him to the Lord all the days of his life" (*1 Sam* 1,11). And God heard the cry of this humiliated woman and gave her Samuel: a living shoot that sprang from the dry trunk (cf. *Is* 11,1); what had been impossible in human eyes had become a tangible reality in that child who was to be consecrated to the Lord.

The hymn of thanksgiving that sprang from the lips of the mother was to be taken up and expressed anew by another Mother, Mary, who while remaining a virgin conceived by the power of the Spirit of God. In fact, in the *Magnificat* of the Mother of Jesus we can perceive an echo of Anna's Canticle which for this reason is known as "the *Magnificat* of the Old Testament".

3. In fact, scholars note that the sacred author has placed on Anna's lips a sort of royal Psalm laced with citations or allusions to other Psalms.

In the foreground, the image of the Hebrew king emerges, assailed by more powerful adversaries, but who in the end is saved and triumphs because the Lord who is at his side breaks the bows of the mighty (cf. *1 Sam* 2,4). The finale of the Canticle is significant, in which the Lord enters the scene in a solemn epiphany: "The adversaries of the Lord shall be broken to pieces; against them he will thunder in heaven. The Lord will judge the ends of the earth; he will give strength to his king, and exalt the power of his anointed" (v. 10). In Hebrew the last word is precisely "messiah", meaning "anointed one", which enables us to transform this royal prayer into a song of messianic hope.

4. We wish to underline in this hymn of thanksgiving two themes that express Anna's feelings. The first will also be dominant in Mary's *Magnificat*: it is the reversal of destinies that God brings about. The bows of the mighty are broken but the feeble "gird on strength". Those who were full have hired themselves out for bread, but those who were hungry sit at a sumptuous banquet with princes; the poor are raised up from the dust and given "a seat of honour" (cf. vv. 4.8).

In this ancient prayer it is easy to follow the thread of the seven actions that Mary sees accomplished in the history of God the Saviour:

"He has shown strength with his arm, he has scattered the proud in the imagination of their hearts, he has put down the mighty from their thrones, and exalted those of low degree; he has filled the hungry with good things, and the rich he has sent empty away. He has helped his servant Israel ..." (*Lk* 1,51-54).

This is a profession of faith spoken by both mothers before the Lord of history, who arrays himself to defend the least, the poor and the suffering, the offended and humiliated.

5. The other theme we would like to highlight is connected even more closely with Anna: "The barren has born seven, but she who has many children is forlorn" (*1 Sam* 2,5). The Lord who reverses destinies is also at the root of life and of death. Anna's sterile womb was like a tomb; yet God was able to make it bring forth life, because "in his hand is the life of every living thing and the breath of all mankind" (*Jb* 12,10). Immediately after, in this connection, Anna sings: "The Lord kills and brings to life, he brings down to Sheol and raises up" (*1 Sam* 2,6).

At this point hope does not only concern the life of the child who is born, but also the life God can bring back after death. Hence an almost "paschal" horizon of resurrection opens. Isaiah was to sing: "Your dead shall live, their bodies shall rise. O dwellers in the dust, awake and sing for joy! For your dew is a dew of light, and on the land of the shades you will let it fall" (*Is* 26,19).

Psalm 96

The Lord is king, let earth rejoice,
let all the coastlands be glad.
Cloud and darkness are his raiment;
his throne, justice and right.

A fire prepares his path;
it burns up his foes on every side.
His lightnings light up the world,
the earth trembles at the sight.

The mountains melt like wax
before the Lord of all the earth.

The skies proclaim his justice;
all peoples see his glory.

Let those who serve idols be ashamed,
those who boast of their worthless gods.
All you spirits, worship him.

Sion hears and is glad;
the people of Judah rejoice
because of your judgments O Lord.

For you indeed are the Lord,
most high above all the earth,
exalted far above all spirits.

The Lord loves those who hate evil:
he guards the souls of his saints;
he sets them free from the wicked.

Light shines forth for the just
and joy for the upright of heart.
Rejoice, you just, in the Lord;
give glory to his holy name.

The glory of the Lord, judge of the world

1. The light, joy and peace that fill the community of the disciples of Christ at Easter and that spread throughout creation, pervade our gathering that is taking place during the joyful days of the Octave of Easter. In these days it is Christ's triumph over evil and death that we celebrate. With his Death and Resurrection the Kingdom of justice and love that God desires is definitively established.

Today we will focus on the Kingdom of God in our catechesis given over to a reflection on Psalm 96 [97]. The Psalm begins with the solemn announcement: *"The Lord reigns; let the earth rejoice; let the many coastlands be glad"*, and is defined as a celebration of the divine King, the Lord of the cosmos and of history. We could say that this is an "Easter" Psalm.

We know the importance that Jesus attached to the proclamation of the Kingdom of God in his preaching. It is not just the creature's recognition of his dependence on his Creator; it is also the conviction that within history there is at work a plan, a design, a strategy of harmony and good desired by God. The Paschal Mystery of the Death and Resurrection of Jesus have brought this to fulfillment.

2. Let us now read through the Psalm that the liturgy presents for our celebration of Lauds. Immediately after the acclamation to the Lord as King that rings out like a trumpet blast, a great divine epiphany unfolds before the person at prayer. Resorting to the use of quotations, allusions to other passages of the Psalms or of the Prophets, especially Isaiah, the Psalmist describes the coming of the great King onto the world scene who appears surrounded by a series of cosmic ministers or attendants: clouds, thick darkness, fire, lightning.

Alongside of them, another series of attendants personifies his action in history: justice, right and glory. Their entry onto the scene makes all creation quake. The earth rejoices everywhere, including the islands, considered the most remote region (cf. *Ps* 96 [97],1). Flashes of light light up the whole world and an earthquake makes the world tremble (cf. v. 4). The mountains, that, according to biblical cosmology, incarnate the most ancient and solid reality, melt like wax (cf. v. 5), as the Prophet Micah sang: "Behold, the Lord is coming forth out of his place ... and the mountains will melt under him and the valleys will be cleft, like wax before the fire" (*Mi* 1,3-4). Angels fill the heavens with songs of praise that exalt justice, the work of salvation brought about by the Lord for the just. Finally, all humanity contemplates the revelation of the divine glory, the mysterious reality of God (cf. *Ps* 96 [97],6), while the "enemies", the wicked and the unjust, give way before the irresistible power of the judgement of the Lord (cf. v. 3).

3. After the theophany of the Lord of the universe, the Psalm describes two kinds of reaction to the great King and his entry into history. On the one hand, idolaters and idols topple to the ground shamed and defeated; on the other, the faithful, who have gathered in Zion for the liturgical celebration in honour of the Lord, joyfully raise a hymn of praise. The scene of the "worshippers of idols" (cf. v. 7-9) is essential; the idols bow down before the one God and their followers are covered with shame. The just exult in the divine judgement that does away with lies and false piety, sources of moral misery and slavery. They intone a profession of clear faith: "For you, O Lord, are most high over all the earth; you are exalted far above all gods" (v. 9).

4. Against the picture showing the victory over the idols and their worshippers there is set the portrayal of what could be called, the splendid day of the faithful (v. 10-12). Indeed a light that dawns for the just person is described (cf. v. 11): it is the rising of a dawn of joy, festivity and hope, because - as is well known - light is a symbol of God (cf. I *Jn* 1,5).

The Prophet Malachi declared, "For you who fear my name, there will arise the sun of justice with its healing rays" (*Ml* 3,20). Light and happiness go together: "Joy for the upright in heart. Rejoice in the Lord, O you righteous, and give thanks to his holy name!" (*Ps* 96 [97],11-12).

The Kingdom of God is a source of peace and serenity that overpowers the empire of darkness. A Jewish community in the time of Jesus sang: "Godlessness draws back before justice, just as darkness shrinks from light; godlessness will vanish forever and justice, like the sun, will be shown to be the beginning of the order of the world" (*Libro dei misteri* di Qumrln [*Book of the Mysteries* of Qumran]: 1Q 27, I, 5-7).

5. However, before we leave Psalm 96 [97], it is important that we rediscover, along with the face of the Lord the King, the profile of the faithful. Seven features are described, the sign of perfection and fullness. Those who await the coming of the great divine King hate evil, love the Lord, are the *hasîdîm*, the faithful (cf. v. 10), who walk in the path of justice, are upright of heart (cf. v. 11), rejoice in the works of God and give thanks to the holy name of the Lord (cf. v. 12). Let us ask the Lord to make these spiritual features shine in our faces.

Thursday

❇

Of the Second Week

Psalm 79

O shepherd of Israel, hear us,
you who lead Joseph's flock,
shine forth from your cherubim throne
upon Ephraim, Benjamin, Manasseh.
O Lord, rouse up your might,
O Lord, come to our help.

God of hosts, bring us back;
let your face shine on us and we shall be saved.

Lord God of hosts, how long
will you frown on your people's plea?
You have fed them with tears for their bread,
an abundance of tears for their drink.
You have made us the taunt of our neighbours,
our enemies laugh us to scorn.

God of hosts, bring us back;
let your face shine on us and we shall be saved.

You brought a vine out of Egypt;
to plant it you drove out the nations.
Before it you cleared the ground;
it took root and spread through the land.

The mountains were covered with its shadow,
the cedars of God with its boughs.
It stretched out its branches to the sea,
to the Great River it stretched out its shoots.

Then why have you broken down its walls?
It is plucked by all who pass by.
It is ravaged by the boar of the forest,
devoured by the beasts of the field.

God of hosts, turn again, we implore,
look down from heaven and see.
Visit this vine and protect it,
the vine your right hand has planted.
Men have burnt it with fire and destroyed it.
May they perish at the frown of your face.

May your hand be on the man you have chosen,
the man you have given your strength.
And we shall never forsake you again:
give us life that we may call upon your name.

God of hosts, bring us back;
let your face shine on us and we shall be saved.

O shepherd of Israel, come to our aid!

1. The Psalm we just heard is a song of lament, a plea from the entire people of Israel.

The first part makes use of a famous biblical symbol, the shepherd. The Lord is invoked as "the shepherd of Israel", who "leads Joseph like a flock" (*Ps* 79,2). From high above the Ark of the Covenant, enthroned among the cherubim, the Lord guides his flock, that is, his people, and protects them in danger.

He did this during the crossing of the desert. Now, however, he seems absent, as though asleep or indifferent. He feeds the flock he must lead and nourish (cf. *Ps* 22) only with the bread of tears (cf. *Ps* 79 [80],6). Enemies scoff at this humiliated, despised people; yet God does not seem to be moved nor "to be stirred up" (v. 3), nor does he reveal his might, arrayed to defend the victims of violence and oppression. The repetition of the antiphonal invocation (cf. vv. 4.8), seeks virtually to rouse God from his detached attitude, so that he will return to be the shepherd and defender of his people.

2. In the second part of the prayer, full of tension and charged with trust, we find another symbol dear to the Bible: the vine. It is an image easy to understand because it belongs to the vision of the Promised Land and is a sign of fruitfulness and joy.

As the Prophet Isaiah teaches in one of his most exalted poetic passages (cf. *Is* 5,1-7), the vine is the incarnation of Israel. It illustrates two fundamental aspects: on the one hand, since it has been planted by God (cf. *Is* 5,2; *Ps* 79 [80],9-10), it represents the gift, grace and love of God; on the other, it demands the labour of the farmer that enables it to produce grapes that yield wine, and thus symbolize the human response: personal effort and the fruit of good deeds.

3. Through the imagery of the vine, the Psalm recalls the major milestones of Hebrew history: their roots, the experience of the Exodus from Egypt, their entry into the promised land. The vine attained its full level of extension, extending over the whole of Palestine and beyond, during Solomon's reign. Indeed, it reached out from the northern mountains of Lebanon with their cedars as far as the Mediterranean Sea, almost to the great River Euphrates (cf. vv. 11-12).

But this splendid flourishing was shattered. The Psalm reminds us that a tempest struck God's vineyard: in other words, Israel suffered a harsh trial, a brutal invasion that devastated the Promised Land. As though he were an invader, God himself broke down the walls surrounding the vineyard, letting the plunderers break in who are represented by the wild boar, held by an ancient tradition to be a fierce and impure animal. Associated with the ferocity of the boar are all wild beasts, the symbol of an enemy horde that ravages everything (cf. vv. 13-14).

4. The Psalmist then directs a pressing appeal to God to come back and defend the victims, to break his silence: "Turn again, O God of hosts! Look down from heaven, and see; have regard for this vine" (v. 15). God will again be the defender of the vital stump of this vine, subjected to such a violent storm, and will scatter all those who have tried to tear it up or set fire to it (cf. vv. 16-17).

At this point, the Psalm opens to messianic hope. Indeed, in verse 18 the Psalmist prays: "Let your hand be upon the man of your right hand, the son of man whom you have made strong for yourself!". Perhaps his first thought is of the Davidic king who, with the Lord's help, will lead the uprising for freedom. But confidence in the future Messiah is implicit, that "Son of Man" who would be sung by the Prophet Daniel (cf. 7,13-14), a title Jesus would choose as his favorite to define his work and messianic being. Indeed, the Fathers of the Church were unanimous in pointing out that the vine that the Psalm describes is a prophetic prefiguration of Christ "the true vine" (*Jn* 15,1), and of his Church.

5. Of course, if the face of the Lord is to shine once again, Israel must be converted through fidelity and prayer to God Our Saviour. This is what the Psalmist says, when he declares: "Then we will never withdraw from you" (Ps 79 [80],19).

So Psalm 79 [80] is a song that is strongly marked by suffering but also by indestructible trust. God is always ready to "return" to his people, but his people must also "return" to him in fidelity. If we turn away from sin, the Lord will be "converted" from his intention to punish: this is the Psalmist's conviction that finds an echo in our hearts and opens them to hope.

———— ※ ————

Canticle   Is 12,1-6

I thank you, Lord, you were angry with me
but your anger has passed and you give me comfort.

Truly, God is my salvation,
I trust, I shall not fear.
For the Lord is my strength, my song,
he is my saviour.

With joy you will draw water
from the wells of salvation.
Give thanks to the Lord, give praise to his name!
Make his mighty deeds known to the peoples.

Declare the greatness of his name,
sing a Psalm to the Lord!
For he has done glorious deeds;
make them known to all the earth.

People of Sion, sing and shout for joy
for great in your midst is the Holy One of Israel

Draw water with joy at the fountain of salvation

1. The hymn just proclaimed appears as a song of joy in the *Liturgy of Lauds*. It is a concluding seal on the sections of the *Book of Isaiah* known for their Messianic reading. It includes chapters 6-12, generally known as the *"Book of Emmanuel"*. In fact, at the centre of those prophetic sayings towers the figure of a sovereign, who while belonging to the historic Davidic dynasty, reveals transfigured features and receives glorious titles: "Wonderful counsellor, Mighty God, Everlasting Father, Prince of Peace" (*Is* 9,6).

The concrete figure of the king of Judah that Isaiah promises as son and successor of Achaz, the sovereign of the time, known to be far removed from the Davidic ideals, is the sign of a higher promise: that of the Messiah-King who will bring to its fullness the name "Emmanuel", namely, "God-with-us", becoming the perfect presence of the divine in human history. It is easy to understand, then, how the New Testament and Christianity did intuit in the profile of the king the personal features of Jesus Christ, Son of God become man in solidarity with us.

2. Scholars now think that the hymn which we are dealing with (cf. *Is* 12,1-6), on account of its literary quality and its general tone, to be a composition written at a time later than that of the Prophet Isaiah who lived in the eighth century before Christ. It is almost like a quotation, a text that resembles a Psalm, thought out, perhaps, for liturgical use, that has been inserted here as the conclusion for the "Book of Emmanuel". In fact, it repeats some of the themes: salvation, trust, joy, divine action, the presence among the people of the "Holy One of Israel", an expression that indicates both the "holy" transcendence of God, and his loving and active closeness on which the people of Israel can rely.

The singer is a person who has lived a bitter experience, felt to be an act of divine judgment. But now the trial is over, the purification has taken place; in the place of the Lord's anger there is a smile, his readiness to save and console.

3. The hymn's two stanzas delineate two moments. In the first (cf. vv.1-3), that begins with the invitation to pray: "You will say on that day", the word "salvation" stands out, it is repeated three times and applied to the Lord: "God indeed is my salvation.... He has become my salvation ... the wells of salvation". Let us recall that the name Isaiah like that of Jesus contains the root of the Hebrew verb *ylsa'*, which alludes to bringing about "salvation". For this reason the one praying has the absolute certainty that divine grace is at the root of his liberation and hope.

It is important to note that he refers implicitly to the great salvific event of the exodus from the slavery of Egypt, as he quotes the words of Moses' song of deliverance, "the Lord God is my strength and my song" (*Ex* 15,2).

4. The salvation granted by God, that can make joy and trust flower even on the dark day of the trial, is portrayed by the classic image in the Bible of water: "You will draw water with joy at the fountain of salvation" (*Is* 12,3). It reminds us of the scene of the Samaritan woman, when Jesus offers her the possibility of having in herself a "spring of water that will well up to eternal life" (*Jn* 4,14).

Cyril of Alexandria commented in a marvelous way: "Jesus calls the life-giving gift of the Spirit living water, the only one through which humanity, even though it was completely abandoned, like the tree trunks on the mountains, and dry, and deprived of every kind of virtue by the deceit of the devil, is restored to the former beauty of its nature.... The Saviour calls the grace of the Holy Spirit water, and if one participates in him, he will have in himself the source of divine teachings, so that he will no longer need the advice of others, and will be able to exhort those who are thirsting for the Word of God. Such were the holy Prophets and apostles of God and their successors in the ministry while they were alive on earth. Of them it is written: "*You will draw water with joy at the fountain of salvation*" (*Commento al Vangelo di Giovanni [Comment on the Gospel of John]*, II, 4, Roma 1994, pp. 272,275).

Unfortunately, humanity often abandons this fountain that will quench the thirst of the entire being of the person, as the Prophet Jeremiah points out with sadness: "They have abandoned me, the fountain of living waters, and hewed out cisterns for themselves, broken cisterns, that cannot hold water" (*Jer* 2,13). Even Isaiah, a few pages before, exalted the "waters of Shiloah, that run slowly", symbol of the Lord present in Zion, and threatened the chastisement of the flooding of the "waters of the river, namely, the Euphrates, great and mighty" (*Is* 8,6-7), symbol of the military and economic might and of idolatry, waters that then fascinated Judah, that would later submerge her.

5. Another invitation, "On that day you will say", begins the second stanza (cf. *Is* 12,4-6), that is a continual call to joyful praise in honour of the Lord. The commands to praise are multiplied: "Praise, invoke, manifest, proclaim, sing, shout, exult".

At the centre of the praise there is a unique profession of faith in God the Saviour who works in history and is beside his creature, sharing his up's and down's: "The Lord has done great works ... great in your midst is the Holy One of Israel" (vv. 5.6). This profession of faith also has a missionary function: "Among the nations make known his deeds ... let this be known throughout all the earth" (vv. 4.5). The salvation that they have obtained must be witnessed to the world, so that all humanity may run to the fountain of peace, joy and freedom.

Psalm 80

Ring out your joy to God our strength,
shout in triumph to the God of Jacob.

Raise a song and sound the timbrel,
the sweet-sounding harp and the lute,
blow the trumpet at the new moon,
when the moon is full, on our feast.

For this is Israel's law,
a command of the God of Jacob.
He imposed it as a rule on Joseph,
when he went out against the land of Egypt.

A voice I did not know said to me:
'I freed your shoulder from the burden;
your hands were freed from the load.
You called in distress and I saved you.

I answered, concealed in the storm cloud
at the waters of Meribah I tested you.
Listen, my people, to my warning,
O Israel, if only you would heed!

Let there be no foreign god among you,
no worship of an alien god.
I am the Lord your God,
who brought you from the land of Egypt.
Open wide your mouth and I will fill it.

But my people did not heed my voice
and Israel would not obey,
so I left them in their stubbornness of heart
to follow their own designs.

O that my people would heed me,
that Israel would walk in my ways!
At once I would subdue their foes,
turn my hand against their enemies.

> The Lord's enemies would cringe at their feet
> and their subjection would last for ever.
> But Israel I would feed with finest wheat
> and fill them with honey from the rock."

A love that frees the oppressed from their burdens

1. "Blow the trumpet at the full moon, on our feast day" (Ps 80 [81],4). These words of Psalm 80 [81], that we just proclaimed, refer to a liturgical celebration according to the lunar calendar of ancient Israel. It is difficult to identify the precise festival to which the Psalm refers; what is certain is that the biblical liturgical calendar, although it is based on the cycle of the seasons and thus of nature, is clearly presented as firmly anchored to the history of salvation and, in particular, to the capital event of the exodus from Egyptian slavery, that is linked to the full moon of the first month (cf. *Ex* 12,2.6; *Lv* 23,5). There, God is revealed as Liberator and Saviour.

As verse 7 of the Psalm poetically states, God himself relieved the Hebrew slave in Egypt of the basket on his back, full of the bricks needed to build the cities of Pithom and Rameses (cf. *Ex* 1,11.14). God had stood beside the oppressed people and with his power removed the bitter sign of slavery, the basket of bricks baked in the sun, a symbol of the forced labour to which the children of Israel were constrained.

2. Let us see how this Canticle of the liturgy of Israel develops. It opens with an invitation to celebrate, to sing, to make music. It is the official convocation of the liturgical assembly according to the ancient precept of worship, already established in Egypt with the celebration of the Passover (cf. *Ps* 80 [81],2-6a). After this call, the voice of the Lord himself is raised through the oracle of the priest in the temple of Zion, and his divine words fill the rest of the Psalm (cf. vv. 6b-17).

The theme developed is simple and rotates round two ideal poles. On the one hand there is the divine gift of freedom offered to Israel, oppressed and wretched: "In distress you called, and I delivered you" (v. 8). The Psalm also mentions the Lord's support of Israel on the journey through the desert, that is, the gift of the waters at Meribah, in a context of hardship and trial.

3. On the other hand, along with the divine gift, the Psalmist introduces another significant element. The Biblical religion is not a solitary monologue of God, an action of God destined not to be performed. Instead, it is a dialogue, a word followed by a response, a gesture of love that calls for acceptance. For this reason ample room is given to the invitations that God addresses to Israel.

The Lord first invites her to observe faithfully the First Commandment, the pillar of the whole Decalogue, that is, faith in the one Lord and Saviour and the rejection of idols (cf. *Ex* 20,3-5). The words of the priest speaking in God's name are punctuated by the verb "to listen", dear to the Book of Deuteronomy, which expresses obedient adherence to the Law of Sinai and is a sign of Israel's response to the gift of freedom. In fact, we hear repeated in our Psalm: "Hear, O my people ... O Israel, if you would but listen to me! ... But my people did not listen to my voice; Israel would have none of me.... O that my people would listen to me...!" (*Ps* 80 [81],9.12.14).

Only through faithful listening and obedience can the people receive fully the gifts of the Lord. Unfortunately, God must attest with bitterness to Israel's many infidelities. The journey through the desert, to which the Psalm alludes, is strewn with these acts of rebellion and idolatry which reach their climax in the representation of the golden calf (cf. *Ex* 32,1-14).

4. The last part of the Psalm (cf. *Ps* 80 [81],14-17) has a melancholic tone. In fact, God expresses a longing that has not yet been satisfied: "O that my people would listen to me, that Israel would walk in my ways!" (v. 14).

However, this melancholy is inspired by love and is united with his deep desire to fill the chosen people with good things. If Israel were to walk in the ways of the Lord, he would soon subdue their enemies (cf. v. 15), feed them "with the finest of the wheat" and satisfy them "with honey from the rock" (v. 17). It would be a joyful feast of fresh bread accompanied by honey that seems to run from the rocks of the Promised Land, representing prosperity and total well-being, a recurrent theme in the Bible (cf. *Dt* 6,3; 11,9; 26,9.15; 27,3; 31,20). In offering this wonderful perspective, the Lord obviously seeks to obtain his people's conversion, a response of sincere and effective love to his own love that is more generous than ever.

In the Christian interpretation, the divine offering is revealed in its fullness. Indeed, Origen gives us this interpretation: the Lord "made them enter into the promised land; there he does not feed them with manna as he did in the desert, but with the wheat that has fallen to the ground (cf. *Jn* 12,24-25) that is risen.... Christ is the wheat; again, he is the rock whose water quenched the thirst of the people of Israel in the desert. In the spiritual sense, he satisfied them with honey and not with water, so that all who believe and receive this food, may taste honey in their mouths" (*Omelia sul Salmo 80, n. 17 [Homily on Psalm 80, n. 17]: Origen-Jerome, 74 Omelie sul Libro dei Salmi, [74 Homilies on the Book of the Psalms]* Milan 1993, pp. 204-205).

5. As is always the case in the history of salvation, the last word in the contrast between God and his sinful people is never judgement and chastisement, but love and pardon. God does not want to judge and condemn, but to save and deliver humanity from evil. He continues to repeat to us the words we read in the *Book of the Prophet Ezekiel*: "Have I any pleasure in the death of the wicked, says the Lord God, and not rather that he should turn from his way and live?... Why will you die, O house of Israel? For I have no pleasure in the death of anyone, says the Lord God; so return and live" (*Ez* 18,23.31-32).

The liturgy becomes the privileged place in which to hear the divine call to conversion and return to the embrace of God "merciful and gracious, slow to anger, and abounding in steadfast love and faithfulness" (*Ex* 34,6).

Friday

Of the Second Week

Psalm 50 - See Friday of the first week (See p. 63 above)

Where sin abounded, grace was more abundant!

1. Every week, in the *Liturgy of Lauds* for Friday, we pray Psalm 50, the *Miserere*, the penitential Psalm, that is so much beloved, sung and meditated upon. It is a hymn raised to the merciful God by the repentant sinner. We have already had the chance in a previous catechesis to give a general overview of this great prayer. First of all, the Psalmist enters the dark region of sin to bring into it the light of human repentance and divine forgiveness (cf. vv. 3-11). Then he goes on to exalt the gift of divine grace, that transforms and renews the repentant sinner's spirit and heart: this is a place of light, full of hope and confidence (cf. vv. 12-21).

In our reflection, we will comment on the first part of Psalm 50 [51] selecting a few key items for comment. Right from the beginning, we want to present the marvellous proclamation of Sinai that is the perfect portrait of God who is praised in the *Miserere*: "The Lord, a God merciful and gracious, slow to anger, and abounding in steadfast love and faithfulness, keeping steadfast love for thousands of generations, forgiving iniquity and transgression and sin" (*Ex* 34,6-7).

2. The person praying prays to God first of all for the gift of purification that, as the Prophet Isaiah said, makes "white as snow" "like wool" our sins even though they are more like "scarlet" and "red as crimson" (cf. *Is* 1,18). The Psalmist confesses his sin candidly, without hesitation: "I know my transgressions.... Against you, you only, have I sinned and done that which is evil in your sight" (*Ps* 50 [51],5-6).

Now there comes into play the personal conscience of the sinner who is ready to perceive his wrongdoing honestly. This experience involves freedom and responsibility, and leads him to admit that he has broken a bond and has preferred to build a life different from that of the divine Word. The result is a radical decision to change. All this is contained in the verb "recognize", that in Hebrew implies not just an intellectual agreement but also a vital choice.

Unfortunately, many do not make this step as Origen warns: "There are some who after sinning are absolutely at peace and give no further thought to their sin; nor are they troubled by the knowledge of the evil they have committed but live as though nothing had happened. Such people would certainly not be able to say: *my sin is ever before me*. Instead, when, after committing a sin, one feels miserable and troubled by it, nagged by remorse, tormented without respite and undergoing inner revolt in his spirit when he tries to deny it, one rightly exclaims: *my sins give my bones no peace*.... Thus when we set before the eyes of our heart the sins we have committed, when we look at them one by one, recognize them, blush and repent for what we have done, then, overcome with remorse and terrified, we can rightly say that there is no peace in our bones on account of *our sins* ..." (*Origen, Omelie sui Salmi*, Florence, 1991, p. 277-279 [Homilies on the Psalms]). The admission and consciousness of sin are the fruit of a sensitivity acquired through the light of God's Word.

3. In the confession of the *Miserere* there is a noteworthy emphasis: the sin is described not only in its personal and "psychological" dimension, but above all what is described is the theological reality. "Against you, against you alone have I sinned" (*Ps* 50 [51],6) exclaims the sinner, whom tradition claims to be David, conscious of his adultery with Bathsheba and of the Prophet Nathan's denunciation of this crime and of the murder of Uriah, her husband (cf. v. 2; *2 Sam*, 11-12).

Sin is not just a psychological and social matter, but an event that corrodes the relationship with God, violating his law, refusing his plan in history and overturning his set of values, "putting darkness for light and light for darkness", in other words, "calling evil good and good evil" (cf. *Is* 5,20).

Before finally injuring man, sin is first and foremost a betrayal of God. The words the prodigal son says to his father, whose love is so abundant, capture it well: "Father, I have sinned against Heaven (that is, against God) and before you" (*Lk* 15,21).

4. At this point the Psalmist introduces an angle that is more directly connected with human reality. It is a sentence that has given rise to many interpretations and has been linked with the doctrine of original sin: "Behold, I was brought forth in iniquity, and in sin did my mother conceive me" (*Ps* 50 [51],7). The praying person wants to indicate the presence of evil in our whole being, as is evident in his mention of conception and birth, as a way of expressing the entirety of existence, beginning with its source. However, the Psalmist does not formally connect his state with the sin of Adam and Eve; he does not speak explicitly of original sin.

It is still clear, according to the text of our Psalm, that evil is rooted in man's innermost depths, it is inherent in his historical reality, so the request for the mediation of divine grace is crucial. The power of God's love exceeds that of sin, the forceful river of evil is less powerful than the fruitful water of forgiveness: "Where sin increased, grace abounded all the more" (*Rom* 5,20).

5. In this way the theology of original sin and the whole biblical vision of man as a sinner are indirectly recalled in a way that at the same time gives an intuition into the light of grace and salvation.

As we will have the chance to discover later on, when we return to this Psalm and the later verses, the confession of sin and the consciousness of one's misery do not lead to terror or the nightmare of judgement, but indeed, to the hope of purification, liberation and the new creation.

In fact God saves us, "not because of deeds done by us in righteousness, but in virtue of his own mercy, by the washing of regeneration and renewal in the Holy Spirit, whom he poured out upon us richly through Jesus Christ our Saviour" (*Ti* 3,5-6).

———— ❈ ————

Canticle   Hab 3,2-4.13a.15-19

Lord, I have heard of your fame,
I stand in awe at your deeds.
Do them again in our days,
in our days make them known!
In spite of your anger, have compassion.

God comes forth from Teman,
the Holy One comes from Mount Paran.
His splendour covers the sky
and his glory fills the earth.
His brilliance is like the light,
rays flash from his hands;
there his power is hidden.

You march out to save your people,
to save the one you have anointed.
You made a path for your horses in the sea,
in the raging of the mighty waters.

This I heard and I trembled with terror,
my lips quiver at the sound.
Weakness invades my bones,
my steps fail beneath me
yet I calmly wait for the doom
that will fall on the people who assail us.

For even though the fig does not blossom,
nor fruit grow on the vine,
even though the olive crop fail,
and fields produce no harvest,
even though flocks vanish from the folds
and stalls stand empty of cattle,

Yet I will rejoice in the Lord
and exult in God my saviour.
The Lord my God is my strength.
He makes me leap like the deer,
he guides me to the high places.

The Lord comes to judge the earth

1. By way of support to the fundamental prayer of the Psalms, the *Liturgy of Lauds* offers us a series of biblical Canticles of great spiritual intensity. Today we heard an example from the third and last chapter of the *Book of Habakkuk*. This prophet lived at the end of the 7th century BC when the kingdom of Judah felt squeezed between two expanding superpowers, Egypt on the one hand, and, Babylon, on the other.

Many scholars hold that this final hymn is a quotation. An authentic liturgical song was added as an appendix to Habakkuk's brief work, to be set "to the tune of a lamentation" and accompanied "by stringed instruments", as two notes at the beginning and the end of the Canticle say (cf. *Hb* 3,1.19b). The *Liturgy of Lauds*, by taking up the thread of the ancient prayer of Israel, invites us to transform this composition into a Christian hymn, choosing some powerful verses (cf. vv. 2-4,13a,15-19a).

2. The hymn, that also shows considerable poetic skill, presents a magnificent image of the Lord (cf. v. 3-4). His figure dominates solemnly the world scene and the universe trembles in the face of his majestic advance. He is coming from the south, from Teman and from Mount Paran (cf. v. 3), from the area of Sinai, the site of the great revelatory epiphany for Israel. In Psalm 67 [68] "the Lord came from Sinai into the holy place" of Jerusalem (cf. v. 18). His appearance, in keeping with a constant biblical tradition, is surrounded by brilliant light (cf. *Hb* 3,4).

It is the radiance of his transcendent mystery that is communicated to humanity. In fact, the light is outside us, we can neither grasp it nor hold on to it; yet it envelops, enlightens and warms us. God is like this, both distant and yet close, someone beyond us yet beside us, in fact willing to be with us and in us. The earth responds with a chorus of praise to the revelation of his majesty: it is a cosmic response, a prayer to which man gives voice.

Christian tradition has lived this interior experience not only in personal spirituality but also in daring artistic creations. Beyond the majestic cathedrals of the Middle Ages, let us mention above all the art of the Christian East, with its wonderful icons and the brilliant architecture of its churches and monasteries.

Of these, the Church of Hagia Sophia in Constantinople remains a kind of archetype as regards the creation of the space for Christian prayer, in which the presence and ethereality of the light enable one to perceive both the closeness and the transcendence of the divine reality. It penetrates the whole praying community to the very marrow of their bones and invites them to go beyond themselves and become entirely immersed in the ineffability mystery of God. Just as important are the artistic and spiritual representations that are the hallmark of the monasteries of that Christian tradition. In those truly sacred spaces - and one immediately thinks of Mount Athos - time contains in itself a sign of eternity. The mystery of God is expressed and hidden in those spaces through the continuous prayer of the monks and hermits who have always been compared to the angels.

3. But let us return to the Prophet Habakkuk's Canticle. For the sacred author, the Lord's entry into the world has a precise meaning. He wills to enter into human history "in the course of the years" as repeated twice in verse 2, to judge and make its affairs better which we conduct in such a confused and at times perverse way.

Then God shows his indignation (cf. v.2c) against evil. And the hymn mentions a series of inexorable divine interventions, but without specifying if these are direct or indirect actions. The Exodus of Israel is evoked, when Pharoah's cavalry were drowned in the sea (cf. v.15). However, in a flash there comes before us a view of what the Lord is about to accomplish in the confrontations with the new oppressors of his people. God's intervention is described in an almost "visible" way through a series of agricultural images: "Though the fig tree do not blossom, nor fruit be on the vines, the produce of the olive fail and the fields yield no food, the flock will be cut off from the fold and there be no herd in the stalls" (v. 17). All signs of peace and fruitfulness are eliminated, and the world looks like a desert. This is a symbol that other Prophets like to use (cf. *Jer* 4,19-26; 12,7-13; 14,1-10) to illustrate the judgement of the Lord who is not indifferent to evil, oppression and injustice.

4. In the face of the divine intervention, the person praying remains terrified (cf. *Hb* 3,16), he trembles, he feels spiritually empty, he is struck with a tremor because the God of justice is infallible, very different from earthly judges.

But the Lord's entry has yet another purpose, which our hymn joyfully praises. In his indignation he does not forget his compassionate mercy (cf. v. 2). He goes forth from the scene of his glory not only to destroy the arrogance of the wicked, but also to save his people and his anointed (cf. v. 13), namely, Israel and its king. He also wants to set free the oppressed, make hope blossom in the victims' hearts, and open a new era of justice.

5. This is why, though our hymn is marked by "a tone of lamentation", it becomes a hymn of joy. The anticipated disasters look forward to the liberation from oppressors (cf. v. 15). So they elicit the joy of the righteous one who exclaims: "yet I will rejoice in the Lord, I will exult in the God of my salvation" (v. 18). The same attitude is suggested by Jesus to his disciples at the time of the apocalyptic cataclysms: "When these things begin to take place, look up and raise your heads, because your redemption is at hand" (*Lk* 21,28).

In Habakkuk's Canticle the final verse that expresses regained serenity is very beautiful. The Lord is defined - as David did in Psalm 17 [18] -

not only as "the strength" of his faithful, but also as the one who gives them agility, freshness and serenity in dangers. David sang: "I love you, O Lord, my strength ... he made my feet like the feet of hinds, and set me secure on the heights" (*Ps* 17 [18], 2.34). Now our singer exclaims "God, the Lord, is my strength; he makes my feet swift as those of hinds, and enables me to go upon the heights" (*Hb* 3,19). When we have the Lord beside us, we no longer fear nightmares and obstacles, but we go forward with a light step and joy on the ever harsh path of life.

Psalm 147

O praise the Lord, Jerusalem!
Sion, praise your God!

He has strengthened the bars of your gates,
he has blessed the children within you.
He established peace on your borders,
he feeds you with finest wheat.

He sends out his word to the earth
and swiftly runs his command.
He showers down snow white as wool,
he scatters hoar-frost like ashes.

He hurls down hailstones like crumbs.
The waters are frozen at his touch;
he sends forth his word and it melts them:
at the breath of his mouth the waters flow.
He makes his word known to Jacob,
to Israel his laws and decrees.
He has not dealt thus with other nations;
he has not taught them his decrees.

Jerusalem, praise your saving God

1. *The Lauda Jerusalem* that we have just proclaimed is dear to Christian liturgy that often used Psalm 147 to refer to the Word of God which "runs swiftly" on the face of the earth, and also to the Eucharist, the true "bread of finest wheat" that God generously gives to "satisfy" human hunger (cf. vv. 14-15).

Origen, who comments on our Psalm in one of his homilies, translated and disseminated by St Jerome in the West, actually interweaves the Word of God with the Eucharist: "We read the Holy Scriptures. I believe that the Gospel is the Body of Christ. I believe that the holy Scriptures are his teaching. And when he says: *he who eats my flesh and drinks my blood* (*Jn* 6,53), although these words can also refer to the [Eucharistic] Mystery, yet the Body and Blood of Christ is truly a word of Scripture, the teaching of God. When we are about to receive the [Eucharistic] Mystery, if even a tiny crumb falls, we feel lost. When we are listening to God's Word, when our ears perceive the Word of God and the body and blood of Christ, what great danger would we not fall into were we to think about something else?" (*74 Omelie sul Libro dei Salmi* [*74 Homilies on the Book of Psalms*], Milano 1993, pp. 543-544).

Biblical scholars point out that this Psalm should be joined to the previous one, so as to form a single composition, as is the case in the original Hebrew. Indeed, we have here a single, coherent Canticle in honour of the creation and redemption brought about by the Lord. It begins with a joyful call to praise: "Praise the Lord! For it is good to sing praises to our God; for he is gracious, and a song of praise is seemly" (*Ps* 146 [147],1).

2. If we focus on the passage we have just heard, we can identify three moments of praise, introduced by an invitation to the Holy City, Jerusalem, to praise and glorify her Lord (cf. *Ps* 147,12).

In the first part (cf. vv. 13-14), God's historical action is referred to. It is described in a series of symbols that represent the Lord's protection and his support of the city of Zion and its children.

First of all, there is a reference to the "bars" that reinforce and make impregnable the gates of Jerusalem. Perhaps the Psalmist is referring to Nehemiah who fortified the holy city, rebuilt after the bitter experience of the Babylonian exile (cf. *Neh* 3,3.6.13-15; 4,1-9; 6,15-16; 12,27-43).

Among other things, the gate is a sign that indicates the whole city in its compactness and tranquillity. Inside the city, likened to a safe womb, live the children of Zion, namely, the citizens, that enjoy peace and serenity, enveloped in the protective mantle of divine blessing.

The image of the joyful, tranquil city is exalted by the highest and precious gift of the peace that makes its borders safe. However, precisely because, for the Bible, peace-*shalôm* is not a negative concept that evokes merely the absence of war, but a positive gift of wellbeing and prosperity, the Psalmist speaks of being satisfied with "the finest of wheat", that is, of excellent grain, with ears full of grains. So the Lord reinforced the ramparts of Jerusalem (cf. *Ps* 86 [87],2), has made his blessing descend (cf. *Ps* 127 [128],5; 133 [134],3), extending it to the whole country, he has given peace (cf. *Ps* 121 [122],6-8) and satisfied his children's hunger (cf. *Ps* 131 [132],15).

3. In the second part of the Psalm (cf. *Ps* 147,15-18), God appears above all as Creator. Indeed twice he connects the work of creation with the words that gave origin to being: "God said, 'Let there be light!' and there was light".... "He sends forth his command to the earth ... he sends forth his word" (cf. *Gn* 1,3; *Ps* 147,15.18).

Here, under the banner of the divine Word, the two fundamental seasons burst forth and are stabilized. On the one hand, the Lord's order makes winter descend on the earth, picturesquely described as snow white as wool, by hoarfrost like ashes, by hail like bread crumbs, and by ice that freezes everything (cf. vv. 16-17). On the other hand, another divine command causes the warm wind to blow, bringing summer and melting the ice: so the rainwater and torrents can run freely, water the earth and make it fruitful.

Therefore, the Word of God is the source of the cold and the heat, of the cycle of the seasons and of the flow of life in nature. Humanity is invited to recognize and thank the Creator for the fundamental gift of the universe that surrounds it, allows it to breathe, feeds and sustains it.

4. We now move on to the third and last part of our hymn of praise (cf. vv. 19-20). We return to the Lord of history with whom we began. The divine Word brings Israel an even more important and precious gift, that of the Law, of Revelation. A specific gift: "He has not dealt thus with any other nation; they do not know his ordinances" (v. 20).

Thus the Bible is the treasure of the Chosen People who must draw on it with love and with faithful devotion. This is what Moses says to the Hebrews in Deuteronomy: "And what great nation is there that has statutes and ordinances so righteous as all this law which I set before you this day?" (*Dt* 4,8).

5. Just as there are two glorious actions of God in creation and in history, so there are also two revelations: one is inscribed in nature itself and open to all; the other given to the Chosen People, who must witness to it and communicate it to all humanity what is contained in Sacred Scripture. Two distinct Revelations, but God is one and his Word is one. All things were made through the Word - as the Prologue of John's Gospel says - and without him nothing was made of all that exists. Yet the Word also became "flesh", namely, he entered history and pitched his tent among us (cf. *Jn* 1,3.14). (See also p. 271 below)

Saturday

Of the Second Week

Psalm 91

It is good to give thanks to the Lord
to make music to your name, O Most High,
to proclaim your love in the morning
and your truth in the watches of the night,
on the ten-stringed lyre and the lute,
with the murmuring sound of the harp.

Your deeds, O Lord, have made me glad;
for the work of your hands I shout with joy.
O Lord, how great are your works!
How deep are your designs!
The foolish man cannot know this
and the fool cannot understand.

Though the wicked spring up like grass
and all who do evil thrive:
they are doomed to be eternally destroyed.
But you, Lord, are eternally on high.
See how your enemies perish;
all doers of evil are scattered.

To me you give the wild-ox's strength;
you anoint me with the purest oil.
My eyes looked in triumph on my foes;
my ears heard gladly of their fall.
The just will flourish like the palm-tree
and grow like a Lebanon cedar.

Planted in the house of the Lord
they will flourish in the courts of our God,
still bearing fruit when they are old,
still full of sap, still green,
to proclaim that the Lord is just.
in him, my rock, there is no wrong.

Sing in praise of Christ's redeeming work

1. Psalm 91 [92] which we have just heard, the song of the righteous man to God the Creator, has a special place in the ancient Hebrew tradition. In fact, the title given to this Psalm indicates that it was sung on the Sabbath (cf. v. 1). Hence, it is the hymn raised to the Most High and Eternal Lord when, at sundown on Friday, we enter the holy day of prayer, contemplation and serene stillness of body and spirit.

The magnificent person of God the Most High is at the centre of the Psalm (cf. v. 9) around whom is arrayed a harmonious and peaceful world. Standing before him is the just person who, in keeping with a favourite Old Testament concept, is filled with well-being, joy and longevity as a natural consequence of his upright and faithful life. This refers to the so-called "theory of retribution", that claims that every crime is punished and every good deed rewarded already on this earth. Although there may be an element of truth to this view, nonetheless - as Job will intuit and Jesus will confirm (cf. *Jn* 9, 2-3) - the reality of human suffering is much more complex and cannot be so easily simplified. Indeed, human suffering must be viewed in the perspective of eternity.

2. Let us now examine this sapiential hymn with liturgical features. It includes an intense call to praise, the joyful song of thanksgiving, the festival of music played on the ten-stringed harp, the lyre and the lute (cf. vv. 2-4). The Lord's love and fidelity must be celebrated in liturgical song that is to be performed "with skill" (Ps 46 [47],8). This invitation can also apply to our celebrations, so that they recover their splendour, not only in the words and rites, but also in the melodies that accompany them.

After this appeal not to break the interior and exterior thread of prayer, the true and constant breath of faithful humanity, Psalm 91 [92] presents, as though in two portraits, the profile of the wicked (cf. vv. 7-10) and of the just person (cf. vv. 13-16). The wicked man, moreover, is brought before the Lord, "the most high for ever" (v. 9), who will make his enemies perish and will scatter all evildoers (cf. v. 10). Indeed, only in the divine light can we understand the depth of good and evil, justice and wickedness.

3. The figure of the sinner is described with images from the vegetable world: "though the wicked sprout like grass, and all evildoers flourish" (v. 8). But this flourishing is destined to shrivel and disappear. In fact, the Psalmist heaps up verbs and words that describe the devastation: "they are doomed to destruction for ever ... Your enemies, O Lord, shall perish, all evildoers shall be scattered" (vv. 8.10).

At the root of this catastrophic outcome is the profound evil that grips the minds and hearts of the wicked: "The dull man cannot know, the stupid cannot understand this" (v. 7). The adjectives used here belong to the language of wisdom and denote the brutality, blindness and foolishness of those who think they can rage over the face of the earth without moral consequences, deceiving themselves that God is absent and indifferent. Instead, the person praying is certain that sooner or later the Lord will appear on the horizon to establish justice and break the arrogance of the fool (cf. *Ps* 13 [14]).

4. Here we stand before the figure of the upright person, sketched as in a vast, richly coloured painting. Here too the Psalmist has used fresh, luxuriant green plant images (*Ps* 91 [92], 13-16). As opposed to the wicked, who is luxuriant but short-lived like the grass of the fields, the upright person rises toward heaven, solid and majestic like the palm tree or a cedar of Lebanon. Besides, the just "flourish in the courts of our God" (v. 14), namely, they have a particularly sound and stable relationship with the temple, hence with the Lord, who has established his dwelling in them.

The Christian tradition also played on the double meaning of the Greek word *phoinix*, used to translate the Hebrew term for "palm tree". *Phoinix* is the Greek word for "palm", but also for the bird we call the "*phoenix*". Everyone knows that the phoenix was a symbol of immortality because it was believed that the bird was reborn from its ashes. Christians have a similar rebirth from ashes, through their participation in the death of Christ, the source of new life (cf. *Rom* 6,3-4). "But God ... even when we were dead through our transgression, brought us to life with Christ", the *Letter to the Ephesians* says, "and raised us up with him" (2,5-6).

5. Another image, taken from the animal kingdom, represents the just man and intends to exalt the strength that God lavishes, even in old age. "You have exalted my horn like that of the wild ox; you have poured rich oil upon me" (*Ps* 91 [92],11). On the one hand, the gift of divine power makes one triumph and gives security (cf. v. 12); on the other, the glorious forehead of the righteous is anointed with oil that radiates energy and a protective blessing. So then, Psalm 91 [92] is an optimistic hymn, strengthened by music and song. It celebrates confidence in God who is the source of serenity and peace, even when one witnesses the apparent success of the wicked. A peace that is intact even in old age (cf. v. 15), a time of life to be lived in security and fruitfulness.

Let us end with the words of Origen, translated by St Jerome, which are inspired by the phrase in which the Psalmist tells God: "You have poured rich oil upon me" (v. 11). Origen comments: "our old age has need of God's oil. Just as when our bodies are tired, we only feel refreshed by anointing them with oil, just as the flame of the lantern is extinguished if we do not add oil to it, so too, the flame of my old age needs to grow with the oil of God's mercy. The Apostles also went up to the Mount of Olives (*Acts* 1,12) to receive the light from the Lord's oil, because they were tired and their lanterns needed the oil of the Lord.... Therefore let us pray the Lord that our old age, our every effort and our darkness may be enlightened by the oil of the Lord" (*74 Omelie sul Libro dei Salmi*, [*Homilies on the Book of Psalms*] Milan 1993, pp. 280-282, *passim*). (See also p. 273 below)

———— ✖ ————

Canticle   Deut 32,1-12

Listen, O heavens, and I will speak,
let the earth hear the words on my lips.
May my teaching fall like the rain,
my speech descend like the dew,
like rain drops on the young green,
like showers falling on the grass.

For I shall praise the name of the Lord.
O give glory to this God of ours!
The Rock - his deeds are perfect,
and all his ways are just,
a faithful God, without deceit,
a God who is right and just.

Those whom he begot unblemished
have become crooked, false, perverse.
Is it thus you repay the Lord,
O senseless and foolish people?
Is he not your father who created you,
he who made you, on whom you depend?

Remember the days of old,
consider the years that are past;
ask your father and he will show you,
ask your elders and they will tell you.

When the Most High gave the nations their heritage
and disposed men according to his plan,
in fixing the boundaries of the nations
he thought first of Israel's sons.
For Israel was the Lord's possession,
Jacob the one he had chosen.

God found him in a wilderness,
in fearful, desolate wastes;
he surrounded him, he lifted him up,
he kept him as the apple of his eye.

Like an eagle that watches its nest,
that hovers over its young,

so he spread his wings; he took him,
placed him on his outstretched wings.
The Lord alone was his guide
and no other god was with him.

Fidelity is the best response to God's benefits

1. *"Then Moses pronounced the words of this song from beginning to end, for the whole assembly of Israel to hear"* (*Dt* 31,30). This is how the Canticle we have just heard begins. It is taken from the last pages of the *Book of Deuteronomy*, to be precise, from chapter 32. The *Liturgy of Lauds* took the first 12 verses, recognizing in them a joyful hymn to the Lord who lovingly protects and cares for his people amid the daylong dangers and difficulties. On examination the Canticle is shown to be an ancient text, later than Moses, that is put on his lips to give it a solemn character. The liturgical Canticle is placed at the root of the history of the people of Israel. On that prayerful page there is no lack of reference and links with a few of the Psalms or the message of the Prophets: hence it was a moving and intense expression of the faith of Israel.

2. Moses' Canticle is longer than the passage used in the *Office of Lauds*, which is only the prelude. Some scholars think they can identify in the composition a literary gender that is technically defined with the Hebrew word "*rîb*", namely, "quarrel", "court litigation". The image of God present in the Bible is not at all that of a dark being, an anonymous and brute energy, an incomprehensible fact.

Instead, he is a person who experiences sentiments, acts and reacts, loves and condemns, participates in the life of his creatures and is not indifferent to their actions. So, in our case, the Lord convokes a sort of trial, in the presence of witnesses, denounces the crimes of the accused people, exacts a punishment, but lets his verdict be permeated by infinite mercy. Let us now follow the traces of this event, even if only reflecting on the verses proposed by the liturgy.

3. First of all he mentions the cosmic spectator-witnesses: "Give ear, O heavens, ... let the earth hearken ..." (*Dt* 32,1). In this symbolic trial Moses acts almost as a public prosecutor. His word is effective and fruitful, like the prophetic word, expression of the divine word. Note the significant flow of the images that define it: They are signs taken from nature like rain, dew, showers, drizzle and the spraying of water that makes the earth green and covers it with grain stalks (cf. v. 2).

The voice of Moses, Prophet and interpreter of the divine word, announces the imminent appearance on the scene of the great judge, the Lord, whose most holy name he pronounces, exalting one of his many attributes. In fact, the Lord is called the Rock (v. 4), a title that is repeated throughout our Canticle (cf. vv. 15.18.30.31.37), an image that exalts God's stable and unchanging fidelity, so different from the instability and infidelity of the people. The topic is developed with a series of affirmations on divine justice: "how faultless are his deeds, how right all his ways. A faithful God, without deceit, how just and upright he is" (v. 4).

4. After the solemn presentation of the supreme Judge, who is also an injured party, the objective of the cantor is directed to the accused. In order to describe this, he takes recourse to an effective representation of God as father (cf. v. 6). His much loved creatures are called his children, but, unfortunately, they are "degenerate children" (cf. v. 5). In fact, we know that already in the Old Testament there is an idea of God as a solicitous father in his meetings with his children who often disappoint him (*Ex* 4,22; *Dt* 8,5; *Ps* 102 [103],13; *Sir* 51,10; *Is* 1,2; 63,16; *Hos* 11,1-4). Because of this, the denunciation is not cold but impassioned: "Is the Lord to be thus repaid by you, O stupid and foolish people? Has he not made and established you?" (*Dt* 32,6). Indeed, rebelling against an implacable sovereign is very different from revolting against a loving father.

In order to make concrete the gravity of the accusation and thus elicit a conversion that flows from the sincerity of the heart, Moses appeals to the memory: "Think back on the days of old, reflect on the years of age upon age" (v. 7). In fact, biblical faith is a "memorial", namely, a rediscovering of God's eternal action spread over time; it is to make present and effective that salvation that the Lord has given and continues to offer man. Hence, the great sin of infidelity coincides with "forgetfulness", which cancels the memory of the divine presence in us and in history.

5. The fundamental event that must not be forgotten is that of the crossing of the desert after the flight from Egypt, major topic of Deuteronomy and of the entire Pentateuch. So the terrible and dramatic journey in the Sinai desert is evoked, "a wasteland of howling desert" (cf. v. 10), as described with an image of strong emotional impact. However, there God bends over his people with amazing tenderness and gentleness. The paternal symbol is intertwined with an allusion to the maternal symbol of the eagle: "He shielded them and cared for them, guarding them as the apple of his eye. As an eagle incites its nestlings forth by hovering over its brood. So he spread his wings to receive them and bore them up on his pinions" (vv. 10-11). Then the way of the desert steppe is transformed into a quiet and serene journey because of the protective mantle of divine love.

The Canticle also refers to Sinai, where Israel became the Lord's ally, his "portion" and "hereditary share", namely, the most precious reality (cf. v. 9; *Ex* 19,5). Thus the Canticle of Moses becomes a collective examination of conscience, so that in the end the response to the divine benefits will no longer be sin but fidelity.

Psalm 8

How great is your name, O Lord our God,
through all the earth!

Your majesty is praised above the heavens;
on the lips of children and of babes
you have found praise to foil your enemy,
to silence the foe and the rebel.

When I see the heavens, the work of your hands,
the moon and the stars which you arranged,
what is man that you should keep him in mind,
mortal man that you care for him?

Yet you have made him little less than a god;
with glory and honour you crowned him,
gave him power over the works of your hand,
put all things under his feet.

All of them, sheep and cattle,
yes, even the savage beasts,
birds of the air, and fish
that make their way through the waters.

How great is your name, O Lord our God,
through all the earth!

How great is your name through all the earth

1. "Man ..., at the heart of this enterprise, is revealed to us as gigantic. He seems to be divine, not in himself, but in his beginning and his end. Honour, therefore, to man, honour to his dignity, to his spirit, to his life". With these words, in July 1969, Paul VI entrusted to the American astronauts leaving for the moon the text of Psalm 8, just proclaimed for us, so that it might enter into the cosmic spaces (cf. *Insegnamenti*, [1969], pp. 493-494, ORE, 17 July 1969, p. 1).

In fact, this hymn celebrates the human person, a minute creature when compared to the immensity of the universe, a fragile "reed" to use a famous image of the great philosopher Blaise Pascal (*Pensieri*, n. 264). And yet he is a "thinking reed" who can understand creation, insofar as he is the lord of creation, "crowned" by God himself (cf. *Ps* 8,6). As is often the case with hymns exalting the Creator, Psalm 8 begins and ends with a solemn antiphon addressed to the Lord, whose magnificence is disseminated in the universe: "O Lord, our God, how great is your name through all the earth" (cf. vv. 2,10).

2. The body of the Canticle itself seems to assume a nocturnal atmosphere, with the moon and the stars that light up in the sky. The first strophe of the hymn (cf. vv. 2-5) is dominated by the comparison between God, the human being and the cosmos. First of all, the Lord appears on the scene, whose glory is sung by the heavens, but also by the lips of humanity. The praise that rises spontaneously on the lips of children cancels and confounds the presumptuous discourses of those who deny God (cf. v. 3). They are described as "foes, enemies, avengers", because they delude themselves by challenging and opposing the Creator with their reason and their actions (cf. *Ps* 13 [14],1).

Then, right afterwards, the impressive scene of a starry night opens. In the face of such an infinite horizon, the eternal question arises, "What are human beings" (*Ps* 8,5). The first and immediate answer speaks of nullity, either in relation to the immensity of the heavens or, above all, with regard to the majesty of the Creator. In fact, the Psalmist says, the heavens are "yours", you set the moon and the stars, they are "the work of your fingers" (cf. v. 4). This last expression is beautiful, rather than the more common "works of your hands" (cf. v. 7): God has created this colossal reality with the ease and refinement of an embroidery or chisel, with the light touch of a harpist who glides his fingers over the cords.

3. The first reaction, there, is of dismay: how can God "remember" and be "mindful" of this creature who is so fragile and so little (cf. v. 5)? But here is the great surprise: God has given the human person, the weak creature, a wonderful dignity: he has made him a little less than the angels or, as the original Hebrew can be translated, a little less than a god (cf. v. 6).

Thus we enter the second strophe of the Psalm (cf. vv. 6-10). Man is seen as the royal lieutenant of the Creator himself. God, indeed, has "crowned" him as a viceroy, giving him a universal lordship. "You have ... put all things under his feet" and the adjective "all" resounds while the various creatures file past (cf. vv. 7-9). However, this dominion is not conquered by man's capacity, fragile and limited reality, nor is it obtained either by a victory over God, as the Greek myth of Prometheus intended. It is a dominion given by God: to the fragile and often egotistic hands of man God entrusts the entire range of creatures so that he will preserve them in harmony and beauty, use them but not abuse them, reveal their secrets and develop their potential.

As the Pastoral Constitution *Gaudium et spes* of the Second Vatican Council states, "man was created in the image of God, is capable of knowing and loving his Creator, and was appointed by him as master of all earthly creatures that he might subdue them and use them for God's glory" (n. 12).

4. Unfortunately, the selfish person, often revealed to be a mad tyrant and not a wise and intelligent ruler, can misunderstand and deform the dominion of the human person, affirmed in Psalm 8. The

Book of Wisdom warns against deviations of this kind, when it specifies that God has "established man to rule the creatures produced by you, to govern the world in holiness and justice" (*Wis* 9,2-3). Although in a different context, Job also refers to our Psalm to recall in particular human weakness, which does not merit so much attention from God: "What is man, that you make much of him, or pay him any heed? You observe him with each new day" (*Jb* 7,17-18). History documents the evil that human freedom disseminates in the world with environmental disasters and the most awful social injustices.

As opposed to human beings who humiliate their own and creation, Christ appears as the perfect man, "*crowned with glory and honour because he suffered death ... that by the grace of God he might taste death for the good of all*" (*Heb* 2,9). He reigns over the universe with that dominion of peace and love that prepares the new world, the new heavens and the new earth (cf. *2 Pt* 3,13). What is more, his royal authority - as the author of the *Letter to the Hebrews* suggests applying Psalm 8 to him - is exercised by the supreme self giving of himself in death "for the good of all".

Christ is not a sovereign who makes himself be served, but who serves and consecrates himself for others: "The Son of Man came not to be served but to serve and give his life as a ransom for the many" (*Mk* 10,45). In this way, he recapitulates in himself "all things ... in heaven and on earth" *(Eph* 1,10). In this Christological light, Psalm 8 reveals all the force of its message and of its hope, inviting us to exercise our sovereignty over creation not as dominion but as love. (See also pp. 278-280 below)

The Third
Week

Sunday

---- ✳ ----

Of the Third Week

Psalm 92

The Lord is king, with majesty enrobed;
the Lord has robed himself with might,
he has girded himself with power.

The world you made firm, not to be moved;
your throne has stood firm from of old.
From all eternity, O Lord, you are.

The waters have lifted up, O Lord,
the waters have lifted up their voice,
the waters have lifted up their thunder.

Greater than the roar of mighty waters,
more glorious than the surgings of the sea,
the Lord is glorious on high.

Truly your decrees are to be trusted.
Holiness is fitting to your house,
O Lord, until the end of time.

God is our strength in the storms of life

1. The essential content of Psalm 92 [93] on which we are reflecting today is evocatively expressed by some verses of the Hymn in the *Liturgy of the Hours* for Vespers of Monday: "O, immense Creator who, in the harmony of the cosmos laid out a path and a limit for the pounding waves of the sea, you gave to the harsh deserts of the parched earth the refreshment of rivers and seas".

Before entering the heart of the Psalm with its powerful image of the waters, let us understand its basic tone, the literary genre that supports it. In fact, our Psalm, like the following Psalms 95-98, is described by Bible scholars as "a song acclaiming Our Lord the King". It exalts the Kingdom of God, the source of peace, truth and love, which we pray for in the "Our Father" when we implore: "Thy Kingdom come!".

Indeed, Psalm 92 [93] opens precisely with a joyful acclamation: "The Lord reigns!" (v. 1). The Psalmist celebrates the active kingship of God, that is, his effective and saving action which creates the world and redeems man. The Lord is not an impassive emperor relegated to his distant heavens, but is present among his people as Saviour, powerful and great in love.

2. The Lord, the King, occupies the first part of this hymn of praise. Like a sovereign, he is seated on a throne of glory, a throne that is indestructible and eternal (cf. v. 2). His mantle is the splendour of transcendence, the belt of his robe is omnipotence (cf. v. 1). The omnipotent sovereignty of God is revealed at the heart of the Psalm, which compares it to the striking image of turbulent waters.

The Psalmist mentions in particular the "voice" of the rivers, in other words, the roaring of their waters. Actually, the thundering of great waterfalls produces a sensation of tremendous force in those whose ears are deafened and whose whole body is seized with trembling. Psalm 41 [42] evokes the same sensation when it says: "Deep is calling on deep, in the roar of waters; your torrents and all your waves swept over me" (v. 8). The human being feels small before this natural force. The Psalmist, however, uses it as a trampoline to exalt the power of the Lord, which is greater by far. The triple repetition of the words: "have lifted up" (cf. *Ps* 92 [93],3) their voice, is answered by the triple affirmation of the superior might of God.

3. The Fathers of the Church like to comment on this Psalm by applying it to Christ, "Lord and Saviour". Origen, translated into Latin by St Jerome, says: "The Lord reigns, he is robed in beauty. That is, he who formerly trembled in the misery of the flesh, now shines in the majesty of divinity". For Origen, the rivers and waters that lift up their voices represent the "authoritative figures of the Prophets and the apostles" who "proclaim the praise and glory of the Lord and announce his judgments for the whole world" (cf. *74 omelie sul libro dei Salmi*, Milan 1993, pp. 666; 669).

St Augustine develops the symbol of the torrents and oceans even further. Like swollen rivers in full spate, that is, filled with the Holy Spirit and strengthened, the Apostles are no longer afraid and finally raise their voice. However, "when many voices begin to announce Christ, the sea starts to get rough". In the ebb and flow of the ocean of the world, Augustine says, the little barque of the Church seems to rock fearfully, menaced by threats and persecutions, but "the Lord is full of wonder on high"; he "walked upon the waters of the sea and calmed the waves" (*Esposizioni sui salmi*, III, Rome 1976, p. 231).

4. Yet God, sovereign of all things, almighty and invincible, is always close to his people, to whom he imparts his teachings. This is the idea that Psalm 92 [93] expresses in the last verse: the highest throne of the heavens is succeeded by the throne of the ark of the temple of Jerusalem, the power of God's cosmic voice is replaced by the sweetness of his holy and infallible words: "Your decrees are very sure; holiness befits your house, O Lord, for ever more" (v. 5).

Thus ends a short hymn, but one with real prayerful breadth. It is a prayer that instils confidence and hope in the faithful who often feel restless, afraid of being overwhelmed by the storms of history and struck by dark, impending forces.

An echo of this Psalm can be detected in the Apocalypse of John when the inspired author, describing the great gathering in heaven that is celebrating the fall of oppressive Babylon says: "I heard what seemed to be the voice of a great multitude, like the sound of many waters and like the sound of mighty thunderpeals, crying, "Alleluia! For the Lord our God the Almighty reigns'" (19,6).

5. Let us end our reflection on Psalm 92 [93] by listening to the words of St Gregory of Nazianzus, "the theologian" *par excellence* among the Fathers: We do so through one of his beautiful poems in which praise to God, Sovereign and Creator, acquires a Trinitarian dimension: "You, [Father], have created the universe, giving everything its rightful place and preserving it through your providence.... Your Word is God the Son: indeed, he is consubstantial with the Father, equal to him in honour. He has harmoniously tuned the universe to reign over all things. And in embracing them all, the Holy Spirit, God, safeguards and cares for all things. I will proclaim You, the living Trinity, the one and only monarch ... steadfast strength that sustains the heavens, a gaze inaccessible to our sight but which contemplates the whole universe and penetrates every secret depth of the earth to its abysses. O Father, be good to me: ... may I find mercy and grace, because glory and grace are to you to the age without end" (*Carm.* 31 in *Poesie/1*, Rome 1994, pp. 65-66).

———— ✖ ————

Canticle Dan 3,57-88.56 - See Sunday of the first week (see p. 18 above)

Give praise and glory to God for Creation

1. A luminous prayer like a litany is included in chapter 3 of the *Book of Daniel*, a real Canticle of the creatures, which the *Liturgy of Lauds* presents to us on several occasions in various fragments.

We have now heard the fundamental part, a grandiose cosmic choir framed by two recapitulatory antiphons: "Bless the Lord, all works of the Lord, sing praise to him and highly exalt him for ever.... Blessed are you [Lord] in the firmament of heaven and to be sung and glorified for ever" (vv. 56.57).

Between these two acclamations a solemn hymn of praise unfolds that is expressed in the repeated invitation: "Bless". This form seems no more than an invitation to all creation to bless God but it is actually a hymn of thanksgiving for all the marvels of the universe which the faithful raise to the Lord. Man gives a voice to all creation, to thank and praise God.

2. This hymn, sung by three young Hebrews who invite all the creatures to praise God, develops in a dramatic situation. The three young men, persecuted by the king of Babylon, are cast into a fiery furnace because of their faith. Yet even facing martyrdom, they do not hesitate to sing, rejoice, and praise God. The pain of their harsh and violent trial disappears, seeming as it were to dissolve in the presence of prayer and contemplation. It is this very attitude of confident abandonment that elicits the divine intervention.

Indeed, as the vivid account in Daniel testifies, "the angel of the Lord came down into the furnace to be with Azariah and his companions, and drove the fiery flames out of the furnace, and made the midst of the furnace like a moist and whistling wind, so that the fire did not touch them at all or hurt or trouble them" (vv. 49-50). Nightmares evaporate like mist in sunshine, fears dissolve and suffering vanishes when the whole human being becomes praise and trust, expectation and hope. This is the strength of prayer when it is pure, intense, and total abandonment to God our provident Redeemer.

3. The Canticle of the three young men depicts a sort of cosmic procession filing past, beginning in heaven, peopled by angels, where sun, moon and stars also shine. From on high, God pours out upon the earth the gift of the waters in heaven above (cf. v. 60); that is, rain and dew (cf. v. 64).

However, the winds then blow, thunder peals ... the chill of winter and the burning summer heat explode, besides ice and cold, frost and snow (cf. vv. 65-70.73). The poet also includes time in his hymn of praise to the Creator: day and night, light and darkness (cf. vv. 71-72). Finally his gaze comes to rest on the mountaintops where earth and sky seem to converge (cf. 74-75).

All things that grow on the earth (cf. v. 76) then join in singing praise to God; the springs that bring life and freshness, and the rivers and seas with their abundant and mysterious waters. Indeed, the poet mentions the "whales" besides marine creatures and fish (cf. v. 79), as a vision of that primordial watery chaos on which God imposed the limits to be observed (cf. *Ps* 92 [93], vv. 3-4; *Jb* 38,8-11; 40,15-41,26).

Then comes the vast and varied animal kingdom that lives and moves in the waters, on the earth and in the sky (cf. *Dn* 3,80-81).

4. The last actor of creation to enter the scene is man. First the poet's gaze broadens and sweeps over all "the sons of man" (cf. v. 82); attention is next focused on Israel, the People of God (cf. v. 83); it is then the turn of those who are fully consecrated to God, not only as priests (cf. v. 84) but also as witnesses to faith, justice and truth. They are the "servants of the Lord", the "spirits and souls of the righteous", the "holy and humble in heart", and from among them emerge the three young men: Hananiah, Azariah, Mishael, who give a voice to all the creatures in a universal and enduring song of praise (cf. vv. 85-88).

Three verbs of divine glorification constantly resound, as in a litany: "Bless, praise, exalt" the Lord. This is the true heart of prayer and song: ceaseless celebration of the Lord with the joy of being part of a choir that includes all creation.

5. Let us end our meditation by listening to the words of the Fathers of the Church such as Origen, Hippolytus, Basil of Caesarea, Ambrose of Milan, who have all commented on the account of the six days of creation (cf. *Gen* 1,1-2,4a) precisely in connection with the Canticle of the three young men.

We shall limit ourselves to the comment of St Ambrose, who, referring to the fourth day of creation (cf. *Gn* 1,14-19), imagines the earth speaking and, in a discourse on the sun, shows all the creatures united in praise of God: "The sun is truly good, for it serves to make me fruitful and ripens my fruits. It was given to me for my own good, and, with me, is subjected to great effort. It groans with me for the adoption of sons and the redemption of the human race, so that we too may be freed from slavery. Beside me, together with me, it praises the Creator; with me it raises a hymn to the Lord our God. Wherever the sun blesses, there the earth blesses, the fruit-trees bless, the animals bless, the birds bless with me" (*I sei giorni della creazione*, SAEMO, I, Milan-Rome 1977-1994, pp. 192-193).

No one is excluded from blessing the Lord, not even our marine creatures (cf. *Dn* 3,79). Indeed, St Ambrose continues: "Snakes also praise the Lord, for their nature and appearance reveal to us a certain beauty, and show that they have their justification" (*ibid.*, pp. 103-104).

This is all the more reason why we, as human beings, should add our own joyful and confident voice to this symphony of praise, and accompany it with a consistent and faithful life.

Psalm 148

Praise the Lord from the heavens,
praise him in the heights.
Praise him, all his angels,
praise him, all his host.

Praise him, sun and moon,
praise him, shining stars.
Praise him, highest heavens
and the waters above the heavens.

Let them praise the name of the Lord.
He commanded: they were made.

He fixed them for ever,
gave a law which shall not pass away.

Praise the Lord from the earth,
sea creatures and all oceans,
fire and hail, snow and mist,
stormy winds that obey his word;

all mountains and hills,
all fruit trees and cedars,
beasts, wild and tame,
reptiles and birds on the wing;

all earth's kings and peoples,
earth's princes and rulers;
young men and maidens,
old men together with children.

Let them praise the name of the Lord
for he alone is exalted.
The splendour of his name
reaches beyond heaven and earth.

He exalts the strength of his people.
He is the praise of all his saints,
of the sons of Israel,
of the people to whom he comes close.

Praise to him who sits upon the throne

1. Psalm 148 that we have just lifted up to God is a true *"Canticle of creatures"*, a kind of Old Testament *Te Deum*, a cosmic "alleluia" that involves everyone and everything in divine praise.

This is how a contemporary exegete has commented on it: "The Psalmist, calling them by name, puts beings in order. Above are the heavens with two heavenly bodies, that move according to time, and then the stars; on the one side are the fruit-trees and on the other the cedars; on one level the reptiles, on the other birds; here the princes, over there the people; in two lines, perhaps holding hands, young men and maidens .... God has established them, giving them their place and role; the human being accepts them, giving them their place in language, and arranged in this way, introduces them into the liturgical celebration. Man is the "shepherd of being' or the liturgist of creation" (L. Alonso Schökel, *Trenta salmi: poesia e preghiera* [*Thirty Psalms, Poetry and Prayer*], Bologna, 1982, p. 499).

Let us too follow this universal chorus that echoes in the apse of heaven and whose temple is the whole cosmos. Let us join in the breathing forth of the praise that all creatures raise to their Creator.

2. We find in the heavens the singers of the starry universe: the remotest heavenly bodies, the choirs of angels, the sun and moon, the shining stars, the "highest heavens" (v. 4), that is, the starry space and the waters above the heavens, which the man of the Bible imagines were stored in reservoirs before falling on the earth as rain.

The "alleluia", that is, the invitation to "praise the Lord", resounds at least eight times, and has as its final goal the order and harmony of the heavenly bodies: "He fixed their bounds which cannot be passed" (v. 6).

We then lift our eyes to the earthly horizon where a procession of at least 22 singers unfolds: a sort of alphabet of praise whose letters are strewn over our planet. Here are the sea monsters and the depths of the sea, symbols of the watery chaos on which the earth is founded (cf. *Ps* 23 [24],2), according to the ancient Semite conception of the cosmos.

St Basil, a Father of the Church observed: "Not even the deep was judged as contemptible by the Psalmist, who included them in the general chorus of creation, and what is more, with its own language completes the harmonious hymn to the Creator" (*Homiliae in hexaemeron*, III 9: PG 29,75).

3. The procession continues with the creatures of the atmosphere: the flash of lightening, hail, snow, frost and stormy winds, thought to be a swift messenger of God (*Ps* 148,8).

Then the mountains and hills appear, popularly held to be the most ancient creatures (cf. v. 9a). The vegetable kingdom is represented by the fruit-trees and cedars (cf. v. 9b). The animal kingdom is represented by the beasts, cattle, reptiles and flying birds (cf. v. 10).

Finally, the human being, who presides over the liturgy of creation, is represented according to all ages and distinctions: boys, youth and the old, princes, kings and nations (cf. vv. 11-12).

4. Let us now entrust to St John Chrysostom the task of casting a comprehensive look upon this immense chorus. He does so in words that refer also to the Canticle of the three young men in the fiery furnace, which we meditated upon in the last catechesis.

The great Father of the Church and Patriarch of Constantinople says: "Because of their great rectitude of spirit, when the saints gather to thank God, they used to invite many to join with them in singing his praise, urging them to take part with them in this beautiful liturgy. This is what the three young men in the furnace also did, when they called the whole of creation to praise and sing hymns to God for the benefit received" (*Dn* 3).

This Psalm does the same calling both parts of the world, that which is above and that which is below, the sentient and the intelligent. The Prophet Isaiah also did this, when he said: "Sing for joy, O heavens, and rejoice, O earth! ... for the Lord has comforted his people and shows mercy to his afflicted" (*Is* 49,13). The Psalter goes on: "When Israel went forth from Egypt, the house of Jacob from a people of strange language ... the mountains skipped like rams, the hills like lambs" (*Ps* 113 [114],1,4); and elsewhere in Isaiah, "Let the heavens rain down justice like dew from above" (*Is* 45,8). Indeed, considering themselves inadequate on their own to sing praise to the Lord, the saints "turn to all sides involving all things in singing a common hymn" (*Expositio in psalmum* CXLVIII: PG 55, 484-485).

5. We are also invited to join this immense choir, becoming the explicit voice of every creature and praising God in the two fundamental dimensions of his mystery. On the one hand, we must adore his transcendent greatness, "for his name alone is exalted; his glory is above earth and heaven" as our Psalm says (v. 13). On the other hand, we should recognize his goodness in coming down to us because God is close to his creatures and comes especially to help his people: "He has raised up a horn for his people ... for the people of Israel who are near to him" (v. 14), as the Psalmist re-affirms.

Before the almighty and merciful Creator, let us take up St Augustine's invitation to praise him, exalt him and celebrate him in his works: "When you observe these creatures and enjoy them and rise up to the Architect of all things and of created things, when you contemplate his invisible attributes intellectually, then a confession rises on earth and in heaven.... If creation is beautiful, how much more beautiful must its Creator be?" (*Esposizioni sui Salmi [Expositions on the Psalms]*, IV, Rome, 1977, pp. 887-889).

Monday

—— ✠ ——

Of the Third Week

Psalm 83

How lovely is your dwelling place,
Lord, God of hosts.

My soul is longing and yearning,
is yearning for the courts of the Lord.
My heart and my soul ring out their joy
to God, the living God.

The sparrow herself finds a home
and the swallow a nest for her brood;
she lays her young by your altars,
Lord of hosts, my king and my God.

They are happy, who dwell in your house,
for ever singing your praise.
They are happy, whose strength is in you,
in whose hearts are the roads to Sion.

As they go through the Bitter Valley
they make it a place of springs,
the autumn rain covers it with blessings.
They walk with ever growing strength,
they will see the God of gods in Sion.

O Lord God of hosts, hear my prayer,
give ear, O God of Jacob.
Turn your eyes, O God, our shield,
look on the face of your anointed.

One day within your courts
is better than a thousand elsewhere.
The threshold of the house of God
I prefer to the dwellings of the wicked.

For the Lord God is a rampart, a shield;
he will give us his favour and glory.
The Lord will not refuse any good
to those who walk without blame.

Lord, God of hosts,
happy the man who trusts in you!

Heaven's peace and life is our destination

1. We continue our journey through the Psalms of the *Liturgy of Lauds*. We heard now Psalm 83 [84], which the Jewish tradition attributes to the "sons of Korah", a family of priests who were in charge of the liturgical service and guarded the threshold of the tent of the Ark of the Covenant (cf. *1 Chr* 9,19).

This is a most charming song, pervaded by mystical longing for the God of life, repeatedly celebrated (cf. *Ps* 83 [84],2.4.9.13) with the name: "Lord of the Armies", that is, Lord of the heavenly hosts, hence of the cosmos. Moreover, this title had a special connection with the ark preserved in the temple that was known as the "ark of the covenant of the Lord of hosts, who is enthroned upon the cherubim" (*1 Sam* 4,4; cf. Ps 79 [80],2). Indeed, it was regarded as the sign of divine protection in times of danger and war (cf. *1 Sam* 4,3-5; *2 Sam* 11,11).

The background of the whole Psalm is represented by the temple toward which the pilgrimage of the faithful is directed. The season seems to be autumn, for the Psalmist mentions the "early rain" that placates the scorching heat of summer (cf. *Ps* 83 [84], 7). This could therefore remind us of the pilgrimage to Zion for the third principal feast of the Hebrew year, the Feast of Tabernacles, which commemorates the Israelites' pilgrimage in the desert.

2. The temple is present in all its fascination at the beginning and end of the Psalm. It opens with the wonderful and delicate imagery of birds who have built their nests in the sanctuary (cf. vv. 2-4), an enviable privilege.

It is a representation of the happiness of all who - like the priests of the temple - dwell permanently in God's House, enjoying its intimacy and peace. In fact, the whole of the believer's being is stretched out to the Lord, impelled by an almost physical and instinctive desire for him: "My soul yearns and pines for the courts of the Lord; my heart and flesh sing for joy to the living God" (v. 3). Then the temple reappears at the end of the Psalm (cf. vv. 11-13). The pilgrim expresses his great happiness at spending some time in the courts of the house of God and compares this spiritual happiness with the idolatrous illusion that pushes a person towards "the tents of wickedness", that is, the infamous temples of injustice and perversion.

3. There is light, life and joy only in the sanctuary of the living God and "blessed are those" who "trust" in the Lord, choosing the path of righteousness (cf. vv. 12-13). The image of the way takes us to the heart of the Psalm (cf. vv. 5-9) where another, more important pilgrimage is made. Blessed are those who dwell in the temple in a stable way and even more blessed are those who decide to undertake a journey of faith to Jerusalem.

In their comments on Psalm 83, the Fathers of the Church give v. 6 a special prominence: "Blessed is he who finds his strength in you, whose heart is set upon the holy pilgrimage". The early translations of the Psalter spoke of the decision to complete the "ascensions" to the Holy City. Therefore, for the Fathers the pilgrimage to Zion became the symbol of the continuous progress of the righteous toward the "eternal tents" where God receives his friends into full joy (cf. *Lk* 16,9).

Let us reflect for a moment on this mystical "ascent" that finds in the earthly pilgrimage an image and a sign. We will do so through the words of a seventh-century Christian writer who was abbot of the monastery on Sinai.

4. This is John Climacus who dedicated an entire treatise - *The Ladder of Divine Ascent* - to illustrating the countless steps by which the spiritual life ascends. At the end of his work, he gives the last word to charity itself, which he sets at the top of the ladder of spiritual progress.

It is charity that invites and exhorts us, proposing sentiments and attitudes already suggested by our Psalm: "Ascend, my brothers, ascend eagerly. Let your hearts' resolve be to climb. Listen to the voice of the one who says: 'Come let us go up to the mountain of the Lord, to the house of our God' (*Is* 2,3), Who makes our feet to be like the feet of the deer, 'Who sets us on the high places, that we may be triumphant on his road' (*Hb* 3,19). Run, I beg you, run with him who said, 'let us hurry until we all arrive at the unity of faith and of the knowledge of God, at mature manhood, at the measure of the stature of Christ's fullness'" (cf. *Eph* 4,13). (*La Scala del Paradiso*, Rome 1989, p. 355. In English, *The Ladder of Divine Ascent*, Paulist Press, Ramsey, N.J. 1982, p. 291).

5. The Psalmist thinks first of all of the concrete pilgrimage that leads to Zion from various places in the Holy Land. The rain that falls seems to be for him a foretaste of the joyful blessings that will envelop him like a mantle (cf. *Ps* 83 [84],7) when he comes face to face with the Lord in the temple (cf. v. 8). The gruelling journey through "the valley of tears" (cf. v. 7) is transfigured by the certainty that God who gives strength is the conclusion (cf. v. 8), that he hears the prayer of the faithful (cf. v. 9) and becomes the "shield" that protects him (cf. v. 10).

The concrete pilgrimage is transformed in this light - as the Fathers intuited - and becomes a parable of the whole of life, set between distance from and intimacy with God, between the mystery of God and his revelation. Even in the desert of daily life, the six workdays are made fruitful, illuminated and sanctified by the meeting with God on the seventh day, through the liturgy and prayer of our ecclesial gathering on Sunday.

Let us walk then, when we are in the "valley of tears", keeping our eyes fixed on the bright goal of peace and communion. Let us repeat in our hearts the final beatitude, which is like an antiphon that seals the Psalm: "O Lord of hosts, blessed is the man who trusts in you!"(v. 13).

———— ✖ ————

Canticle   Is 2,2-5

It shall come to pass in the latter days
that the mountain of the house of the Lord
shall be established as the highest of the mountains,
and shall be raised above the hills;
and all the nations shall flow to it,

And many peoples shall come, and say:
Come, let us go up to the mountain of the Lord,
to the house of the God of Jacob,
that he may teach us his ways,
and that we may walk in his paths.
For out of Sion shall go forth the law,
and the word of the Lord from Jerusalem.

He shall judge between the nations,
and shall decide for many peoples;
and they shall beat their swords into ploughshares,
and their spears into pruning hooks;
nation shall not lift up sword against nation,
neither shall they learn war anymore.

O house of Jacob, come,
Let us walk in the light of the Lord.

They shall beat their swords into ploughshares

1. The daily *Liturgy of Lauds,* in addition to the Psalms, always offers a Canticle from the Old Testament. Indeed, it is well known that besides the Psalter, the true prayer book of Israel and later of the Church, another sort of "Psalter" exists, found among the various historical, prophetic and sapiential pages of the Bible. It also consists in hymns, supplications, praises and invocations, often of great beauty and spiritual intensity.

In our spiritual pilgrimage through the prayers of the *Liturgy of Lauds,* we have already seen many of these songs that are scattered through the pages of the Bible. We will now examine one that is really admirable, the work of Isaiah, one of Israel's greatest Prophets, who lived in the eighth century before Christ. He was the witness of the difficult times lived by the Kingdom of Judah, but also sang of messianic hope in deeply poetic language.

2. This is the case with the Canticle we have just heard, which is placed very near the beginning of the *Book of Isaiah,* in the first verses of chapter two. It is introduced by a later editorial note which says: "The Vision of Isaiah, the son of Amoz, which he saw concerning Judah and Jerusalem" (*Is* 2,1). The hymn is conceived as a prophetic vision describing a goal towards which the history of Israel moves in hope. It is not by accident that the first words: "In the last days" (v. 2), that is, in the fullness of time. It is therefore an invitation not to be fixed on the present that is so wretched, but to sense beneath the surface of daily events the mysterious presence of divine action leading history towards a very different horizon of light and peace.

This Messianic "vision" will be taken up again in chapter 60 of the same Book in a broader perspective, a sign of the rethinking of the Prophet's essential and incisive words, those of the Canticle we have just heard. The Prophet Micah (cf. 4,1-3) will take up the same hymn, although his ending (cf. 4,4-5) differs from that of the oracle of Isaiah (cf. Is 2,5).

3. At the heart of Isaiah's "vision" rises Mount Zion, which speaking figuratively will rise above all the other mountains, since it is God's dwelling place and so the place of contact with heaven (cf. 1 Kgs 8,22-53). From here according to Isaiah's saying in 60,1-6, a light will emanate that will rend and disperse the darkness and toward it will move processions of nations from every corner of the earth.

The power of attraction of Zion is based on two realities that emanate from the Holy Mountain of Jerusalem: the Law and the Word of the Lord. In truth, they constitute a single reality which is the source of life, light and peace, an expression of the mystery of the Lord and of his will. When the nations reach the summit of Zion where the temple of God rises, then the miracle will take place which humanity has always awaited and for which it longs. The peoples will drop their weapons which will then be collected and made into tools for peaceful work: swords will be beaten into ploughshares, spears into pruning hooks. Thus will dawn a horizon of peace, of *shalôm* in Hebrew (cf. Is 60,17), a word particularly cherished by Messianic theology. At last the curtain falls forever on war and hatred.

4. Isaiah's saying ends with an appeal, in harmony with the spirituality of the hymns of pilgrimage to Jerusalem: "O house of Jacob, come, let us walk in the light of the Lord" (Is 2,5). Israel must not be a mere a spectator of this radical historical transformation; she cannot dissociate herself from the invitation that rang out in the opening, on the peoples' lips: "Come, let us climb the mountain of the Lord" (v. 3).

We Christians are also challenged by this Canticle of Isaiah. In commenting on it, the Fathers of the Church of the fourth and fifth centuries (Basil the Great, John Chrysostom, Theodoret of Cyr, Cyril of Alexandria) saw it fulfilled with the coming of Christ. Consequently they identified the Church with the "mountain of the house of the Lord ... established as the highest of the mountains", from which came the Word of the Lord and to which the pagan peoples streamed, in the new era of peace inaugurated by the Gospel.

5. Already the martyr St Justin, in *The First Apology*, written about the year 153, announced that the verse of the Canticle which says: "the word of the Lord [would go forth] from Jerusalem" (cf. v. 3) had come to pass. He wrote "For twelve illiterate men, unskilled in the art of speaking, went out from Jerusalem into the world, and by the power of God they announced to the men of every nation that they were sent by Christ to teach everyone the word of God; and we, who once killed one another, [now] not only do not wage war against our enemies, but, in order to avoid lying or deceiving our examiners, we even meet death cheerfully, confessing Christ". (*Prima Apologia*, 39,3: *Gli apologeti greci*, Rome 1986, p. 118. *The First Apology*, chapter 39, pp. 75-76, CUA Press).

For this reason, in a special way let us Christians welcome the Prophet's appeal and seek to lay the foundations of the civilization of love and peace in which there will be no more war, "and death will be no more, neither shall there be mourning, nor pain any more for the former things have passed away" (*Apoc* 21,4).

Psalm 95

O sing a new song to the Lord,
sing to the Lord all the earth.
O sing to the Lord, bless his name.

Proclaim his help day by day,
tell among the nations his glory
and his wonders among all the peoples.

The Lord is great and worthy of praise,
to be feared above all gods;
the gods of the heathens are naught.

It was the Lord who made the heavens,
his are majesty and state and power
and splendour in his holy place.

Give the Lord, you families of peoples,
give the Lord glory and power,
give the Lord the glory of his name.

Bring an offering and enter his courts,
worship the Lord in his temple.
O earth, tremble before him.

Proclaim to the nations: "God is king."
The world he made firm in its place;
he will judge the peoples in fairness.

Let the heavens rejoice and earth be glad,
let the sea and all within it thunder praise,
let the land and all it bears rejoice,
all the trees of the wood shout for joy

at the presence of the Lord for he comes,
he comes to rule the earth.
With justice he will rule the world,
he will judge the peoples with his truth.

The Lord reigns from the cross

1. "Say among the nations "the Lord reigns!"". This exhortation of Psalm 95 (v. 10), just proclaimed, sets the tone that colours the whole hymn. Indeed, it is one of the "Psalms of the Lord's Kingship" that include Psalms 95-98 [96-99] as well as 46 [47] and 92 [93].

In the past we have already had the chance to pray and comment upon Psalm 92 [93] and we know that these Canticles are centred on the great figure of God who rules the whole universe and governs human history.

Psalm 95 [96] exalts both the Creator of beings and the Saviour of the peoples: God "establishes the world, it shall never be moved; he will judge the peoples with equity" (v. 10). Indeed, in the original Hebrew, the verb translated as "judge" means "govern": thus we are certainly not left to the mercy of the dark forces of chaos or chance, but are always in the hands of a just and merciful Sovereign.

2. The Psalm begins with a joyful invitation to praise God, that opens immediately on to a universal perspective: "Sing to the Lord, all the earth!" (v. 1). The faithful are invited to "declare his glory among the nations", and then to tell "of his marvellous deeds" (v. 3). Indeed, the Psalmist directly calls on the "families of the peoples" (v. 7) to invite them to glorify the Lord. Lastly, the Psalmist asks the faithful to "say among the nations, "the Lord reigns!"" (v. 10), and explains that the Lord "judges the peoples" (v. 10), and the whole "world" (v. 13). This universal opening on the part of a small nation squeezed between two great empires is very important. This people know that their Lord is God of the universe and that "all the gods of the nations are nothing" (v. 5).

The Psalm is substantially composed of two scenes. The first part (cf. vv. 1-9) portrays a solemn epiphany of the Lord "in his sanctuary" (v. 6), that is, the Temple of Zion. It is preceded and followed by the songs and sacrificial rites of the congregation of the faithful. The current of praise flows steadily before the divine majesty: "Sing to the Lord a new song ... sing ... sing ... bless ... tell of his salvation ... tell God's glory ... declare his marvellous works ... ascribe to the Lord glory and power ... give to the Lord the glory ... bring offerings ... bow down before him!" (vv. 1-3.7-9).

The fundamental gesture before the Lord King who manifests his glory in the history of salvation is therefore the hymn of adoration, praise and blessing. These attitudes must also be present in our daily liturgy and in our personal prayer.

3. At the heart of this choral song of praise, we find an anti-idolatrous declaration. Thus prayer is revealed as a way of reaching the purity of faith, according to the well known affirmation *lex orandi, lex credendi*: the norm of true prayer is also the norm of faith and is a lesson on divine truth. Indeed, the latter can really be discovered through the intimate communion with God achieved in prayer.

The Psalmist proclaims: "Great is the Lord and greatly to be praised, he is to be feared above all gods. For all the gods of the peoples are nothing; but the Lord made the heavens" (vv. 4-5). Through the liturgy and prayer, the faith of every generation is purified, the idols to which one sacrifices so easily in daily life are abandoned, and we pass from fear of the transcendent justice of God to a living experience of his love.

4. So we come to the second scene, the one that opens with the prolamation of the Lord's kingship (cf. vv. 10-13). It is now the universe that sings, even through its most mysterious and dark elements, such as the sea, in accord with the ancient biblical concept: "Let the heavens be glad, and let the earth rejoice, let the sea and what fills it resound; let all the plains exult, and all that is in them! Then let all the trees of the forest sing for joy before the Lord, for he comes, for he comes to judge the earth" (vv. 11-13).

As St Paul will say, even nature with the human person, "waits with eager longing ... [to] be set free from slavery to corruption and share in the glorious freedom of the sons of God" (*Rom* 8,19.21).

And at this point we would like to make room for the Christian re-reading (*rilettura*) of the Psalm by the Fathers of the Church, who saw in it a prefiguration of the Incarnation and Crucifixion, a sign of the paradoxical lordship of Christ.

5. Thus at the beginning of his address in Constantinople, on Christmas Day in 379 or 380, St Gregory Nazianzen uses some expressions of Psalm 95: "Christ is born: glorify him! Christ comes down from heaven: go to meet him! Christ is on earth: Be exalted! "Sing to the Lord, all the earth!' (v. 1) and, to combine the two concepts, "Let the heavens be glad, and let the earth rejoice' (v. 11), because of Him who is of heaven and then of earth" (*Omelie sulla natività*, Discorso 38, 1, Rome 1983, p. 44; *Oration 38 on the Birthday of Christ*, 1., *Nicene and Post-Nicene Fathers*, vol 7, p. 345, reprinted by Eerdmans March, 1989).

In this way the mystery of the divine lordship is manifested in the Incarnation. Indeed, he who reigns by "becoming earthly", reigns precisely in humiliation on the Cross. It is significant that many of the ancients interpreted v. 10 of this Psalm with a thought-provoking Christological integration: "The Lord reigned from the tree".

Thus the *Letter of Barnabas* taught that "the kingdom of Jesus is on the wood [of the cross]" (VIII, 5: *I Padri Apostolici*, Rome 1984, p.

198; *The Apostolic Fathers*, p. 282, Thomas Nelson, 1978) and the martyr St Justin, quoting almost the whole of the Psalm in his *First Apology*, ended by inviting all the Gentiles to rejoice because "the Lord hath reigned from the tree" of the Cross (*Gli apologeti greci*, Rome 1986, p. 121; The First Apology, chapter 41, p.78, *Writings of St Justin Martyr*, CUA Press).

From this terrain sprang the hymn *Vexilla regis* (*The Royal Banners of the King*, used in Passion week) written by the Christian poet, Venantius Fortunatus, that exalts Christ who reigns from the height of the Cross - a throne of love and not of dominion: *Regnavit a ligno Deus* (*God has reigned from the tree*). Indeed, already during his earthly life, Jesus warned: "Whoever wishes to be great among you must be your servant, and whoever wishes to be first among you will be the slave of all. For indeed, the Son of Man came not to be served but to serve and to give his life as a ransom for many" (*Mk* 10,43-45).

Tuesday

---- ✖ ----

Of the Third Week

Psalm 84

O Lord, you once favoured your land
and revived the fortunes of Jacob,
you forgave the guilt of your people
and covered all their sins.
You averted all your rage,
you calmed the heat of your anger.

Revive us now, God, our helper!
Put an end to your grievance against us.
Will you be angry with us for ever,
will your anger never cease?

Will you not restore again our life
that your people may rejoice in you?
Let us see, O Lord, your mercy
and give us your saving help.

I will hear what the Lord God has to say,
a voice that speaks of peace,
peace for his people and his friends
and those who turn to him in their hearts.
His help is near for those who fear him
and his glory will dwell in our land.

Mercy and faithfulness have met;
justice and peace have embraced.
Faithfulness shall spring from the earth
and justice look down from heaven.

The Lord will make us prosper
and our earth shall yield its fruit.
Justice shall march before him
and peace shall follow his steps.

Show us, O Lord, your mercy; grant us your salvation

1. Psalm 84 [85], which we have just heard sung, is a joyful hymn full
of hope in the future of our salvation. It reflects the happy moment of
Israel's return from the Babylonian Exile to the land of the fathers. The
life of the nation begins again in that beloved homeland, burnt-out
and destroyed in the conquest of Jerusalem by the army of King
Nebuchadnezzar in 586 B.C.

Indeed, in the original Hebrew of the Psalm one hears repeated the
verb *shûb*, which refers to the return of the deported but it also means
a spiritual "return", or a "conversion". The rebirth, therefore, does not
only refer to the nation, but also to the community of the faithful who
regarded the exile as a punishment for the sins they had committed,
and now see their repatriation and new freedom as a divine blessing
that is the result of their conversion.

2. We can follow the Psalm in its development according to two
fundamental stages. The first is articulated by the subject of "return",
with the two meanings we mentioned.

Israel's physical return is celebrated first of all. "Lord ... you did
restore the fortunes of Jacob" (v. 2); "Restore us again, O God of our
salvation.... Will you not revive us again?" (vv. 5.7). This is a precious
gift of God, who is concerned to deliver his People from oppression

and promotes their prosperity. Indeed, you "love all things that exist
... spare all things, for they are yours, O Lord who love the living"
(cf. *Wis* 11,24.26).

However, besides this "return" that concretely unifies those who
were scattered, there is another more interior and spiritual "return".
The Psalmist allows it ample room, attributing a special importance to
it that applies not only to ancient Israel, but to the faithful of all time.

3. In this "return" the Lord acts effectively, revealing his love in forgiving
the iniquity of his People, pardoning all their sins, withdrawing all his
wrath and putting an end to his anger (cf. *Ps* 84 [85],3-4).

In fact, their deliverance from evil, the pardon of their faults and the
purification of sins create the new People of God. This is expressed
in an invocation that has also entered the Christian liturgy: "Show us,
O Lord, your mercy and grant us your salvation" (v. 8).

However, to the "return" of God who forgives must correspond the
"return", that is, the "conversion", of the one who repents. In fact, the
Psalm says that peace and salvation are offered "to those who turn to
him in their hearts" (v. 9). Those who set out with determination on
the path of holiness receive the gifts of joy, freedom and peace.

It is well known that biblical terms for sin often refer to a mistaken
direction, a missed goal, a deviation from the straight path.
Conversion is, precisely, a "return" to the straight road that leads to
the house of the Father who waits to embrace us, pardon us and make
us happy (cf. *Lk* 15,11-32).

4. Thus we come to the second part of the Psalm (cf. *Ps* 84 [85],10-
14), so dear to Christian tradition. It describes a new world in which
God's love and his faithfulness embrace each other as if they were
persons. Similarly, justice and peace meet and kiss each other. Truth
sprouts up as if in a new springtime and justice, which for the Bible
also means salvation and holiness, appears from heaven to begin its
journey in the midst of humanity.

All the virtues, at first expelled from the earth by sin, now re-enter
history and meet, drawing the map of a world of peace. Mercy, truth,
justice and peace become the four cardinal points of this geography
of the spirit. Isaiah also sings: "Let justice descend, O heavens, like
dew from above, like gentle rain let the skies drop it down. Let the

earth open and salvation bud forth; let justice also spring up. I, the Lord, have created this" (*Is* 45,8).

5. The Psalmist's words, already in the second century, were re-read by St Irenaeus of Lyons as a proclamation of the "generation of Christ from the Virgin" (*Adversus haereses*, III, 5, 1). Indeed, Christ's coming is the source of mercy, the springing up of truth, the flowering of justice, the splendour of peace.

For this reason, especially in the last part, the Psalm is reread by Christian tradition in terms of Christmas. This is how St Augustine interprets it in a discourse for Christmas. Let us allow him to conclude our reflection. ""Truth, then, is sprung out of the earth: Christ who said, 'I am the truth', is born of a virgin. And justice looked down from heaven: man, believing in him who has been born, has been justified not by himself, but by God. Truth is sprung out of the earth, for the Word was made flesh. And justice looked down from heaven, for every best gift, and every perfect gift, is from above. Truth is sprung out of the earth - flesh born of Mary. And justice looked down from heaven, for a man cannot receive anything, unless it be given him from heaven" (*Discorsi*, IV/1, Rome 1984, p. 11; Sermon 185, [*Roman Breviary,* 24 December, Second Reading]).

Canticle

Is 26,1-4.7-9.12

We have a strong city;
he sets up salvation as walls and bulwarks.
Open the gates,
that the righteous nation which keeps faith may enter in.

You keep him in perfect peace,
whose mind is stayed on you,
because he trusts in you.
Trust in the Lord for ever,
for the Lord God is an everlasting rock.

The way of the righteous is level;
you make smooth the path of the righteous.
In the path of your judgments, O Lord,
we wait for you.

My soul yearns for you in the night,
my spirit within me earnestly seeks you;
For when your judgments are in the earth,
the inhabitants of the world learn righteousness.

O Lord, you will ordain peace for us,
you have wrought for us all our works.

My peace I give to you, my peace I leave you

1. In the Book of the Prophet Isaiah, over a broad span of time various voices converge, all of them under the name and inspiration of this great witness of the Word of God, who lived in the 8th century B.C.

Within this long scroll of prophecies, which Jesus also opened and read in the synagogue of his village Nazareth (cf. *Lk* 4,17-19), is a series of chapters, from 24 to 27, generally known by scholars as "the great apocalypse of Isaiah". A second and minor apocalypse can be found in chapters 34-35. In pages that are often passionate and packed with symbols a powerful, poetic description is given of the divine judgment of history that exalts the expectation of salvation on the part of the just.

2. Often, as happens in the Apocalypse of John, two opposing cities are contrasted with each other: the rebellious city, incarnated in some of the historical cities of the time, and the holy city where the faithful gather.

The Canticle we have just heard proclaimed, which is taken from the 26th chapter of Isaiah is the joyful celebration of the city of salvation. It stands strong and glorious, for the Lord himself laid its foundations and fortified it, making it a safe and peaceful dwelling-place (cf. v. 1). He now opens wide the gates to welcome the people of the just (cf. v. 2), who seem to repeat the Psalmist's words when, standing before the Temple of Zion, he exclaims: "Open to me the gates of justice, that I may enter through them and give thanks to the Lord. This is the gate of the Lord; the just shall enter through it (*Ps* 117 [118],19-20).

3. There is one fundamental prerequisite for those who enter the city of salvation: "firm purpose ... trust in you ... trust" (cf. *Is* 26,3-4). It is faith in God, a solid faith based on Him who is the "everlasting rock" (v. 4).

Confidence, already expressed in the etymological root of the Hebrew word *"amen"*, sums up the profession of faith in the Lord, who - as

King David sang - is "my strength, my rock, my fortress, my deliverer; my God, my rock, in whom I take refuge; my shield, and the horn of my salvation, my stronghold" (*Ps* 17 [18], 2-3; cf. *2 Sam* 22,2-3).

The gift that God offers to the faithful is peace (cf. *Is* 26,3), *the messianic gift par excellence*, the synthesis of life in justice, freedom and the joy of communion.

4. This gift is forcefully confirmed in the last verse of the Canticle of Isaiah. "O Lord, you will ordain peace for us, you have wrought for us all our works" (v. 12). This is the verse that attracted the attention of the Fathers of the Church: in that promise of peace they glimpsed the words of Christ that would resound centuries later: "Peace I leave with you; my peace I give to you" (*Jn* 14,27).

In his *Commentary on the Gospel of John*, St Cyril of Alexandria reminds us that in giving us peace, Jesus gives us his Spirit. He does not, therefore, leave us orphans, but through his Spirit remains with us. St Cyril comments: The Prophet "prays for the gift of the divine Spirit, through whom we have been readmitted to friendship with God the Father who were previously far from him because of the sin that held sway in us". His commentary then becomes a prayer: "Grant us peace, O Lord. Then we will acknowledge that we have all things, and we will realize that those lack nothing who have received the fullness of Christ. Indeed, it is the fullness of every good that God dwells in us through the Spirit (cf. *Col* 1,19)" (*Commento al Vangelo di Giovanni*, vol. III, Rome 1994, p. 165).

5. Let us give a last look at Isaiah's text. It presents a reflection on the "way of the just" (v. 7) and a declaration of adherence to the just decisions of God (cf. vv. 8-9). The dominant image is that of the way, a classical biblical image, already used by Hosea, a Prophet who lived just before Isaiah: "whoever is wise, let him understand these things ... for the ways of the Lord are right and the just walk in them, but sinners stumble in them" (*Hos* 14,9-10).

The Canticle of Isaiah contains another theme that is also eloquent, also in its liturgical use in the *Office of Lauds*. Indeed, the dawn is mentioned, that is awaited after a night spent seeking God: "My soul yearns for you in the night, my spirit within me earnestly seeks you" (v. 9).

At daybreak, when work begins and the hum of daily life can already be heard in the city streets, the faithful must once again be resolved to walk "in the path of your judgments, O Lord" (v. 8), hoping in him and in his Word, our only source of peace.

Now the words of the Psalmist come to his lips, who has professed his faith since dawn: "O God, you are my God, for you I long, my soul thirsts for you ... your merciful love is better than life" (Ps 62 [63],2.4). His soul refreshed, he can face the new day.

Psalm 66

O God, be gracious and bless us
and let your face shed its light upon us.
So will your ways be known upon earth
and all nations learn your saving help.

Let the peoples praise you, O God;
let all the peoples praise you.

Let the nations be glad and exult
for you rule the world with justice.
With fairness you rule the peoples,
you guide the nations on earth.

Let the peoples praise you, O God;
let all the peoples praise you.

The earth has yielded its fruit
for God, our God, has blessed us.
May God still give us his blessing
till the ends of the earth revere him.

Let the peoples praise you, O God;
let all the peoples praise you.

God is offering his salvation to the whole world

1. Now we have just heard the voice of the ancient Psalmist, who sang a joyful song of thanksgiving to the Lord. It is a brief but compelling text, which opens out on an immense horizon, to embrace in spirit all the peoples of the earth.

This universal openness probably reflects the prophetic spirit of the age that followed the Babylonian exile, when it was hoped that God would also lead foreigners to his holy mountain to fill them with joy. Their sacrifices and burnt offerings would be pleasing to him, for the temple of the Lord would become "a house of prayer for all peoples" (*Is* 56,7).

In our Psalm, 66 [67] too, the universal chorus of the nations is invited to join in the praise that Israel raises in the temple of Zion. Indeed, this antiphon is repeated twice: "Let the peoples praise you O God; let all the peoples praise you" (vv. 4-6).

2. Even those who do not belong to the community chosen by God receive a vocation from him: indeed, they are called to know the "way" revealed to Israel. The "way" is the divine plan of salvation, the kingdom of light and peace in whose realization the pagans are also involved since they are invited to listen to the voice of the Lord (cf. v. 3). The result of this obedient listening is the fear of the Lord "to the ends of the earth" (v. 8), an expression that does not evoke fear but rather adoring reverence for the transcendent and glorious mystery of God.

3. At the beginning and end of the Psalm there is an insistent desire for the divine blessing: "May God be gracious to us and bless us, may God's face shed its light upon us ... God, our God, has blessed us. May God still give us his blessing" (vv. 2.7-8).

In these words it is easy to hear the echo of the famous priestly blessing which, in God's name, Moses taught Aaron and the descendants of the priestly tribe: "The Lord bless you and keep you: The Lord make his face shine upon you, and be gracious to you: the Lord lift up his countenance upon you, and give you peace" (*Nm* 6,24-26).

Well, according to the Psalmist, this blessing of Israel was to be like a seed of grace and salvation planted in the soil of the whole world and of history, ready to sprout and become a flourishing tree.

We turn in thought to the promise the Lord made to Abraham on the day of his election: "I will make of you a great nation, and I will bless you; I will make your name great, so that you will be a blessing ... and by you all the families of the earth shall bless themselves" (*Gn* 12,2-3).

4. In the biblical tradition, one of the effects of the divine blessing that was experienced is the gift of life, of fruitfulness and fertility.

In our Psalm there is an explict reference to this concrete reality, that is precious for existence: "The earth has yielded its fruit" (v. 7). This observation has led scholars to link the Psalm with the rite of thanksgiving for an abundant harvest, the sign of divine favour and a witness for other peoples of the Lord's closeness to Israel.

The same sentence attracted the attention of the Fathers of the Church, who moved from the agricultural horizon to the symbolic perspective. Thus Origen applied the verse to the Virgin Mary and the Eucharist, that is, to Christ who came from the flower of the Virgin and becomes fruit that can be eaten. In this perspective, "the earth is the Blessed Virgin Mary, who comes from our earth, from our seed, from this mud, from this clay, from Adam". This earth has borne its fruit: what it lost in paradise, it has recovered in the Son. "The earth has borne its fruit: first it produced a flower ... then, this flower became a fruit, so that we could eat it, so that we could eat his flesh. Do you want to know what this fruit is? It is the Virgin from the Virgin, the Lord from the handmaid, God from man, the Son from the Mother, the fruit from the earth" (*74 Omelie sul libro dei Salmi*, Milan 1993, p. 141).

5. Let us conclude with St Augustine's words in his commentary on our Psalm. He identifies the fruit that sprouted on earth with the newness that is produced in the human being thanks to the coming of Christ, a newness of conversion, a fruit of praise to God.

Indeed, he describes "the earth as full of thorns". But "there came the hand of One rooting them up, there came a calling by His majesty and mercy, the earth began to confess; now the earth gives her fruit". Certainly, would she give her fruit "unless first she were rained on", "unless first the mercy of God had come from above?" Now we see a mature fruit in the Church thanks to the preaching of the Apostles: Then "by his sending rain through the clouds, by the sending of the Apostles and by their preaching the truth, 'the earth has given her fruit' more abundantly, and that harvest has now filled the whole world" (*Esposizioni sui Salmi*, II, Rome, 1970, p. 551 [*Exposition on the Psalms by St Augustine*, Oxford 1849, vol. 3, pp. 308-309]).

Wednesday

※

Of the Third Week

Psalm 85

Turn your ear, O Lord, and give answer
for I am poor and needy.
Preserve my life, for I am faithful:
save the servant who trusts in you.

You are my God, have mercy on me, Lord
for I cry to you all the day long.
Give joy to your servant, O Lord,
for to you I lift up my soul.

O Lord, you are good and forgiving,
full of love to all who call.
Give heed, O Lord, to my prayer
and attend to the sound of my voice.

In the day of distress I will call
and surely you will reply.
Among the gods there is none like you, O Lord;
nor work to compare with yours.

All the nations shall come to adore you
and glorify your name, O Lord:
for you are great and do marvellous deeds,
you who alone are God.

Show me, Lord, your way
so that I may walk in your truth.
Guide my heart to fear your name.

I will praise you, Lord my God, with all my heart
and glorify your name for ever;
for your love to me has been great:
you have saved me from the depths of the grave.

The proud have risen against me;
ruthless men seek my life:
to you they pay no heed.

But you, God of mercy and compassion,
slow to anger, O Lord,
abounding in love and truth,
turn and take pity on me.

O give your strength to your servant
and save your handmaid's son.
Show me a sign of your favour
that my foes may see to their shame
that you console me and give me your help.

All nations shall come and adore you, O Lord

1. Psalm 85 [86] just recited, which will be the theme of our reflection, offers an impressive description of the Psalmist. He comes before God with these words: I am "your servant" and "the son of your handmaid" (v. 16). Certainly, the expression can belong to the language of court ceremonial, but was used to indicate the servant adopted as a son by the head of a family or tribe. In this light the Psalmist, who defines himself as "the faithful" of the Lord (cf. v. 2), feels he is bound to God by a bond, not just of obedience, but also of familiarity and communion. For this reason his prayer expresses confident abandonment and hope.

Let us now follow this prayer which the *Liturgy of Lauds* sets out for us at the beginning of a day that will probably bring with it not just work and fatigue, but also misunderstanding and problems.

2. The Psalm begins with an intense appeal which the Psalmist directs to the Lord, trusting in his love (cf. vv. 1-7). At the end he expresses again the certainty that the Lord is a "God of mercy, compassionate, slow to anger, full of love, faithful God" (v. 15; cf. *Ex* 34,6). The repeated and convinced expressions of confidence reveal a faith that is intact and pure with an act of abandonment to the "Lord, good ... full of love to all who call on him" (*Ps* 85 [86],5).

At the centre of the Psalm, a hymn is sung to the Lord that alternates feelings of thanksgiving with a profession of faith in the works of salvation that God displays before the peoples (cf. vv. 8-13).

3. Against every temptation to idolatry, the Psalmist proclaims the absolute uniqueness of God (cf. v. 8). In the end he expresses the bold hope that one day "all the nations" shall adore the God of Israel (v. 9). This wonderful prospect finds its fulfillment in the Church of Christ because he sent his apostles to teach "all nations" (*Mt* 28,19). No one but the Lord can offer a full liberation because all depend on him as creatures and all must turn to him in an attitude of adoration (cf. *Ps* 85 [86],9). In fact, he manifests in the cosmos and in history his wonderful works, that give witness to his absolute lordship (cf. v. 10).

At this point the Psalmist presents himself before God with an intense and pure appeal: "Show me, Lord, your way so that I may walk in your truth; give me a simple heart to fear your name" (v. 11).

The petition to be able to know the will of God is wonderful as is the prayer to obtain the gift of "a simple heart" like that of a child, who without duplicity and calculation entrusts himself fully to the Father to direct him on the path of life.

4. Then, from the lips of the faithful flows praise of the merciful God who does not allow him to fall into despair and death, evil and sin (cf. vv. 12-13; *Ps* 15,10-11).

Psalm 85 [86] is a prayer that is dear to Judaism, that inserted it into the liturgy of one of the most important solemnities, *Yom Kippur* or the Day of Atonement. The Book of the Apocalypse, in turn, extracted a verse from it (cf. v. 9), placing it in the glorious heavenly liturgy at the heart of the "song of Moses, the servant of God, and the song of the Lamb": "All nations shall come and worship you" and the Apocalypse adds: "for your [just] judgments have been revealed" (*Apoc* 15,4).

St Augustine dedicated a long and passionate commentary to our Psalm in his *Expositions on the Psalms* transforming it into a song of Christ and of the Christian. The Latin translation, in v. 2, in conformity with the Greek version of the Septuagint instead of the term "faithful" uses the word "holy one": "Preserve my life for I am holy". In reality, only Christ is holy. However, St Augustine reasons, even the Christian can apply these words to himself: "I am holy for you have sanctified me; because I received, not because I had [it of myself]; because you gave it to me, not because I merited it". Therefore, "every Christian by himself, therefore also the whole Body of Christ may say it, may cry everywhere, while it bears tribulations, many temptations and offences: "Preserve my soul because I am holy. Save your servant, my God, who hopes in you'. See, this holy man is not proud since he puts his trust in God" (*Esposizioni sui Salmi*, vol. II, Rome 1970, p. 1251. For an English translation, cf. *Expositions on the Book of Psalms*, vol. IV, Oxford 1850, p. 189).

5. The holy Christian opens himself to the universality of the Church and prays with the Psalmist: "All the nations that you have created shall come and adore you, O Lord" (*Ps* 85 [86],9). Augustine comments: "All the nations in the one Lord are one people, this is true oneness. As there is the Church and churches, and those are churches which are also the Church, so that is a "people' which was peoples; formerly, peoples, many peoples, now only one people. Why only one people?

Because one faith, one hope, one charity, one expectation. Finally, why one people if only one country? Our country is heavenly, our country is Jerusalem.... This people from east to west, from north to the sea, is extended through the four quarters of the whole world" (*ibid.*, p. 1269).

In this universal light our liturgical prayer is transformed into a breath of praise and a hymn of glory to the Lord in the name of every creature.

Canticle   Is 33,13-16

Hear, you who are far off,
what I have done;
and you who are near,
acknowledge my might.

The sinners in Sion are afraid;
trembling has seized the godless:
'Who among us can dwell with the devouring fire?
Who among us can dwell with everlasting burnings?'

He who walks righteously and speaks uprightly,
who despises the gain of oppressions,
who shakes his hands lest they hold a bribe,
who stops his ears from hearing of bloodshed,
and shuts his eyes from looking upon evil,

He will dwell on the heights;
his place of defence will be the fortresses of rocks;
his bread will be given him;
his water will be sure.

The Lord will judge with justice

1. We find the brief text proclaimed today among the biblical Canticles that are interwoven with the Psalms in the *Liturgy of Lauds*. It is taken from the 33rd chapter of the Book of the Prophet Isaiah, his extensive and wonderful collection of divine oracles.

In the verses that precede those quoted (cf. vv. 10-12), the Canticle begins by proclaiming God's powerful and glorious entry onto the stage of human history: "'Now I will arise', says the Lord, 'now I will lift myself up; now I will be exalted'" (v. 10). God's words are addressed to those who are "far off" and to those who are "near", that is, to all the nations of the earth, even the most remote, and to Israel, the people "close" to the Lord, because of the Covenant (cf. v. 13).

Another passage of the *Book of Isaiah* says: "I will place on my lips: peace, peace, to the far and to the near, says the Lord; and I will heal them" (*Is* 57,19). Now, instead, the Lord's words grow harsh and acquire the tone of judgment on the evil of both the "far off" and the "near".

2. In fact see how immediately after, fear spreads among the inhabitants of Zion in whom sin and wickedness have taken root (*Is* 33,14). They are conscious of living alongside the Lord who dwells in the temple, who has chosen to walk with them through history and has transformed himself into the "Emmanuel", "God-with-us" (cf. *Is* 7,14). But the just and holy Lord cannot tolerate unholiness, corruption, injustice. As a "consuming fire" and "everlasting flame" (*Is* 33,14), he lashes out against evil to destroy it.

Isaiah had already warned in chapter 10: "The light of Israel will become a fire, and his Holy One a flame; and it will burn and devour" (v. 17). The psalmist also sang: "As wax melts before fire, so the wicked will perish before God" (*Ps* 67,3). In the context of the economy of the Old Testament, this means that God is not indifferent to good and evil and shows himself to be indignant and angry in the face of wickedness.

3. Our Canticle does not end with this dark scene of judgment. On the contrary, its principal and most intense part is devoted to holiness, received and lived as a sign of the conversion and of reconciliation brought about with God. In continuity with some Psalms, such as 14 and 23, that bring to light the conditions the Lord requires for living in joyful communion with him in the liturgy of the temple, Isaiah lists six moral duties for the true believer who is faithful and just (cf. *Is* 33,15) and can dwell unharmed in the divine fire, that is for him a source of benefits.

The first duty consists of "walking in justice", that is, of seeing divine law as the lamp that lights the path of life. The second one coincides with loyal and sincere speech, the sign of correct and genuine social relations. As the third duty, Isaiah suggests "spurning what is gained by oppression", thus combatting the oppression of the poor, as well as unjust riches. The believer then is determined to condemn political and judicial corruption, "brushing his hands free of contact with a bribe", a provocative image that illustrates the refusal of gifts made to deflect the application of the law and the course of justice.

4. The fifth moral duty is expressed with the meaningful gesture of "stopping your ears", when acts of bloodshed or of violence to be performed are proposed. The sixth and last commitment is expressed with an image which at first sight we find disconcerting. When we speak of "turning a blind eye", we want to say "to pretend not to see so as not to have to intervene"; instead, the Prophet says that the honest person "closes his eyes in order not to see evil" as a sign of his complete refusal to have anything to do with evil.

In his commentary on Isaiah, St Jerome develops this concept with a reflection that takes in the entire passage: "Every iniquity, oppression and injustice is a decision for bloodshed: if one does not kill with the sword, one kills by intention 'and shuts one's eyes, to blot out the evil': happy the conscience that does not listen to nor contemplate evil! Whoever is like this will dwell 'on high', that is, in the Kingdom of Heaven, or in the highest cavern of the soundest Rock, in Christ Jesus" (*In Isaiam prophetam*, 10,33: *PL* 24, 437, p. 367).

Thus Jerome introduces us to a correct understanding of that "closing of the eyes" referred to by the Prophet: it is an invitation to reject absolutely any complicity with evil. As it is easy to perceive, the principal senses of the body are challenged: indeed, the hands, feet, eyes, ears and tongue are involved in human moral behaviour.

5. Whoever chooses to follow this path of honesty and justice will have access to the temple of the Lord where he will receive the security of the exterior and interior well-being which God gives to those who are in communion with Him. The Prophet uses two images to describe this happy ending (cf. v. 16): security in impregnable fortresses and the abundance of bread and water, symbols of the prosperous and happy life.

Tradition has spontaneously interpreted the symbol of water as an image of Baptism (cf. for example, the *Letter of Barnabas*, 11,5), whereas the bread is transfigured, for Christians, into the sign of the Eucharist. This is what we read, for example, in the commentary of St Justin the Martyr, who sees Isaiah's words as prophesying the Eucharistic "bread", the "memorial" of Christ's redeeming death (cf. *Dialogo con Trifone*, Paoline 1988, p. 242; *Dialogue with Trypho*, chapter 70, p. 262, CUA Press, 1948).

---- ✠ ----

Psalm 97

Sing a new song to the Lord
for he has worked wonders.
His right hand and his holy arm
have brought salvation.

The Lord has made known his salvation;
has shown his justice to the nations.
He has remembered his truth and love
for the house of Israel.

All the ends of the earth have seen
the salvation of our God.
Shout to the Lord all the earth,
ring out your joy.

Sing psalms to the Lord with the harp
with the sound of music.
With trumpets and the sound of the horn
acclaim the King, the Lord.

Let the sea and all within it, thunder;
the world, and all its peoples.
Let the rivers clap their hands
and the hills ring out their joy.

Rejoice at the presence of the Lord:
for he comes to rule the earth.
He will rule the world with justice
and the peoples with fairness.

May your kingdom come

1. Psalm 97 [98], just proclaimed, belongs to a kind of hymn we have already met during the spiritual journey we are undertaking in the light of the Psalter.

This is a hymn to the Lord King of the universe and of history (cf. v. 6). It is described as a "new song" (cf. v. 1), which, in biblical language, means a perfect, full, solemn song accompanied by festive music. In fact, in addition to the choral song, the Psalmist evokes "the melodious sound" of the lyre (cf. v. 5), the trumpet and the horn (cf. v. 6), and also a kind of cosmic applause (cf. v. 8).

Moreover, the name of the "Lord" resounds repeatedly (six times), invoked as "our God" (v. 3). Hence, God is at the centre of the scene in all his majesty, while he carries out salvation in history and is awaited to "govern" the world and the peoples (cf. v. 9). The Hebrew verb that indicates "judgment" also means "to govern": so all await the effective action of the Sovereign of the entire earth who will usher in peace and justice.

2. The Psalm opens with the proclamation of divine intervention at the heart of the history of Israel (cf. vv. 1-3). The images of the "right hand" and the "holy arm" refer to Exodus, to the deliverance from the slavery of Egypt (cf. v. 1). Instead, the covenant with the chosen people is remembered through the two great divine perfections: "love" and "faithfulness" (cf. v. 3).

These signs of salvation are revealed "before the eyes of the peoples" and to "all the ends of the earth" (vv. 2.3) so that all humanity may be attracted to God the Saviour and open to his word and to his saving work.

3. The reception reserved for the Lord, who intervenes in history is marked by a universal praise: in addition to the orchestra and the hymns of the Temple of Zion (cf. vv. 5-6), the universe, as a kind of cosmic temple, also participates.

There are four singers of this immense choir of praise. The first is the roaring sea, that seems to be the constant basso of this grandiose hymn (cf. v. 7). The earth and the entire world (cf. vv. 4.7) with all its inhabitants follow united in solemn harmony. The third personification is that of the rivers, that are considered the arms of the sea which, with their rhythmic flow, seem to clap hands in applause (cf. v. 8). Finally, there are the mountains that seem to dance for joy before the Lord, even though they are the most massive and imposing creatures (cf. v. 8; *Ps* 28 [29],6; 113 [114],6).

So we have a colossal choir that has only one purpose: to exalt the Lord, King and just Judge. As mentioned, the end of the Psalm, in fact, presents God, "who comes to govern (and to rule) the earth ... with justice and equity" (*Ps* 97 [98],9).

This is our great hope and our petition: "Your Kingdom come" - a kingdom of peace, justice, and serenity, that will re-establish the original harmony of creation.

4. In this Psalm, with deep joy the Apostle Paul has recognized a prophecy of the work of God in the mystery of Christ. Paul made use of verse 2 to express the theme of his important Letter to the Romans: in the Gospel, the "justice of God is revealed" (cf. *Rom* 1,17), "is manifested" (cf. *Rom* 3,21).

Paul's interpretation confers on the Psalm a greater fullness of meaning. Read in the perspective of the Old Testament, the Psalm proclaims that God saves his people and that all the nations, seeing this, are in admiration. However, in the Christian perspective, God works salvation in Christ, Son of Israel; all the nations see him and are invited to benefit from this salvation, since the Gospel "is the power of God for salvation to everyone who has faith, for the Jew first, and then for the Greek", namely the pagan (*Rom* 1,16). Moreover, "all the ends of the earth" not only "have seen the victory of our God" (Ps 97 [98],3), but have received it.

5. In this perspective, Origen, a Christian writer of the third century, in a text quoted by St Jerome, interprets the "new song" of the Psalm as an anticipated celebration of the Christian newness of the crucified Redeemer. Now let us listen to his commentary in which he combines the song of the Psalmist with the proclamation of the Gospel.

"A new song is the Son of God who was crucified - something that had never before been heard of. A new reality must have a new song. 'Sing to the Lord a new song'. He who suffered the Passion is in reality a man; but you sing to the Lord. He suffered the Passion as a man, but saved as God". Origen continues: Christ "did miracles in the midst of the Jews: he healed paralytics, cleansed lepers, raised up the dead. But other Prophets also did this. He changed a few loaves into an enormous number, and gave countless people something to eat. But Elisha did this. Now, what new thing did he do to merit a new song? Do you want to know what new thing he did? God died as a man so that men might have life; the Son of Man was crucified to raise us up to heaven" (*74 Omelie sul libro dei Salmi* [*74 Homilies on the Book of Psalms*], Milan, 1993, pp. 309-310).

Thursday

———— ❈ ————

Of the Third Week

Psalm 86

On the holy mountain is his city
cherished by the Lord.
The Lord prefers the gates of Sion
to all Jacob's dwellings.
Of you are told glorious things,
O city of God!

'Babylon and Egypt I will count
among those who know me;
Philistia, Tyre, Ethiopia,
these will be her children
and Sion shall be called "Mother"
for all shall be her children.'

It is he, the Lord Most High,
who gives each his place.

In his register of peoples he writes:
'These are her children'
and while they dance they will sing:
'In you all find their home.'

Jerusalem, mother of all peoples

1. The hymn to Jerusalem, city of peace and universal mother, which we have just heard is unfortunately at variance with the historical experience the city is living. But the task of prayer is to sow confidence and give birth to hope.

The universal perspective of Psalm 86 [87] can call to mind the hymn of the *Book of Isaiah,* who sees all the nations converging toward Zion to hear the Word of the Lord and rediscover the beauty of peace, beating their "swords into ploughshares" and their "spears into pruning hooks" (cf. 2,2-5).

In reality, the Psalm is placed in a very different perspective: that of a movement, that instead of converging on Zion, goes out from Zion. The Psalmist sees in Zion the origin of all peoples. After declaring the primacy of the Holy City, not for its historical or cultural merits, but only because of the love God poured out on it (cf. Ps 86 [87],1-3), the Psalm opens to a real celebration of this universality, which makes all peoples brothers and sisters.

2. Zion is sung as mother, not just of Israel, but of all humanity. Such an affirmation is extremely daring. The Psalmist is aware of this and draws attention to it: "Glorious things are spoken of you, O city of God" (v. 3). How could the modest capital of a small nation be portrayed as the origin of peoples who are far more powerful? How can Zion make this immense claim? The answer is given in the same sentence: Zion is mother of all humanity because she is the "city of God"; she is at the foundation of God's plan.

All the cardinal points of the earth are situated in relation with this mother: *Rahab*, that is, Egypt, the great western state; Babylon, the well-known eastern power; Tyre, which personifies the commercial people of the north, while Ethiopia represents the deep south and Palestine, the central area, also a daughter of Zion.

In the spiritual register of Jerusalem, all the peoples of the earth are registered: three times the formula is repeated "This one was born there;

that one [was] born in her" (vv. 4.5.6). It is the official juridical expression which at that time declared that a person was a native of a specific city, and as such, entitled to enjoy all the civil rights of that people.

3. It is striking to observe even nations considered hostile to Israel going up to Jerusalem and to be welcomed not as foreigners but as "relatives". Indeed, the Psalmist transforms the procession of these peoples towards Zion into a choral song and a joyful dance: they rediscover their "source" (cf. v. 7) in the city of God from which a river of living water flows that makes the whole world fruitful, in line with what the Prophets proclaimed (cf. *Ez* 47,1-12; *Zec* 13,1; 14,8; *Apoc* 22,1-2).

In Jerusalem, all people must discover their spiritual roots, feel they are in their homeland, meet again as members of the same family and embrace one another as brothers and sisters who have come back home.

4. A passage of true interreligious dialogue, Psalm 86 [87] sums up the universal heritage of the Prophets (cf. *Is* 56,6-7; 60,6-7; 66,21; *Jos* 4,10-11; *Mal* 1,11, etc.) and anticipates the Christian tradition that applies this Psalm to the "Jerusalem above", which St Paul proclaims, "is free and she is our mother" and has more sons than the earthly Jerusalem (cf. *Gal* 26-27). The *Apocalypse* says the same when it sings of "Jerusalem coming down out of heaven from God" (*Apoc* 21,2.10).

Along the lines of Psalm 86 [87], the Second Vatican Council sees in the universal Church the place in which "all the just from the time of Adam" are reunited, "from Abel the just one to the last of the elect". The Church will be brought to "glorious completion at the end of time" (*Lumen gentium*, n. 2).

5. This ecclesial interpretation of the Psalm is open, in the Christian tradition, to a reinterpretation in a Mariological key. Jerusalem, for the Psalmist, was a real "metropolis" that is, a "mother-city", in which the Lord himself was present (cf. *Zep* 3,14-18). In this light, Christianity sings of Mary as the living Zion in whose womb is conceived the Incarnate Word, and consequently the children of God reborn. The voices of the Fathers of the Church - from Ambrose of Milan to Athanasius of Alexandria, from Maximus Confessor to John

Damascene, from Chromatius of Aquileia to Germanus of Constantinople - agree on this Christian re-reading of Psalm 86 [87].

Let us now listen to a teacher of the Armenian tradition, Gregory of Narek (c. 950-1010), who in his *Panegyric Address to the Blessed Virgin Mary* says to her: "Taking refuge under your most worthy and powerful intercession, we are protected, O holy Mother of God, finding refreshment and repose under the shadow of your protection as if we were protected by a heavily fortified wall: an ornate wall, gracefully inset with the purest diamonds; a wall encircled by fire, therefore impenetrable to the assaults of thieves; sparkling, blazing, insurmountable and inaccessible to cruel traitors; a wall surrounded on all sides, according to David, whose foundations were laid by the Most High (cf. *Ps* 86 [87], 1.5); a mighty wall of the heavenly city, according to Paul (cf. *Gal* 4,26; *Heb* 12,22), where you welcome everyone as its inhabitants because through the corporeal birth of God, you made the children of Jerusalem on earth into children of the heavenly Jerusalem.

Therefore their lips bless your virginal womb and all profess you as the dwelling place and temple of the One who is consubstantial with the Father. Justly, then, what the Prophet said rightly applies to you: "You were for us a house of refuge and our help against the torrents on the days of anguish' (cf. Ps 45 [46],2)" *Testi mariani del primo millennio*, IV, Rome 1991, p. 589).

Canticle   Is 40,10-17

Behold, the Lord God comes with might,
and his arm rules for him;
behold, his reward is with him,
and his recompense before him.

He will feed his flock like a shepherd,
he will gather the lambs in his arms,
he will carry them in his bosom,
and gently lead those that are with young.

Who has measured the waters in the hollow of his hand
and marked off the heavens with a span,

enclosed the dust of the earth in a measure
and weighed the mountains in scales
and the hills in a balance?

Who has directed the Spirit of the Lord,
or as his counsellor has instructed him?
Whom did he consult for his enlightenment,
and who taught him the path of justice,
taught him knowledge,
and showed him the way of understanding?

Behold, the nations are like a drop from a bucket,
and are accounted as the dust on the scales;
behold, he takes up the isles
like fine dust.

Lebanon would not suffice for fuel,
nor are its beasts enough for a burnt offering.
All the nations are as nothing before him,
they are accounted by him as less than nothing and emptiness.

Almighty God, omniscient Lord, loving shepherd

1. The book of the great Prophet Isaiah, who lived in the eighth century B.C., also contains the voices of other Prophets who were his disciples and successors. This is the case of the one whom Biblical scholars have called "Deutero-Isaiah", the Prophet of Israel's return from the Babylonian exile which took place in the sixth century B.C. His work forms the chapters 40-55 of the *Book of Isaiah* and it is from one of these chapters that the Church has taken the Canticle just proclaimed that has become part of the *Liturgy of Lauds*.

This Canticle consists of two parts: the first two verses come from the end of a magnificent oracle of consolation that proclaims the return of the exiles to Jerusalem, under the leadership of God himself (cf. *Is* 40,1-11). The subsequent verses form the beginning of an apologetic discourse that exalts God's omniscience and omnipotence and also subjects to harsh criticism the makers of idols.

2. Thus at the beginning of the liturgical text, the powerful figure of God appears, who returns to Jerusalem preceded by his trophies, just as Jacob had returned to the Holy Land preceded by his flocks (cf. *Gn* 31,17;

32,17). God's trophies are the exiled Hebrews whom he snatched out of the hands of their conquerors. God is then depicted "like a shepherd" (*Is* 40,11). Frequently in the Bible and in other ancient traditions, this image evokes the idea of leadership and kingship, but here his traits are above all gentle and cherishing, for the shepherd is also the travelling companion of his sheep (cf. *Ps* 22 [23]). He cares for his flock, not only by feeding it and caring that it does not go stray, but also tenderly bending over his lambs and his ewes with their young (cf. *Is* 40,11).

3. When the description of the entry of the Lord, King and Shepherd onto the scene is over, there is a reflection on his way of acting as Creator of the universe. No one can match him in this grandiose, colossal work: certainly no man and even less so the idols, dead and impotent beings. The Prophet then makes use of a series of rhetorical questions which already contain their answers.

They are uttered in a kind of public trial: no one can compete with God nor claim for himself his immense power, his unlimited wisdom.

No one can measure the vast universe created by God. The Prophet makes us understand how human instruments are ridiculously inadequate for the task. Furthermore, God was a solitary architect; no one was able to help or advise him in so immense a project as the creation of the cosmos (cf. vv. 13-14).

In his 18th *Baptismal Catechesis*, on the basis of our Canticle, St Cyril of Jerusalem suggests that we not measure God with the measure of our human limitations: "To you, poor weak man that you are, India is far from the land of the Goths, Spain from Persia. But to God, who holds the whole earth in the hollow of His hand, all things are near". (*Le catechesi*, Rome 1993, p. 408; *Catechesis* 18, *The Works of St Cyril of Jerusalem,* vol. 2, p. 121, CUA Press, 1970).

4. After celebrating God's omnipotence in creation, the Prophet describes his lordship over history, namely, over the nations, over humanity who populates the earth. The inhabitants of the known territories, but also those of the remote regions that the Bible calls the distant "isles", are a microscopic reality in relation to the Lord's infinite greatness. The images are brilliant and intense: the nations are compared to "a drop in the bucket", the "rust on the scales", "powder" (in Italian, a grain of dust) (*Is* 40,15).

No one would be able to offer a sacrifice worthy of this grandiose Lord and King: all the sacrificial victims of the earth would not suffice, nor all the forests of the cedars of Lebanon to fuel the fire of this holocaust (cf. v. 16). The Prophet brings the human being to the consciousness of his limitations before the infinite grandeur and sovereign omnipotence of God. The conclusion is lapidary: "All the nations are as nothing before him, as nothing and emptiness are they accounted by him" (v. 17).

5. The faithful person is therefore invited from the beginning of the day to adore the Almighty Lord. St Gregory of Nyssa, a Father of the Church of Cappadocia (fourth century) meditated on the Canticle of Isaiah this way: "When we hear the word "almighty', our conception is this, that God sustains in being all intelligible things as well as all things of a material nature. For this reason he sits upon the circle of the earth, for this reason, he holds the ends of the earth in his hands, for this reason he measures out heaven with the span and measures the waters in the hollow of his hand.

For this reason he comprehends in himself all the intelligible creation, that all things may remain in existence controlled by His encompassing power" (*Teologia trinitaria*, Milan 1994; *Against Eunomius*, p. 120, col. 1, *Nicene and Post-Nicene Fathers*, Wm. B Eerdmans, reprinted 1979).

For his part, St Jerome halts with wonder before another amazing truth: that of Christ who, "though he was in the form of God ... emptied himself, taking the form of a servant, being born in the likeness of man" (*Phil* 2,6-7). The infinite, all-powerful God, he remarks, made himself small and finite. St Jerome contemplates him in the stable of Bethlehem and exclaims: "He within whose closed fist the whole world is held, is contained by the narrow confines of a manger" (Lettera 22,39 in: *Opere scelte*, I, Turin 1971, p. 379; *The Letters of St Jerome*, vol. 1, Letters 1-22, p. 176, Newman Press Paulist Press, Ramsey NJ, 1963).

------ ❋ ------

Psalm 98

The Lord is king; the peoples tremble.
He is throned on the cherubim; the earth quakes.
The Lord is great in Sion.

He is supreme over all the peoples.
Let them praise his name, so terrible and great.
He is holy, full of power.

You are a king who loves what is right;
you have established equity, justice and right;
you have established them in Jacob.

Exalt the Lord our God;
bow down before Sion, his footstool.
He the Lord is holy.

Among his priests were Aaron and Moses,
among those who invoked his name was Samuel.
They invoked the Lord and he answered.

To them he spoke in the pillar of cloud.
They did his will; they kept the law,
which he, the Lord, had given.

O Lord our God, you answered them.
For them you were a God who forgives;
yet you punished all their offences.

Exalt the Lord our God;
bow down before his holy mountain
for the Lord our God is holy.

Holy is the Lord our God

1. "The Lord reigns". The acclamation that opens Psalm 98 [99], that we have just heard, reveals its basic theme and literary genre. It is a lofty song of the People of God to the Lord who governs the world and history as transcendent, supreme sovereign. It reminds us of other similar hymns - Psalms 95-97, which we have already reflected upon - which the *Liturgy of Lauds* sets forth as an ideal morning prayer.

In fact, as the faithful person starts his day, he knows that he is not left to the mercy of blind and dark chance, nor given over to the uncertainty of his freedom, nor dependent on the decisions of others, nor dominated by the events of history. He knows that the Creator and Saviour in his greatness, holiness and mercy, is above every earthly reality.

2. Experts have put forward several hypotheses on the use of this Psalm in the liturgy of the Temple of Zion. In any case, it has the character of a contemplative praise that rises to the Lord, enthroned in heavenly glory before all the peoples and the earth (cf. v. 1). Yet God makes himself present in a place and in the midst of a community, namely, in Jerusalem (cf. v. 2), showing that he is "God-with-us".

In the first verses the Psalmist attributes seven solemn titles to God: he is king, great, supreme, terrible, holy, powerful, just (cf. vv. 1-4). Further on, God is also described as "patient" (cf. v. 8). Above all, the emphasis is put on the holiness of God. Indeed, "he is holy" is repeated three times - almost in the form of an antiphon - (vv. 3.5.9). In biblical language this term indicates above all divine transcendence. God is superior to us, and he is infinitely above every one of his creatures.

This transcendence, however, does not make him an impassive and distant sovereign: when he is called upon, he responds (cf. v. 6). God is He who can save, the only One who can free humanity from evil and death. Indeed, "he loves justice" and has "established equity and justice in Jacob" (v. 4).

3. The Fathers of the Church have reflected at great length on the theme of the holiness of God, celebrating his divine inaccessibility. However, this transcendent, holy God drew near to humanity. Indeed, as St Irenaeus says, he already became "accustomed" to being with the human person in the Old Testament, showing himself in appearances and speaking through the Prophets, while man "became accustomed" to God learning to follow and obey him. Indeed, in one of his hymns, St Ephrem stressed that through the Incarnation "the Holy One dwelt in the [Mary's] womb in a bodily manner, and behold, he dwells in the mind in a spiritual manner" (St Ephrem, *Inni sulla Natività*, 4, 130 Ephrem the Syrian, *Hymns on the Nativity*, 4, 130, p. 99, Paulist Press, Mahwah, N.J., 1989). Moreover, through the gift of the Eucharist, in analogy with the Incarnation, "The Medicine of Life came down from above/ to dwell in those who are worthy of him./ After entering them,/ he set up his dwelling among us,/ so that we can be sanctified in him" (*Inni conservati in armeno*, [*Hymns preserved in Armenian*], 47,27.30).

4. This deep bond between the "holiness" and closeness of God is also developed in Psalm 98 [99]. In fact, after contemplating the absolute perfection of the Lord, the Psalmist reminds us that God was in constant touch with his people through Moses and Aaron, his mediators, and through Samuel, his Prophet. He spoke and was heard, he punished offenses but also forgave.

The sign of his presence among his people was "his footstool", namely, the throne of the Ark of the Temple of Zion (cf. vv. 5-8). The holy and invisible God also made himself available to his people through Moses, the legislator, Aaron the priest and Samuel the Prophet. He revealed himself in words and deeds of salvation and judgment. He was present in Zion in the worship celebrated in the temple.

5. So we can say that today Psalm 98 [99] is fulfilled in the Church, the centre of the presence of the holy and transcendent God. The Lord did not withdraw into the inaccessible realm of his mystery, indifferent to our history and our expectations. He "comes to judge the earth. He will judge the world with justice, and the peoples with equity" (*Ps* 97 [98],9).

God came among us above all in his Son, who became one of us, to instil in us his life and his holiness. This is why we now approach God with confidence not terror. Indeed, in Christ we have the High Priest, holy, innocent and unblemished. He "is able for all time to save those who draw near to God through him, since he always lives to make intercession for them" (*Heb* 7,25). Our hymn, then, is full of serenity and joy: it exalts the Lord, the King, who dwells among us, wiping every tear from our eyes (cf. *Apoc* 21,3-4).

Friday

Of the Third Week

Psalm 50 - See Friday of the first week (see p. 63 above)

Take not your Holy Spirit from me

1. Every week the *Liturgy of Lauds* repeats Psalm 50 [51], the famous *Miserere*. We have already reflected on sections of it on other occasions. Now also, we will reflect in a particular way on a section of this grandiose plea for forgiveness: verses 12-16.

First of all, it is important to note that in the original Hebrew the word "spirit" is repeated three times, invoked of God as a gift and received by the human creature who has repented of his sin: "Renew in me a steadfast spirit.... Do not deprive me of your holy spirit.... Sustain in me a generous spirit" (vv. 12.13.14). One could say, taking recourse to a liturgical term, that it is an "epiclesis", that is, a triple invocation of the Spirit who, as in creation hovered over the waters (cf. *Gn* 1,2), now penetrates the soul of the faithful, infusing it with new life and raising it from the kingdom of sin to the heaven of grace.

2. The Church Fathers, in the "spirit" invoked by the Psalmist, see the effective presence of the Holy Spirit. Thus, St Ambrose is convinced that it is about the Holy Spirit, who is one "who was active in the Prophets, was breathed upon the Apostles and was joined with the Father and the Son in the sacrament of Baptism" (*Lo Spirito Santo* I, 4, 55: SAEMO 16, p. 95; *The Holy Spirit* in St Ambrose, *Theological and Dogmatic Works*, CUA Press, reprinted 1977). The same conviction is expressed by other Fathers, such as Didymus the Blind of Alexandria, Egypt, and Basil of Caesarea in their respective treatises on the Holy Spirit (Didymus the Blind, *Lo Spirito Santo*, Rome 1990, p. 59; Basil of Caesarea, *Lo Spirito Santo*, X, 24, Rome 1993).

Again, St Ambrose, observing that the Psalmist speaks of the joy that invades the soul once it has received the generous and powerful Spirit of God, comments: "Joy and delight are fruits of the Spirit and really the sovereign Spirit is the one on whom we are founded. Thus whoever is brought to life by the sovereign Spirit is not subject to slavery, is not enslaved by sin, is not indecisive, does not wander here and there, is not uncertain in his choices, but standing on the rock, he is firm with feet that do not waver" (*Apologia del profeta David a Teodosio Augusto*, 15,72 *[Defence of the Prophet David for the Emperor Theodosius]*: SAEMO 5, 129).

3. With this triple mention of the "spirit", after describing in the preceding verses the dark prison of guilt, Psalm 50 [51] opens onto the bright realm of grace. It is an important turning point, comparable to a new creation. As in the beginning God breathed his spirit into matter and created the human person (cf. *Gn* 2,7), so now the same divine Spirit recreates (cf. *Ps* 50 [51],12), renews, transfigures and transforms the repentant sinner, embraces him again (cf. v. 13) making him share in the joy of salvation (cf. v. 14). Now the human being, animated by the divine Spirit, sets out on the path of justice and love, as is said in another Psalm: "Teach me to do your will, for you are my God! Let your good spirit guide me on a level path!" (cf. *Ps* 142 [143],10).

4. Having experienced this inner rebirth, the person praying becomes a witness; he promises God to "teach the erring your ways" of good (*Ps* 50 [51],15), so that, like the Prodigal Son, they may be able to return to the house of the Father. In the same way, St Augustine, after experiencing the dark paths of sin, in his *Confessions* felt the need to witness to the freedom and the joy of salvation.

Whoever has experienced God's merciful love, becomes a passionate witness of it, especially in dialogue with those who are still caught in the nets of sin. Let us think of the person of Paul, dazzled by Christ on the road to Damascus, who became an untiring missionary of divine grace.

5. For one last time, the person praying looks at his dark past and cries out to God: "Free me from blood guilt, O God, my saving God (cf. NAB version of v. 16). The "blood", to which he refers is variously interpreted in Scripture. Here on the lips of King David, it refers to the killing of Uriah, the husband of Bathsheba, the woman who was the object of the king's passion. In a more general sense, the invocation indicates the desire for purification from evil, violence and hatred always present in the human heart with dark and malicious force. Now the lips of the faithful person, purified from sin, sing praise to the Lord.

In fact, the passage of Psalm 50 [51] which we have just commented on ends with the promise to proclaim the "justice" of God. The term "justice" in this context, as so often in biblical language, does not actually indicate God's punitive action of evil by God, but rather indicates the sinner's rehabilitation, since God reveals his justice by making sinners just (cf. *Rom* 3,26). God derives no pleasure from the death of the wicked, but only that he give up his behaviour and live (cf. *Ez* 18,23).

Canticle   Jer 14,17-21

Let my eyes run down with tears night and day,
and let them not cease,
for the virgin daughter of my people is smitten with a great wound,
with a very grievous blow.

If I go out into the field,
behold, those slain by the sword!
And if I enter the city,
behold, the diseases of famine!
For both prophet and priest ply their trade through the land,
and have no knowledge.

Have you utterly rejected Judah?
Does your soul loathe Sion?
Why have you smitten us
so that there is no healing for us?

We looked for peace,
but no good came;
for a time of healing,
but behold, terror.

We acknowledge our wickedness, O Lord,
and the iniquity of our fathers,
for we have sinned against you.
Do not spurn us, for your name's sake;
do not dishonour your glorious throne;
remember and do not break your covenant with us.

Show us O Lord your mercy

1. The Prophet Jeremiah raises to heaven from within his own historical context a bitter and deeply felt song (14,17-21). We have just heard it recited as an invocation, which the *Liturgy of Lauds* presents to us on the day when we commemorate the Lord's death: Friday. The context in which this lamentation arises is represented by a scourge that often strikes the land of the Middle East: drought. However, with this natural disaster, the Prophet interweaves another, the tragedy of war which is equally appalling: "If I walk out into the field, look! those slain by the sword; if I enter the city look! those consumed by hunger". Unfortunately, the description is tragically present in so many regions of our planet.

2. Jeremiah enters the scene with his face bathed in tears: he weeps uninterruptedly for "the daughter of his people", namely for Jerusalem. Indeed, according to a well-known biblical symbol, the city is represented with a feminine image, "the daughter of Zion". The Prophet participates intimately in the "great destruction" and in the "incurable wound" of his people (v. 17). Often, his words are marked by sorrow and tears, because Israel does not allow herself to be involved in the mysterious message that suffering brings with it. In another passage, Jeremiah exclaims: "If you do not listen to this in your pride, I will weep in secret many tears; my eyes will run with tears for the Lord's flock, led away to exile" (13,17).

3. The reason for the Prophet's heart-rending prayer is to be found, as has been said, in two tragic events: the sword and hunger, that is, war and famine (*Jer* 14,18). We are therefore in a tormented historical situation and the portrait of the Prophet and the priest, guardians of the Lord's Word who "wander about the land distraught" (*ibid.*) is striking.

The second part of the Canticle (cf. vv. 19-21) is no longer an individual lament in the first person singular, but a collective supplication addressed to God: "Why have you struck *us* a blow that cannot be healed?" (v. 19). In fact, in addition to the sword and hunger, there is a greater tragedy, that of the silence of God who no longer reveals himself and seems to have retreated into his heaven, as if disgusted with humanity's actions. The questions addressed to him are therefore tense and explicit in a typically religious sense: "Have you cast off Judah completely?", or "Is Zion loathsome to you?" (v. 19). Now they feel lonely and forsaken, deprived of peace, salvation and hope. The people, left to themselves, feel as if they were isolated and overcome by terror.

Isn't this existential solitude perhaps the profound source of all the dissatisfaction we also perceive in our day? So much insecurity, so many thoughtless reactions originate in our having abandoned God, the rock of our salvation.

4. Now comes the turning-point: the people return to God and raise an intense prayer to him. First of all, they recognize their own sin with a brief but heartfelt confession of guilt: "We recognize, O Lord, our wickedness,... that we have sinned against you" (v. 21). Thus God's silence was provoked by man's rejection. If the people will be converted and return to the Lord, God will also show himself ready to go out to meet and embrace them.

Finally, the Prophet uses two fundamental words: "remember" and "covenant" (v. 21). God is asked by his people to "remember", that is, to return to the line of his generous kindness, which he had so often shown in the past with crucial interventions to save Israel. God is asked to remember that he bound himself to his people by a covenant of fidelity and love. Precisely because of this covenant, the people can be confident that the Lord will intervene to set them free and save them.

The commitment he assumed, the honour of his "name" and the fact that he was present in the temple, "the throne of his glory", impel God - after his judgment of sin and his silence - to draw close to his people once again to give them life, peace and joy.

With the Israelites, therefore, we too can be sure that the Lord will not give us up for good but, after every purifying trial, will return to make "his face to shine upon us, and be gracious to us ... and give us peace" as the priestly blessing mentioned in *Numbers* says (6,25-26).

5. To conclude, we can associate Jeremiah's plea with the moving exhortation that St Cyprian, Bishop of Carthage in the third century, addressed to the Christians of that city. In a time of persecution, St Cyprian exhorted his faithful to implore the Lord. This prayer is not identical to the Prophet's supplication for it does not include a confession of sin as the persecution is not so much a punishment for sin, but a participation in Christ's Passion. Nevertheless, it is as urgent an entreaty as Jeremiah's. St Cyprian writes, "What we must do is beg the Lord with united and undivided hearts, without pause in our entreaty, with confidence that we shall receive, seeking to appease Him with cries and tears as befits those who find themselves amid the lamentations of the fallen and the trembling of the remnant still left, amidst the host of those who lie faint and savaged and the tiny band of those who stand firm. We must beg that peace be promptly restored, that help be quickly brought to our places of concealment and peril, that those things be fulfilled which the Lord vouchsafes to reveal to his servants: the restoration of His church, the certitude of our salvation, bright skies after rain, after darkness light, after wild storms a gentle calm. We must beg that the Father send his loving aid to his children, that God in his majesty perform now as he has so often His wonderful works" (*cf. Letter* 11,8 in *The Letters of St Cyprian of Carthage*, vol. I, p. 80, in the series *Ancient Christian Writers*, Newman Press, Ramsay, N.J. 1984).

Psalm 99

Cry out with joy to the Lord, all the earth.
Serve the Lord with gladness.
Come before him, singing for joy.

Know that he, the Lord, is God.
He made us, we belong to him,
we are his people, the sheep of his flock.

Go within his gates, giving thanks.
Enter his courts with songs of praise.
Give thanks to him and bless his name.

Indeed, how good is the Lord,
eternal his merciful love.
He is faithful from age to age.

In prayer we abandon ourselves to God's embrace

1. In the spirit of joy and celebration that continues in this last week of the Christmas season, we want to resume our meditation on the *Liturgy of Lauds*. Today we reflect on Psalm 99 [100], just proclaimed, which is a joyful invitation to praise the Lord, the shepherd of his people.

Seven imperatives are scattered throughout the Psalm and call the faithful community to celebrate and worship the God of love and of the covenant: *extol, serve, come before, acknowledge, enter his gates, praise him, bless him*. One thinks of a liturgical procession that is about to enter the Temple of Zion to perform a rite in honour of the Lord (cf. *Ps* 14; 23; 94).

In the Psalm certain characteristic terms are repeated for exalting the bond of the covenant that exists between God and Israel. Above all, there emerges the assertion of a complete belonging to God: "we belong to him, we are his people" (*Ps* 99 [100],3), an affirmation full of both pride and humility, since Israel is presented as "the sheep of his pasture" (*ibid.*). We later find an expression of relationship: "For he [the Lord] is our God" (*Ps* 94 [95],7). Then we discover the richness of the relationship of love, his "mercy" and "fidelity", joined with his "goodness" (cf. *Ps* 99 [100],5), which, in the original Hebrew are formulated with the typical terms of the covenant that binds Israel to her God.

2. The coordinates of space and time are also reviewed. In fact, on the one hand, the entire earth is presented to us as joined in the praise of God (cf. v. 2); then the horizon shifts to the sacred area of the Temple of Jerusalem with its courts and gates (cf. v. 4), where the community is gathered in prayer. On the other hand, reference is made to time in its three basic dimensions: the past of creation ("the Lord our God, he made us", v. 3), the present of the covenant and worship ("we belong to him, we are his people, the sheep of his pasture", *ibid.*) and finally, the future, in which the Lord's merciful fidelity extends "from age to age" revealing itself to be "eternal" (v. 5).

3. We will now reflect briefly on the seven imperatives that make up the long invitation to praise God and take up the whole Psalm (vv. 2-4) before we discover, in the last verse, their motivation in the exaltation of God, contemplated in his intimate and profound identity.

The first appeal consists in the festive acclamation that involves the whole earth in the song of praise to the Creator. When we pray, we should feel in tune with all those who pray exalting the one Lord in different languages and ways. As the Prophet Malachi says, "For from the rising of the sun even to its setting, my name is great among the nations, and in every place incense is offered to my name, and everywhere they bring sacrifice to my name and a pure offering; for my name is great among the nations, says the Lord of hosts" (1,11).

4. Then come several calls using liturgical and ritual terms "serve", "come before" and "go within the gates" of the temple. These are verbs which in alluding to royal audiences, describe the various gestures the faithful perform when they enter the sanctuary of Zion to take part in the community's prayer. After the cosmic hymn, the liturgy is celebrated by the people of God "the sheep of his pasture", his "possession among all peoples" (*Ex* 19,5).

The invitation to "go within his gates, giving thanks" and to "enter his courts with songs of praise" reminds us of a passage from *The Mysteries* of St Ambrose, in which he describes the baptized as they approach the altar: "The cleansed people, [rich in these insignia], hasten to the altar of Christ, saying: 'I will go to the altar of God, the God who gives joy to my youth' (*Ps* 42 [43],4). For the people, having put aside the defilements of ancient error, renewed in their youth as an eagle, hasten to approach the heavenly banquet. So they come, and, when they see the sacred altar properly prepared, they exclaim: ['You have prepared a table in my sight'. David introduces these people as speaking when he says], 'The Lord is my shepherd, I shall not want; he makes me lie down in green pastures. He leads me beside still waters; he restores my soul' (*Ps* 22 [23],1-2)" (St Ambrose, *Theological and Dogmatic Works*, pp. 20-21, CUA Press, 1963).

5. The other imperatives that enrich the Psalm repeat the fundamental religious attitudes of the person at prayer: *acknowledge, praise, bless*. The verb *to acknowledge* expresses the content of the profession of faith in the one God. In fact, we must proclaim that only "the Lord is God" (*Ps* 99 [100],3), combatting all idolatry, pride and human power opposed to him.

The object of the other verbs praise and bless, is also "the name" of the Lord (cf. v. 4), or his person, his effective and saving presence.

In this light the Psalm leads in the end to a solemn exaltation of God, that is a kind of profession of faith: the Lord is good and his fidelity never abandons us because He is always ready to sustain us with his merciful love. With this confidence the person praying abandons himself to the embrace of his God: "Taste and see that the Lord is good!" and the Psalmist also says, "happy are those who take refuge in him" (*Ps* 33 [34],9; cf. *1 Pt* 2,3).

Saturday

———— ✖ ————

Of the Third Week

Psalm 118 - See Saturday of the first week (see p. 73 above)

Begin the day with prayer: let Christ be the light of day

1. In our already long journey through the Psalms that the *Liturgy of Lauds* presents, we come to one strophe - to be precise, the 19th - of the longest prayer of the Psalter, Psalm 118 [119]. It is a part of an immense alphabetical hymn. In a play on style, the Psalmist divides his work into 22 strophes corresponding to the sequence of the 22 letters of the Hebrew alphabet. Each strophe has eight verses and the first word of each verse uses a Hebrew word that begins with the same letter of the alphabet.

The stanza we have just heard is a strophe marked by the Hebrew letter *qôf*, that portrays the person at prayer who expresses his intense life of faith and prayer to God (cf. vv. 145-152).

2. The invocation of the Lord is relentless because it is a continuing response to the permanent teaching of the Word of God. On the one hand, in fact, the verbs used in prayer are multiplied: "I cry to you", "I call upon you", "I cry for help", "hear my voice". On the other hand, the Psalmist exalts the word of the Lord that proposes *decrees, teachings, the word, promises, judgment, the law, the precepts and testimonies* of God. Together they form a constellation that is like the polar star of the Psalmist's faith and confidence. Prayer is revealed as a dialogue that begins when it is night before the first gleam of dawn (cf. v. 147), and continues through the day, particularly in the difficult trials of life. In fact, at times the horizon is dark and stormy: "In betrayal my persecutors turn on me, they are far from your law" (v. 150). But the person praying has a steadfast certainty: the closeness of God, with his word and his grace: "But you, O Lord, are close" (v. 151). God does not abandon the just in the hands of persecutors.

3. At this point, having outlined the simple but incisive message of the stanza of Psalm 118 [119] - a suitable message for the beginning of the day - we will turn for our meditation to a great Father of the Church, St Ambrose who, in his *Commentary on Psalm 118* [*119*], devotes 44 paragraphs to explaining the stanza we have just heard.

Taking up the ideal invitation to sing praise of God from the early hours of the morning, he reflects in particular on verses 147-148: "I rise before dawn and cry for help.... My eyes greet the night watches". From the Psalmist's declaration, St Ambrose intuits the idea of a constant prayer that embraces all the hours of the day: "Whoever calls upon the Lord must act as if he does not know the existence of any special time to be dedicated to implore the Lord, but always remains in that attitude of supplication. Whether we eat or drink, let us proclaim Christ, pray to Christ, think of Christ, speak of Christ! May Christ be ever in our heart and on our lips!" (*Commentary on Psalm 118* [*119*],2: SAEMO 10, p. 297).

Referring to the verses that speak of the specific moment of the morning, and alluding to the expression of the *Book of Wisdom* that prescribes that we are "to give [the Lord] thanks before the sunrise" (16,28), St Ambrose comments: "It would be serious indeed if the rays of the rising sun were to surprise you lying lazily in bed with insolent impudence and if an even brighter light wounded your sleepy eyes, still sunk in torpor. It is a disgrace for us to spend so long a period of time without even the least devotional practice, without offering a spiritual sacrifice during a night with nothing to do" (*ibid.*, op. cit., p. 303).

4. Then St Ambrose, contemplating the rising sun - as he did in another of his famous hymns, "at the crack of dawn", *Aeterne rerum conditor*, included in the *Liturgy of the Hours*, counsels us in this way: "Perhaps, you do not know, O man, that every day you owe to God the first fruits of your heart and voice? The harvest ripens every day; every day the fruit ripens. So run to meet the rising sun.... The sun of justice wishes to be anticipated and does not expect anything else.... If you rise before the sun you will receive Christ as your light. He Himself will be the first light that shines in the secret of your heart. He Himself will be ... who will make the light of dawn shine for you in the hours of the night, if you will meditate on God's Word. While you meditate, the light rises.... Early in the morning hasten to church and in homage take the first fruits of your devotion. And then, if the affairs of the world call you, nothing will prevent you from saying: 'My eyes anticipate the watches of the night to meditate on your promises'; and, with a good conscience, you will betake yourself to your affairs. How beautiful it is to begin the day with hymns and songs, with the beatitudes you read in the Gospel! How promising that the Lord's words should descend on you as a blessing; and that as you sing, you repeat the blessings of the Lord, that you be gripped by the need to practice some virtue, if you also want to perceive within you something that makes you feel worthy of the divine blessing!" (*ibid.*, *op. cit.*, pp. 303.309.311.313).

Let us respond to St Ambrose's call, and every morning open our eyes to daily life, to its joys and worries, calling on God to be close to us and guide us with his words that ensure serenity and grace.

———— ❊ ————

Canticle   Wis 9,1-6.9-11

O God of my fathers and Lord of mercy,
who have made all things by your word,
and by your wisdom have formed man
to have dominion over the creatures you have made,
and rule the world in holiness and righteousness,
and pronounce judgment in uprightness of soul,
give me the wisdom that sits by your throne,
and do not reject me from among your servants.

For I am your slave
and the son of your maidservant,
a man who is weak and short-lived,
with little understanding of judgment and laws;
for even if one is perfect among the sons of men,
yet without the wisdom that comes from you
he will be regarded as nothing.

With you is wisdom, who knows your works
and was present when you made the world,
and who understands what is pleasing in your sight
and what is right according to your commandments.

Send her forth from the holy heavens,
and from the throne of your glory send her,

that she may be with me and toil,
and that I may learn what is pleasing to you;
for she knows and understands all things,
and she will guide me wisely in my actions
and guard me with her glory.

True wisdom is a participation in the mind of God

1. The Canticle we just heard now presents a great part of a long prayer placed on the lips of Solomon, who in the biblical tradition is considered *the just and wise king par excellence*. It is offered to us in the ninth chapter of the *Book of Wisdom*, an Old Testament work that was written in Greek, perhaps at Alexandria, Egypt, at the dawn of the Christian era. In it we can perceive tones of the lively, open Judaism of the Jewish Diaspora in the Hellenistic world.

This Book offers us three currents of theological thought: blessed immortality as the final end of the life of the just (cf. cc. 1-5); wisdom as a divine gift and guide of life and of the decisions of the faithful (cf. cc. 6-9); the history of salvation, especially the fundamental event of the Exodus from Egyptian oppression, as a sign of that struggle between good and evil that leads to full salvation and redemption (cf. cc. 10-19).

2. Solomon lived about ten centuries before the inspired author of the *Book of Wisdom*, but has been considered the founder and ideal author of all later sapiential thought. The prayer in the form of a hymn placed on his lips is a solemn invocation addressed to "the God of my fathers, Lord of mercy" (9,1), that he would grant the precious gift of wisdom.

In our text there is a clear allusion to the scene narrated in the *First Book of Kings* when Solomon, at the beginning of his reign, goes up on the heights of Gibeon where there was a sanctuary. After celebrating a grandiose sacrifice, he has a revelation in a dream at night. To the request of God himself, who invited him to ask for a gift, he replies: "Give your servant, therefore, an understanding heart to judge your people and to distinguish right from wrong" (*1 Kgs* 3,9).

3. The starting point offered by Solomon's prayer is developed in our Canticle in a series of appeals to the Lord to grant the irreplaceable treasure of wisdom.

In the passage presented by the *Liturgy of Lauds* we find these two prayers: "Give me Wisdom ... send her forth from your holy heavens and from your glorious throne" (*Wis* 9,4.10). Without this gift we are conscious that we lack a guide, as if we were without a polar star to direct us in the moral choices of life: "I am ... a man weak and short-lived and lacking in comprehension of judgment and of laws ... if Wisdom, which comes from you be not with [me] [I] shall be held in no esteem" (vv. 5-6).

It is easy to intuit that this "wisdom" is not mere intelligence or practical ability, but rather a participation in the very mind of God who "with his wisdom [has] established man" (cf. v. 2). Thus it is the ability to penetrate the deep meaning of being, of life and of history, going beyond the surface of things and events to discover their ultimate meaning, willed by the Lord.

4. Wisdom is a lamp that enlightens the moral choices of daily life and leads us on the straight path "to understand what is pleasing in [the] eyes [of the Lord] and what is comfortable with your commands" (cf. v. 9). For this reason the Liturgy makes us pray with the words of the *Book of Wisdom* at the beginning of the day, so that God may be close to us with his wisdom and "assist us and support us in our (daily) toil" (cf. v. 10), revealing to us the good and evil, the just and unjust.

Taking the hand of divine Wisdom, we go forward confidently in the world. We cling to her loving her with a spousal love after the example of Solomon who, according to the *Book of Wisdom*, confessed: "I loved and sought after her from my youth; I sought to take her for my bride and was enamoured of her beauty" (*Wis* 8,2).

The Fathers of the Church identified Christ as the Wisdom of God, following St Paul who defined Christ as "the power of God and the wisdom of God" (*1 Cor* 1,24).

Let us conclude with the prayer St Ambrose addresses to Christ: "Teach me words rich in wisdom for you are Wisdom! Open my heart, you who have opened the Book! Open the door that is in Heaven, for you are the Door! If we are introduced through you, we will possess the eternal Kingdom. Whoever enters through you will not be deceived, for he cannot err who enters the dwelling place of Truth" (*Commento al Salmo* 118/1 [*Comment on Psalm 118*]: SAEMO 9, p. 377).

———— ✖ ————

Psalm 116 - See Saturday of the first week (see p. 79 above)

Prayer is a ray of light in a self-sufficient world

1. Continuing our meditation on the texts of the *Liturgy of Lauds*, we consider again a Psalm already presented, the shortest of all the Psalms. It is Psalm 116 [117] which we have just heard, a short hymn or an aspiration that becomes a universal praise of the Lord. It proclaims what is expressed in two fundamental words: *covenant love and faithfulness* (cf. v. 2).

With these terms the Psalmist describes synthetically the Covenant between God and Israel, stressing the deep, loyal and trusting relationship between the Lord and his people. We hear the echo of the words that God himself spoke on Mount Sinai when he appeared to Moses: "The Lord, the Lord, a merciful and gracious God, slow to anger, and abounding in steadfast love and faithfulness" (*Ex* 34,6).

2. Despite its brevity and conciseness, Psalm 116 [117] captures the essence of prayer, which consists in coming together and entering into lively personal conversation with God. In such an event, the mystery of the Divinity is revealed as faithfulness and love.

The Psalmist adds a special aspect of prayer: the experience of prayer should be radiated in the world and become a witness for those who do not share our faith. Indeed, it begins by expanding the horizon to embrace "all peoples" and "all nations" (cf. *Ps* 116 [117],1), so that before the beauty and joy of faith, they too may be overcome by the desire to know, meet and praise God.

3. In a technological world menaced by an eclipse of the sacred, in a society that delights in a certain self-sufficiency, the witness of the person at prayer is like a ray of light in the darkness.

Initially, it can only awaken curiosity; then it can induce the thoughtful person to wonder about the meaning of prayer, and, finally, it can give rise to the growing desire to have the experience. For this reason, prayer is never an isolated event, but tends to expand until it involves the whole world.

4. Let us now accompany Psalm 116 [117] with the words of a great Father of the Eastern Church, St Ephrem the Syrian, who lived in the fourth century. In one of his Hymns on Faith, the 14th, he expresses his desire to praise God without ceasing, involving "all who understand the (*divine*) truth".

This is his witness:

"How can my harp, O Lord, cease to praise you?

How could I teach my tongue infidelity?

Your love has given confidence to my embarrassment, but my will is still ungrateful" (*strophe 9*).

"It is right that man should recognize your divinity, it is right for heavenly beings to praise your humanity; the heavenly beings were astonished to see how much you emptied yourself, and those on earth to see how you were exalted" (*strophe 10*: *L'Arpa dello Spirito [The Harp of the Spirit]*, Rome 1999, pp. 26-28).

5. In another hymn (*Hymns on Nisibis*, 50), St Ephrem confirms his task of unceasing praise and finds the reason for it in God's love and compassion for us, just as our Psalm suggests.

"In you, Lord, may my mouth make praise come from silence. May our mouths not be lacking in praise, may our lips not be lacking in confessing; may your praise vibrate in us!" (*strophe 2*).

"Since it is on the Lord that the root of our faith is grafted, although he is far-removed, yet he is near in the fusion of love. May the roots of our love be fastened to him, may the full measure of his compassion be poured out upon us" (*strophe 6*: *ibid.*, pp. 77.80).

The Fourth
Week

Sunday

———— ✖ ————

Of the Fourth Week

Psalm 117 - See Sunday of the second week (see p. 85 above)

In all our trials, God has the last word

1. The sequence of Psalms from 111 [112] to 117 [118] was sung during the most important and joyful feasts of ancient Judaism, especially during the celebration of the Passover. This series of hymns of praise and thanksgiving to God were called the "Egyptian *Hallel*" because, in one of them, Psalm 113A [114], the exodus of Israel from the land of oppression, Pharaonic Egypt, and the marvelous gift of the divine covenant are recalled in a visual, poetic way. The last Psalm that seals this "Egyptian *Hallel*" is the Psalm 117 [118], just proclaimed, which we have already meditated on in an earlier commentary (cf. *General Audience,* 5 December 2001; *ORE,* 12 December 2001, p. 11).

2. This hymn clearly reveals its liturgical use in the Temple of Jerusalem. In fact, as it unfolds, we see a procession going forward, from among "the tents of the just" (v. 15), that is, the homes of the faithful. They exalt the protection of the divine hand, that can protect the just and believing, even when invaded by cruel adversaries. The Psalmist uses expressive imagery: "They compassed me about like bees; they blazed like a fire among the thorns. In the Lord's name I crushed them" (v. 12).

After escaping from this danger, the people of God break into "shouts of joy and victory" (v. 15) in honour of the Lord's right hand [which] was raised and has done wonders (cf. v. 16). Thus there is a consciousness that we are never alone, left to the mercy of the storm unleashed by the wicked. In truth, the last word is always God's, who, even if he permits the trial of his faithful, never hands him over to death (cf. v. 18).

3. At this point it seems that the procession reaches the end the Psalmist suggests with the image of "the gates of holiness" (v. 19), that is the Holy Door of the Temple of Zion. The procession accompanies the hero to whom God has granted victory. He asks that the gates be opened to him, so that he may "give thanks to the Lord" (v. 19). With him "the just enter" (v. 20). To express the harsh trial that he has overcome and his consequent glorification, he compares himself to a "stone which the builders rejected" that then "has become the cornerstone" (v. 22).

Christ will use this image and verse, at the end of the parable of the murderous vinedressers, to announce his passion and glorification (cf. *Mt* 21,42).

4. By applying the Psalm to himself, Christ opens the way for the Christian interpretation of this hymn of confidence and gratitude to the Lord for his *hesed,* his loving fidelity, that echoes throughout the Psalm (cf. *Ps* 117 [118],1.2.3.4.29).

The Fathers of the Church made use of two symbols. First of all, that of the "gate of justice" on which St Clement of Rome commented in his *Letter to the Corinthians:* "For many gates stand open: the gate of justice is the gate of Christ, and all are blessed who enter by it and direct their way "in holiness and justice', accomplishing all things without disorder" (48,4: *I Padri Apostolici,* Rome 1976, p. 81; *The Apostolic Fathers, Letter of Clement of Rome to Corinth,* Thomas Nelson and Co. 1978, p. 44).

5. The other symbol, linked to the previous one, is the "rock". We will therefore let St Ambrose guide our meditation with his *Exposition of the Gospel according to Luke.* Commenting on Peter's profession of faith at Cesarea Philippi, he recalls that "Christ is the Rock" and that "Christ did not refuse to give this beautiful name to his disciple so that he too might be Peter, and find in the rock the firmness of perseverance, the steadfast solidity of the faith".

Ambrose then introduces the exhortation: "Try hard also to be a rock. However, to do this, do not seek the rock outside yourself but within yourself. Your rock is your actions, your rock is your thoughts. On this rock your house is built, so that it may never be battered by any storm of the evil spirits. If you are a rock, you will be inside the Church because the Church is on the rock. If you are inside the Church, the gates of hell will not prevail against you" (VI, 97-99: *"Opere Esegetiche"* IX/II *[Exegetical Works],* Milan/Rome, 1978: *Saemo* 12, p. 85).

———— �֍ ————

Canticle Dan 3,52-57 - See Sunday of the second week (see p. 89 above)

Bless the Lord, all you works of the Lord

1. *"These three [young men] in the furnace with one voice sang, glorifying and blessing God..."* (*Dn* 3,51). This sentence introduces the famous Canticle that we just heard in a fundamental passage. It is found in the *Book of Daniel,* in the section that has come down to us only in Greek, and is intoned by courageous witnesses of the faith, who did not wish to bow down in adoration to a statue of the king and preferred to face a tragic death: martyrdom in the fiery furnace.

They are three young Jewish men, whom the sacred author places in the historical context of the reign of Nebuchadnezzar, the terrible Babylonian sovereign who destroyed the holy city of Jerusalem in 586 B.C. and deported the Israelites to "the streams of Babylon" (cf. *Ps* 136 [137]). Even in extreme danger, when the flames are already licking their bodies, they find the strength to "praise, glorify and bless God", certain that the Lord of the cosmos and history will not abandon them to death and nothingness.

2. The biblical author, who wrote several centuries later, portrays this heroic event to encourage his contemporaries to hold high the banner of the faith during the persecutions of the Syrian-Hellenistic kings of the second century B.C. Precisely then the courageous reaction of the Maccabees took place, combatants for the freedom of the faith and of the Hebrew tradition.

The Canticle, traditionally known as "of the three young men", is similar to a flame that lights up the darkness of the time of oppression and persecution, a time that has often been repeated in the history of Israel and of Christianity itself. We know that the persecutor does not always assume the violent and grim face of an oppressor, but often delights in isolating the just person with mocking and irony, asking him sarcastically: "Where is your God?" (*Ps* 41 [42],4.11).

3. All creatures are involved in the blessing that the three young men raise to the Almighty Lord from the crucible of their trial. They weave a sort of multicoloured tapestry where the stars shine, the seasons flow, the animals move, the angels appear, and, above all, "servants of the Lord" sing, the "holy" and "the humble of heart" (cf. *Dan* 3,85.87).

The passage that was just proclaimed precedes this magnificent evocation of all creation. It constitutes the first part of the Canticle, that evokes the glorious presence of the Lord, transcendent yet close. Yes, because God is in heaven, where "he looks into the depths" (cf. 3,55), and he is also "in the temple of holy glory" of Zion (cf. 3,53). He is seated on the "throne" of his eternal and infinite "kingdom" (cf. 3,54) but is also "throned upon the cherubim" (cf. 3,55) in the ark of the covenant placed in the Holy of Holies in the Temple of Jerusalem.

4. He is a God who is above us, capable of saving us with his power; but also a God close to his People, in whose midst he willed to dwell in his "glorious holy temple", thus manifesting his love. A love that he will reveal fully in making his Son "full of grace and truth", "dwell among us" (cf. *Jn* 1,14). He will reveal the fullness of his love by sending his Son among us to share, in all things except sin, our condition marked by trials, oppression, loneliness and death.

The praise of the three young men to God our Saviour continues in various ways in the Church. For example, at the end of his *Letter to the Corinthians,* St Clement of Rome includes a long prayer of praise and confidence. It is woven throughout with biblical references and, perhaps echoes the early Roman liturgy. It is a prayer of thanksgiving to the Lord who, despite the apparent triumph of evil, guides history to a happy end.

Prayer of thanksgiving of St Clement of Rome

5. "You have opened the eyes of our hearts (*Eph* 1,18) to recognize that you alone (*Jn* 17,3) are highest in the highest heavens, ever remaining holy among the holy. You humble the violence of the arrogant (cf. *Is* 13,11), overthrow the calculations of the nations (cf. *Ps* 32 [33],10), raise up the humble and humble the proud (cf. *Jb* 5,11); you make rich and make poor, kill and make alive (cf. *Dt* 32,39); you alone are the benefactor of spirits and the God of all flesh You fathom the depths (cf. *Dn* 3,55) and observe men's deeds; you are the aid of those in peril, Saviour of those in despair (cf. *Jdt* 9,11), the Creator of every spirit and its Custodian. You multiply the nations upon the earth and from them all you have chosen those who love you through Jesus

Christ your beloved Servant, through whom you have educated, sanctified, and honoured us" (Clement of Rome, *Letter to the Corinthians,* 59,3, in *The Apostolic Fathers,* 1978, Thomas Nelson Inc., Nashville, Tennessee, USA, p. 50).

Psalm 150 - See Sunday of the second week (see p. 92 above)

Music, hymnody should be worthy of the greatness of the Liturgy

1. Psalm 150, which we have just proclaimed, rings out for the second time in the *Liturgy of Lauds:* a festive hymn, an "alleluia" to the rhythm of music. It sets a spiritual seal on the whole Psalter, the book of praise, of song, of the liturgy of Israel.

The text is marvelously simple and transparent. We should just let ourselves be drawn in by the insistent call to praise the Lord: "Praise the Lord ... praise him ... praise him!". The Psalm opens presenting God in the two fundamental aspects of his mystery. Certainly, he is transcendent, mysterious, beyond our horizon: his royal abode is the heavenly "sanctuary", "his mighty heavens", a fortress that is inaccessible for the human being. Yet he is close to us: he is present in the "holy place" of Zion and acts in history through his "mighty deeds" that reveal and enable one to experience "his surpassing greatness" (cf. vv. 1-2).

2. Thus between heaven and earth a channel of communication is established in which the action of the Lord meets the hymn of praise of the faithful. The liturgy unites the two holy places, the earthly temple and the infinite heavens, God and man, time and eternity.

During the prayer, we accomplish an ascent towards the divine light and together experience a descent of God who adapts himself to our limitations in order to hear and speak to us, meet us and save us. The Psalmist readily urges us to find help for our praise in the prayerful encounter: sound the musical instruments of the orchestra of the temple of Jerusalem, such as the trumpet, harp, lute, drums, flutes and cymbals. Moving in procession was also part of the ritual of Jerusalem (cf. *Ps* 117 [118],27). The same appeal echoes in Psalm 46 [47],8: "Sing praise with all your skill!".

3. Hence, it is necessary to discover and to live constantly the beauty of prayer and of the liturgy. We must pray to God with theologically correct formulas and also in a beautiful and dignified way.

In this regard, the Christian community must make an examination of conscience so that the beauty of music and hymnody will return once again to the liturgy. They should purify worship from ugliness of style, from distasteful forms of expression, from uninspired musical texts which are not worthy of the great act that is being celebrated.

In this connection in the *Epistle to the Ephesians* we find an important appeal to avoid drunkenness and vulgarity, and to make room for the purity of liturgical hymns: "Do not get drunk with wine, for that is debauchery; but be filled with the Spirit, addressing one another in Psalms and hymns and spiritual songs, singing and making melody to the Lord with all your heart, always and for everything giving thanks in the name of our Lord Jesus Christ to God the Father" (5,18-20).

4. The Psalmist ends with an invitation to "every living being" (cf. *Ps* 150,5), to give praise, literally "every breath", "everything that breathes", a term that in Hebrew means "every being that breathes", especially "every living person" (cf. *Dt* 20,16; *Jos* 10,40; 11,11.14). In the divine praise then, first of all, with his heart and voice, the human creature is involved. With him all living beings, all creatures in which there is a breath of life (cf. *Gn* 7,22) are called in spirit, so that they may raise their hymn of thankgiving to the Creator for the gift of life.

Following up on this universal invitation, St Francis left us his thoughtful *"Canticle of Brother Sun"*, in which he invites us to praise and bless the Lord for all his creatures, reflections of his beauty and goodness (cf. *Fonti Francescane [Franciscan Sources]*, 263).

5. All the faithful should join in this hymn in a special way, as the *Epistle to the Colossians* suggests: "Let the Word of Christ dwell in you richly, as you teach and admonish one another in all wisdom, and as you sing Psalms and hymns and spiritual songs with thankfulness in your hearts to God" (*Col* 3,16).

On this subject, in his *Expositions on the Psalms (Enarrationes in Psalmos)*, St Augustine sees the musical instruments as symbolizing the saints who praise God: "You are the trumpet, lute, harp, tambourine, choir, strings, organ, and cymbals of jubilation sounding well, because sounding in harmony. You are all of these. Do not here think of anything vile, anything transitory or anything ridiculous"... "every spirit (who) praises the Lord" is a voice of song to God (cf. *Exposition on the Psalms,* vol. VI, Oxford, 1857, p. 456).

So the highest music is what comes from our hearts. In our liturgies this is the harmony God wants to hear.

Monday

——— ✖ ———

Of the Fourth Week

Psalm 89

O Lord, you have been our refuge
from one generation to the next.
Before the mountains were born
or the earth or the world brought forth,
you are God, without beginning or end.

You turn men back into dust
and say: 'Go back, sons of men.'
To your eyes a thousand years
are like yesterday, come and gone,
no more than a watch in the night.

You sweep men away like a dream,
like grass which springs up in the morning.
In the morning it springs up and flowers:
by evening it withers and fades.

So we are destroyed in your anger,
struck with terror in your fury.
Our guilt lies open before you;
our secrets in the light of your face.

All our days pass away in your anger.
Our life is over like a sigh.
Our span is seventy years
or eighty for those who are strong.

And most of these are emptiness and pain.
They pass swiftly and we are gone.
Who understands the power of your anger
and fears the strength of your fury?

Make us know the shortness of our life
that we may gain wisdom of heart.
Lord, relent! Is your anger for ever?
Show pity to your servants.

In the morning, fill us with your love;
we shall exult and rejoice all our days.
Give us joy to balance our affliction
for the years when we knew misfortune.

Show forth your work to your servants;
let your glory shine on their children.
Let the favour of the Lord be upon us:
give success to the work of our hands,
give success to the work of our hands.

Teach us to number our days aright

1. The verses that have just echoed in our ears and in our hearts are a sapiential meditation which, however, has the tone of a supplication. In fact, in Psalm 89 [90] the one who prays the Psalm puts at the heart of his prayer one of the topics most explored by philosophy, most sung by poetry and most felt by human experience in all ages and in all the regions of the earth: human frailty and the passing of time.

It is enough to think of certain unforgettable pages of the *Book of Job,* which present our frailty. In fact, we are like those who "dwell in houses of clay, whose foundation is in the dust, who are crushed more easily than the moth. Between morning and evening they are destroyed; they perish for ever without anyone regarding it" (cf. *Job* 4,19-20). Our life on earth is "but a shadow" (*Job* 8,9). Again, Job continues to confess: "My days are swifter than a runner; they flee away, they see no happiness. They shoot by like skiffs of reed, like an eagle swooping on its prey" (*Job* 9,25-26).

2. At the beginning of his song, which is akin to an elegy (cf. *Ps* 89 [90],2-6), the Psalmist insistently contrasts the eternity of God with the fleeting time of humanity. This is his most explicit declaration: "For a thousand years in your sight are but as yesterday when it is past, or as a watch of the night" (v. 4).

As a consequence of original sin, by divine command, man returns to the dust from which he was taken, as already affirmed in the account of *Genesis:* "You are dust, and to dust you shall return" (*Gn* 3,19; cf. 2,7). The Creator, who shapes the human creature in all his beauty and complexity, is also the One who "turns men back into dust" (cf. *Ps* 89 [90],3). And "dust" in biblical language is also a symbolic expression for death, the lower regions, the silence of the tomb.

3. The sense of human limitation is intense in this entreaty. Our existence has the frailty of the grass that springs up at dawn; suddenly it hears the whistle of the sickle that reduces it to a heap of hay. The freshness of life all too soon gives way to the aridity of death (cf. vv. 5-6; cf. *Is* 40,6-7; *Job* 14,1-2; *Ps* 102 [103],14-16).

As often occurs in the Old Testament, the Psalmist associates this radical weakness with sin. In us there is finiteness but also culpability. For this reason, the Lord's anger and judgment seem to overshadow our lives. "Truly we are consumed by your anger, filled with terror by your wrath. Our guilt lies open before you.... All our days pass away in your anger" (*Ps* 89 [90],7-9).

4. At the dawn of the new day, with this Psalm, the *Liturgy of Lauds* rouses us from our illusions and our pride. Human life is limited: "Our span is seventy years or eighty for those who are strong", the Psalmist affirms. Moreover the passing of the hours, days, and months is marked by "sorrow and toil" (cf. v. 10) and the years themselves turn out to be like a "sigh" (v. 9).

This, then, is the great lesson: the Lord teaches us to "count our days" so that by accepting them with healthy realism "we may gain wisdom of heart" (v. 12). But the person praying asks something more of God: that his grace support and gladden our days, even while they are so fragile and marked by affliction. May he grant us to taste the flavour of hope, even if the tide of time seems to drag us away. Only the grace of the Lord can give our daily actions consistency and perpetuity: "Let the favour of the Lord our God be upon us: give success to the work of our hands, give success to the work of our hands" (v. 17).

In prayer let us ask God that a reflection of eternity penetrate our brief lives and actions. With the presence of divine grace in us, a light will shine on the passing of our days, misery will be turned into glory, what seems not to make sense will acquire meaning.

5. Let us conclude our reflection on Psalm 89 [90] by leaving the word to early Christian tradition, which comments on the Psalter having in the background the glorious figure of Christ. Thus for the Christian writer Origen, in his *Treatise on the Psalms* which has been handed down to us in the Latin translation of St Jerome, the Resurrection of Christ gives us the possibility, perceived by the Psalmist, to "rejoice and be glad all our days" (cf. v. 14). This is because Christ's Paschal Mystery is the source of our life beyond death: "After being gladdened by the Resurrection of Our Lord, through whom we believe we have been redeemed and will also rise one day, we now live in joy the days that remain of our life, exulting because of this confidence, and with hymns and spiritual chants we praise God through Jesus Christ Our Lord" (Origen Jerome, *"74 Omelie sul libro dei Salmi"* [74 Homilies on the Book of the Psalms], Milan 1993, p. 652).

Canticle   Is 42,10-16

Sing to the Lord a new song,
his praise to the end of the earth!

Let the sea roar and all that fills it,
the coastlands and their inhabitants;
let the desert and its cities lift up their voice,
the villages that Kedar inhabits.

Let the inhabitants of Sela sing for joy,
let them shout from the top of the mountains.
Let them give glory to the Lord,
and declare his praise in the coastlands.
The Lord goes forth like a mighty man,
like a man of war he stirs up his fury;
he cries out, he shouts aloud,
he shows himself mighty against his foes.

For a long time I have held my peace,
I have kept still and restrained myself;
now I will cry out like a woman in travail,
I will gasp and pant.

I will lay waste mountains and hills,
and dry up all their herbage;
I will turn the rivers into islands,
and dry up the pools.

And I will lead the blind
in a way that they know not;
in paths that they have not known
I will guide them.
I will turn the darkness before them into light,
the rough places into level ground.

Sing to the Lord a new song!

1. In the Book that bears the Prophet Isaiah's name, scholars have identified various voices all of which are placed under the patronage of this great Prophet who lived in the eighth century B.C. This is the case with the vigorous hymn of joy and victory that has just been proclaimed as part of the *Liturgy of Lauds* of the Fourth Week. Exegetes refer to it as the so-called "Second Isaiah", a Prophet who lived in the sixth century B.C., at the time of the return of the Hebrews from the Babylonian Exile. The hymn begins with an appeal to "sing to the Lord a new song" (cf. *Is* 42,10), as in other Psalms (cf. 95 [96],1 and 97 [98],1).

The "newness" of the song that the Prophet invites the Hebrews to sing certainly refers to the unfolding horizon of freedom, a radical turning-point in the history of a people which experienced oppression and exile in a foreign land (cf. *Ps* 136 [137]).

2. In the Bible, "newness" often has the flavour of a perfect and definitive reality. It is almost the sign of the beginning of an era of saving fullness that seals humanity's tormented history. The Canticle of Isaiah has this exalted tone that is well suited to Christian prayer.

The whole world, including the earth, sea, coastlands, deserts and cities, is invited to sing to the Lord a "new song" (cf. *Is* 42,10-12). All space is involved, even its furthest horizons that also contain the unknown, and its vertical dimension, which rises from the desert plain, the dwelling place of the nomadic tribes of Kedar (cf. *Is* 21,16-17), and soars to the mountains. High up, in the territory of the Edomites, we can locate the city of Sela which many people have identified with Petra, a city placed between the rocky peaks.

All the earth's inhabitants are invited to become like an immense choir to acclaim the Lord with exultation and to give him glory.

3. After the solemn invitation to sing (cf. vv. 10-12), the Prophet brings the Lord onto the scene, represented as the God of the Exodus, who has set his people free from slavery in Egypt: "The Lord goes forth like a mighty man, like a warrior" (v. 13). He sows terror among his foes, who oppress others and commit injustice.

The Canticle of Moses also portrays the Lord during the Red Sea crossing as a "man of war", ready to stretch out his right hand and destroy the enemy (cf. *Ex* 15,3-8). With the return of the Hebrews from the deportation to Babylon, a new exodus is about to take place, and the faithful must be assured that history is not at the mercy of destiny, chaos or oppressive powers: the last word rests with God who is just and strong. The Psalmist had already sung: "Grant us help against the foe, for vain is the help of man!" (*Ps* 59 [60],13).

4. Having entered on the scene, the Lord speaks and his vehement words (cf. *Is* 42,14-16) combine judgment and salvation. He begins by recalling that "for a long time" he has "held [his] peace": in other words, he has not intervened. The divine silence is often a cause of perplexity to the just, and even scandalous, as Job's long lamentation attests (cf. *Jb* 3,1-26). However, it is not a silence that suggests absence as if history had been left in the hands of the perverse, or the Lord were indifferent and impassive. In fact, that silence gives vent to a reaction similar to a woman in labour who gasps and pants and screams with pain. It is the divine judgment on evil, presented with images of aridity, destruction, desert (cf. v. 15), which has a living and fruitful result as its goal.

In fact, the Lord brings forth a new world, an age of freedom and salvation. The eyes of the blind will be opened so that they may enjoy the brilliant light. The path will be levelled and hope will blossom (cf.

v. 16), making it possible to continue to trust in God and in his future of peace and happiness.

5. Every day the believer must be able to discern the signs of divine action even when they are hidden by the apparently monotonous, aimless flow of time. As a highly-esteemed modern Christian author has written: "The earth is pervaded by a cosmic ecstasy: in it is an eternal reality and presence which, however, usually sleeps under the veil of habit. Eternal reality must now be revealed, as in an epiphany of God, through all that exists" (R. Guardini, *Sapienza dei Salmi,* Brescia, 1976, p. 52).

Discovering this divine presence, with the eyes of faith, in space and time but also within ourselves, is a source of hope and confidence, even when our hearts are agitated and shaken "as the trees of the forest shake before the wind" (*Is* 7,2). Indeed, the Lord enters the scene to govern and to judge "the world with righteousness, and the peoples with his truth" (*Ps* 95 [96],13).

———— ✠ ————

Psalm 134   vv. 1-12

Praise the name of the Lord,
praise him, servants of the Lord,
who stand in the house of the Lord,
in the courts of the house of our God.

Praise the Lord for the Lord is good.
Sing a psalm to his name for he is loving.
For the Lord has chosen Jacob for himself
and Israel for his own possession.

For I know the Lord is great,
that our Lord is high above all gods.
The Lord does whatever he wills,
in heaven, on earth, in the seas.
He summons clouds from the ends of the earth;
makes lightning produce the rain;
from his treasuries he sends forth the wind.

The first-born of the Egyptians he smote,
of man and beast alike.

Signs and wonders he worked
in the midst of your land, O Egypt,
against Pharaoh and all his servants.

Nations in their greatness he struck
and kings in their splendour he slew.
Sihon, king of the Amorites,
Og, the king of Bashan,
and all the kingdoms of Canaan.
He let Israel inherit their land;
on his people their land he bestowed.

Praise the name of the Lord!

1. *The Liturgy of Lauds,* whose development we are following in our catecheses, presents to us the first part of Psalm 134 [135] which we have just heard the choir sing. The text reveals a closely-packed series of allusions to other biblical passages, and it seems to be pervaded by an Easter atmosphere. Not for nothing has the Judaic tradition linked our Psalm to the next one, Psalm 135 [136], considering the whole as the "Great *Hallel*", the solemn, festive praise to be raised to the Lord at Easter.

Indeed, the Psalm brings the Exodus to the fore with its mention of the "plagues" of Egypt and its evocation of the entry into the promised land. But let us now look at the subsequent stages which Psalm 134 [135] reveals in the development of the first 12 verses: it is a reflection that we would like to turn into a prayer.

2. The Psalm opens with the characteristic invitation to praise, a typical feature of the hymns addressed to the Lord in the Psalter. The appeal to sing the *Alleluia* is addressed to the "servants of the Lord" (cf. v. 1), who in the original Hebrew "stand" in the sacred area of the temple (cf. v. 2), that is, in the ritual attitude of prayer (cf. *Ps* 133 [134],1-2).

The first to be involved in this praise are the ministers of worship, priests and Levites, who live and work "in the courts of the house of our God" (cf. *Ps* 134 [135],2). However, all the faithful are associated, in spirit, with these "servants of the Lord". In fact, immediately after the mention of the election of all Israel to be ally and witness of the Lord's love follows: "For the Lord has chosen Jacob for himself, Israel as his own possession" (v. 4). In this perspective, two basic qualities of God are celebrated: he is "good" and he is "gracious" (cf. v. 3). The bond between us and the Lord is marked by love, intimacy and joyful adherence.

3. After the invitation to praise, the Psalmist continues with a solemn profession of faith that starts with the words "I know", that is, I recognize, I believe (cf. v. 5). Two articles of faith are sung by a soloist on behalf of the entire people, assembled for the liturgy. He first exalts God's work in the whole universe: He is the Lord of the cosmos *par excellence:* "The Lord does whatever he wills, in heaven and on earth" (v. 6). He even commands the seas and the depths, which are the emblem of chaos, of negative forces, of limitation and the void.

Again, it is the Lord, with recourse to his "storehouses" (cf. v. 7), who produces the clouds, lightning, rain and winds. In ancient times, people in the Near East imagined that the elements were stored in special containers, rather like heavenly caskets, from which God drew them and scattered them on earth.

4. The other element of the profession of faith concerns the history of salvation. God the Creator is now recognized as the redeeming Lord, calling to mind the fundamental events of Israel's liberation from slavery in Egypt. The Psalmist initially cites the "plague" of the first-born (cf. *Ex* 12,29-30) that sums up all the "signs and miracles" that God the Liberator worked during the epic of the Exodus (cf. *Ps* 134 [135],8-9). Immediately afterwards are recalled the sensational victories that enabled Israel to overcome the difficulties and obstacles with which its path was strewn (cf. vv. 10-11). Finally, the promised land, which Israel receives as "a heritage" from the Lord, can be discerned on the horizon (cf. v. 12).

All these signs of the covenant, more broadly expressed in the following Psalm, 135 [136], testify to the basic truth, announced in the first Commandment of the Decalogue. God is one and he is a person who works and speaks, loves and saves: "the Lord is great... our God is above all gods" (v. 5; cf. *Ex* 20,2-3; *Ps* 94 [95],3).

5. Following this profession of faith, we too raise our praise to God. Pope St Clement I, in his *Letter to the Corinthians,* addresses this invitation to us: "Let us gaze upon the Father and Creator of the whole universe. Let us cherish his gifts and benefits of peace, magnificent and sublime. Let us contemplate him with our minds and turn the eyes of our soul to the greatness of his will! Only think how just he is to all his creatures. The heavens that move as he orders obey him in harmony. Day and night take the course he has established and are not confused with each other. The sun and moon and the multitudes of stars revolve harmoniously according to his directions, never deviating from the orbits he has assigned to them. The earth, made fertile through his will, produces abundant food for men and women, for wild beasts and for all the animals that live on it, without reluctance and changing none of his orders" (19,2-20,4: *I Padri Apostolici,* Rome, 1984, pp. 62-63). Clement I concludes observing: "The Creator and Lord of the universe disposes that all these things should be in peace and concord, beneficient to all and especially to us who call on his mercy through Our Lord Jesus Christ. To him be glory and majesty for ever and ever. Amen" (20,11-12: *ibid.,* p. 63).

Tuesday

———— ❦ ————

Of the Fourth Week

Psalm 100

My song is of mercy and justice;
I sing to you, O Lord.
I will walk in the way of perfection.
O when, Lord, will you come?

I will walk with blameless heart
within my house;
I will not set before my eyes
whatever is base.

I will hate the ways of the crooked;
they shall not be my friends.
The false-hearted must keep far away;
the wicked I disown.

The man who slanders his neighbour in secret
I will bring to silence.

The man of proud looks and haughty heart
I will never endure.

I look to the faithful in the land
that they may dwell with me.
He who walks in the way of perfection
shall be my friend.

No man who practises deceit
shall live within my house.
No man who utters lies shall stand
before my eyes.

Morning by morning I will silence
all the wicked in the land,
uprooting from the city of the Lord
all who do evil.

I will sing of loyalty and of justice!

1. After the two catecheses on the meaning of the Easter celebrations, let us return to our reflection on the *Liturgy of Lauds*. For Tuesday of the Fourth Week it offers us Psalm 100 [101], which we have just heard.

It is a meditation that paints the portrait of the ideal politician whose model of life must be divine action in the governance of the world: an action dictated by perfect moral integrity and a resolute commitment to combating all forms of injustice. This text is now proposed anew as a programme of life for the faithful who are beginning their working day and relations with their neighbour. It is a programme of "loyalty and of justice" (cf. v. 1), which is expressed in two great moral paths.

2. The first is called the way "of the blameless" and aims at exalting personal choices in life, made with an "integrity of heart", that is, with a perfectly clear conscience (cf. v. 2).

On the one hand, there are positive remarks about the great moral virtues that brighten the "house", that is, the family of the just man: the wisdom that helps us understand and judge properly; the innocence that is purity of heart and of life; and lastly, the integrity of conscience that tolerates no compromise with evil.

On the other hand, the Psalmist introduces a negative task. This is the struggle against every form of wickedness and injustice, in order to keep his own house and his own decisions free of every perversion of the moral order (cf. vv. 3-4).

As St Basil, a great Father of the Eastern Church, writes in his work *De Baptismo,* "Not even the momentary pleasure that contaminates thought should trouble the one who is mourned with Christ in a death like his" (*Opere Ascetiche,* Turin 1980, p. 548).

3. The second path unfolds in the last part of the Psalm (cf. vv. 5-8) and explains the importance of the most typically public and social talents. In this case too are listed the essential references for a life that is set on rejecting evil with force and determination.

First of all, [there is] the fight against slander and spying in secret, a fundamental commitment in a society with an oral tradition that gave special importance to the function of words in interpersonal relations. The king, who also acts as judge, announces that he will use the utmost severity in this fight: he will "destroy" the slanderer (cf. v. 5). Then he rejects all arrogance and haughtiness; he spurns the company and counsel of those who always practise deceit and utter lies. Lastly, the king declares the way in which he wants to choose the "people who serve him" (cf. v. 6), that is, his ministers. He will be careful to choose them from among the "faithful in the land". He wants to surround himself with people of integrity and to avoid contact with "those who practise deceit" (cf. v. 7).

4. The last verse of the Psalm is particularly forceful. It can make the Christian reader uncomfortable, for it proclaims destruction: "Morning by morning I will destroy all the wicked in the land, cutting off the evildoers from the city of the Lord" (v. 8). It is important, however, to remember one thing: the person speaking these words is not just any individual but a king, the supreme authority responsible for justice in the land. In this sentence he expresses, with exaggeration, his implacable commitment to fight crime, which is only right and is shared by all who have civil authority.

Of course, it is not up to every citizen to mete out punishment! If, therefore, individual members of the faithful wish to apply this sentence of the Psalm to themselves, they must do so by analogy, that is, by deciding to uproot *from their own hearts and conduct,* every morning, the evil sown by corruption and violence, by perversion and wickedness, as well as by every form of selfishness and injustice.

5. Let us end our meditation by returning to the first verse of the Psalm: "I will sing of loyalty and of justice..." (v. 1). In his *Comments on the Psalms,* an ancient Christian author, Eusebius of Caesarea, stresses the primacy of mercy over justice, albeit necessary: "I will sing of your mercy and your judgment, showing your usual approach: not to judge first and then to have mercy, but first to have mercy and then to judge and pass sentences with clemency and compassion.

"Thus treating my neighbour with mercy and discretion, I dare to come close to sing you Psalms of praise. Conscious, therefore, that we must act like this, I keep my paths immaculate and innocent, convinced that in this way, through good works, my songs of praise will be pleasing to you" (*PG* 23,1241).

———— �֍ ————

Canticle   Dan 3,3.4.6.11-18

Blessed are you, O Lord, God of our fathers,
and worthy of praise,
and your name is glorified for ever.

You are just
in all that you have done to us,
for we have sinned
and lawlessly departed from you,
and have sinned in all things.
For your name's sake
do not give us up utterly,
and do not break your covenant.

Do not withdraw your mercy from us
for the sake of Abraham your beloved,
and for the sake of Isaac your servant
and Israel your holy one, to whom you promised
to make their descendants as many as the stars of heaven
and as the sand on the shore of the sea.

For we, O Lord, have become fewer than any nation,
and are brought low this day in all the world
because of our sins;
and at this time there is no prince, or prophet, or leader,
no burnt offering, or sacrifice, or oblation, or incense,
no place to make an offering before you
or to find mercy.

Yet with a contrite heart and a humble spirit
may we be accepted,
as though it were with burnt offerings of rams and bulls
and with tens of thousands of fat lambs.

Such may our sacrifice be in your sight this day,
and may we wholly follow you,
for there will be no shame
for those who trust in you.

And now with all our heart we follow you,
we fear you and seek your face.

We trust in your merciful love!

1. The Canticle that has just been proclaimed is part of the Greek text of the *Book of Daniel,* presented as a fervent and sincere supplication raised to the Lord. It is the voice of Israel, experiencing the harsh trial of exile and of the diaspora among the peoples. Indeed, it is an Israelite, Azariah, who intones the Canticle, set in the Babylonian panorama at the time of the exile of Israel after the destruction of Jerusalem by King Nebuchadnezzar.

Azariah, with two other faithful Israelites, is "in the midst of the fire" (*Dn* 3,25), like a martyr ready to suffer death in order not to betray his conscience and his faith. He was condemned to death for refusing to worship the imperial image.

2. The persecution is considered in this Canticle as a just punishment with which God purifies his sinful people: "In truth and justice you have brought all this upon us", Azariah confesses, "because of our sins" (v. 28). We are therefore in the presence of a penitential prayer that does not give way to discouragement or fear but to hope.

Of course, the starting point is sorrowful, the despair deep, the trial burdensome, and the divine judgment on the people's sin severe: "At this time there is no prince, or Prophet, or leader, no burnt offering, or sacrifice, or oblation, or incense, no place to make an offering before you or to find mercy" (v. 38). The temple of Zion is destroyed and it seems as though the Lord no longer dwells among his people.

3. In the present tragic situation, hope seeks its roots in the past, that is, in the promises made to the fathers. It goes back, therefore, to Abraham, Isaac and Jacob (cf. v. 35), to whom God assured blessings and fruitfulness, a land and importance, life and peace. God is faithful and will not be untrue to his promises. Even if justice demands that Israel be punished for its sins, the certainty that mercy and pardon will always have the last word endures. The Prophet Ezekiel previously mentioned these words of the Lord: "Have I any pleasure in the death of the wicked... and not rather that he should turn from his way and live?... For I have no pleasure in the death of any one" (*Ez* 18,23.32). Now, of course, is the time of humiliation: "For we, O Lord, have become fewer than any nation and are brought low this day in all the world because of our sins" (*Dn* 3,37). Yet we do not have an expectation of death, but of new life, after purification.

4. The man praying approaches the Lord, offering him the most precious and acceptable sacrifice: a "contrite heart" and "humbled spirit" (v. 39; cf. *Ps* 50 [51],19). Indeed, it is the centre of existence, the "I" renewed by the trial that it offers to God, so that he might accept it as a sign of conversion and dedication to do good.

By this inner disposition, fear is overcome, confusion and shame are put to flight (cf. *Dn* 3: 40), and the spirit opens to confidence in a better future, when the promises made to the fathers will be fulfilled.

The last sentence of Azariah's entreaty, as it is proposed by the liturgy, has a strong emotional impact and deep spiritual intensity: "now with all our heart we follow you, we fear you and seek your face..." (v. 41). In these words lingers an echo of another Psalm: "My heart says to you, 'Your face, Lord, do I seek'" (*Ps* 26 [27],8).

The time has now come when our journey is leaving behind the perverse routes of evil, the crooked paths and devious ways (*Prv* 2,15). We are beginning to follow the Lord, moved by the desire to find his face. And his face is not angry but filled with love, as was the merciful father's for his prodigal son (cf. *Lk* 15,11-32).

5. Let us conclude our reflection on the *Canticle of Azariah* with the prayer written by St Maximus the Confessor in his *Discorso Ascetico* (37-39), inspired by the text of the Prophet Daniel. "For your name's sake do not abandon us forever, do not break your covenant, nor withdraw your mercy from us (cf. *Dn* 3,34-35), through your mercy, O, Our Father in Heaven, through the compassion of your Only-begotten Son and the mercy of your Holy Spirit.... Do not be deaf to our plea, O Lord, and do not abandon us for ever.

"Let us not trust in our own works of justice but in your mercy, through which you preserve our race.... Do not despise our unworthiness, but have pity on us in accordance with your great mercy, and take away our sins through the fullness of your mercy, so that, without condemnation, we may come close to your holy glory and be deemed worthy of the protection of your Only-begotten Son".

St Maximus ends: "Yes, O Lord, Almighty Master, hear our plea, for we recognize none other than you" (*Umanità e Divinità di Cristo,* Rome 1979, pp. 51-52).

———— ✖ ————

Psalm 143   vv. 1-10

Blessed be the Lord, my rock
who trains my arms for battle,
who prepares my hands for war.

He is my love, my fortress;
he is my stronghold, my saviour,
my shield, my place of refuge.
He brings peoples under my rule.

Lord, what is man that you care for him,
mortal man, that you keep him in mind;
man, who is merely a breath
whose life fades like a shadow?

Lower your heavens and come down;
touch the mountains; wreathe them in smoke.

Flash your lightnings; rout the foe,
shoot your arrows and put them to flight.

Reach down from heaven and save me;
draw me out from the mighty waters,
from the hands of alien foes
whose mouths are filled with lies,
whose hands are raised in perjury.

To you, O God, will I sing a new song;
I will play on the ten-stringed harp
to you who give kings their victory,
who set David your servant free.

Blessed be the Lord, my rock!

1. We have just heard the first part of Psalm 143 [144]. It appears to be a royal *hymn,* interwoven with other biblical texts so as to give life to a new prayerful composition (cf. *Ps* 8,5; 17 [18],8-15; 32 [33],2-3; 38 [39],6-7). The Davidic sovereign himself, speaking in the first person, recognizes the divine origin of his success.

The Lord is portrayed in martial images, in accordance with the ancient use of symbols: indeed, he is seen as a military instructor (cf. *Ps* 143 [144],1), an impregnable fortress, a protective shield, a victor (cf. v. 2). It is desired in this way to exalt the personality of God, who battles against the evil in history: he is neither a dark or fateful power, nor an imperturbable sovereign indifferent to human vicissitudes. The citations and tone of this celebration of the divine echo the hymn of David preserved in Psalm 17 [18] and in chapter 22 of the *Second Book of Samuel.*

2. Compared with the mightiness of God, the Jewish king recognizes that he is as frail and weak as all human creatures. To express his feeling, the royal person in his prayer makes use of two sentences, found in Psalms 8,4 and 38 [39],5 and, interweaving them, produces a powerful new effect: "O Lord, what is man that you regard him, or the son of man that you think of him? Man is like a breath, his days are like a passing shadow" (vv. 3-4). Here the firm conviction emerges that like a puff of wind we have no substance, if the Creator does not keep us alive, the One in whose "hand", as Job says, "is the life of every living thing and the breath of all mankind" (12,10).

Only with divine support can we overcome the dangers and difficulties which beset our daily life. Only by counting on help from Heaven will we have the determination to set out, like the ancient king of Israel, on the way towards freedom from every form of oppression.

3. Divine intervention is pictured in the traditional cosmic and historical images in order to illustrate the divine supremacy over the universe and human events. Here, then, are the mountains smoking in sudden volcanic eruptions (cf. 143 [144],5). Here are the flashes of lightning that seem like arrows released by the Lord, ready to destroy evil (cf. v. 6). Here, lastly, are the "many waters" which in biblical language symbolize chaos, evil and the void, in a word, the negative elements within history (cf. v. 7). These cosmic images are juxtaposed with others of a historical kind: like the "enemies" (cf. v. 6), the "aliens" (cf. v. 7), the liars and perjurers, that is, idolaters (cf. v. 8).

This is a very concrete and Oriental way of portraying wickedness, perversion, oppression and injustice: terrible realities from which the Lord frees us as we make our way in the world.

4. Psalm 143 [144], which the *Liturgy of Lauds* presents to us, ends with a short hymn of thanksgiving (cf. vv. 9-10). It is inspired by the certainty that God will not abandon us in the fight against evil. For this reason, the person praying intones a melody, accompanying it with his ten-stringed harp, in the certainty that the Lord "gives victory to kings" and "rescues David [his anointed] servant" (vv. 9-10).

In Hebrew, the word "consecrated" is "Messiah": thus, we are looking at a royal Psalm, transformed into a messianic hymn, as was the liturgical custom of ancient Israel. We Christians should repeat it as we keep our gaze fixed on Christ, who frees us from every evil and sustains us in the battle against the hidden powers of wickedness. Indeed, "we are not contending against flesh and blood, but against the principalities, against the powers, against the rulers of this dark world, against the spiritual hosts of wickedness in the heavenly places" (cf. *Eph* 6,12).

5. Let us therefore conclude with a thought suggested to us by St John Cassian, a monk who lived in Gaul in the fourth to fifth century. In his work *The Incarnation of the Lord,* inspired by verse 5 of our Psalm, "Bow your heavens, O Lord, and come down!", he sees in these words the expectation of Christ's coming into the world.

He continues: "The Psalmist implored... the Lord to manifest himself in the flesh, to appear visibly in the world, to be visibly taken up in glory (cf. *1 Tm* 3: 16) and lastly, to enable the saints to see, with their own eyes, all that they had spiritually foreseen" (*L'Incarnazione del Signore,* V, 13, Rome 1991, pp. 208-209). It is precisely this that every baptized person witnesses to in the joy of faith.

Wednesday

Of the Fourth Week

Psalm 107

My heart is ready, O God;
I will sing, sing your praise.
Awake, my soul;
awake, lyre and harp.
I will awake the dawn.

I will thank you, Lord, among the peoples,
among nations I will praise you,
for your love reaches to the heavens
and your truth to the skies.
O God, arise above the heavens;
may your glory shine on earth!

O come and deliver your friends;
help with your right hand and reply.
From his holy place God has made this promise:
'I will triumph and divide the land of Shechem;
I will measure out the valley of Succoth.

Gilead is mine and Manasseh.
Ephraim I take for my helmet,
Judah for my commander's staff.
Moab I will use for my washbowl,

on Edom I will plant my shoe.
Over the Philistines I will shout in triumph.'

But who will lead me to conquer the fortress?
Who will bring me face to face with Edom?
Will you utterly reject us, O God,
and no longer march with our armies?

Give us help against the foe:
for the help of man is vain.
With God we shall do bravely
and he will trample down our foes.

My heart is steadfast, O God!

1. Psalm 107 [108], which has just been presented to us, is part of the sequence of Psalms in the *Liturgy of Lauds,* the topic of our catechesis. It has a characteristic which at first sight is surprising: it is merely composed of two pre-existing Psalm fragments fused together, one from Psalm 56 [57] (vv. 8-12) and the other from Psalm 59 [60] (vv. 7-14). The first fragment is reminiscent of a hymn, the second seems to be a supplication but includes a divine oracle which instils serenity and trust in the person praying.

This fusion gives rise to a new prayer, and this fact provides us with a model. Actually, the Christian liturgy frequently combines different biblical passages, transforming them into a new text destined to illuminate new situations. Yet the link with the original source is preserved. In practice, Psalm 107 [108] - (but it is not the only one; for further proof, see Psalm 143 [144]) - shows that Israel, already in the Old Testament, was re-using and bringing up-to-date the Word of God revealed.

2. The Psalm resulting from this fusion is therefore something more than the mere combination or juxtaposition of two pre-existing passages. Instead of beginning with a humble plea like Psalm 56 [57]: "Be merciful to me, O God, be merciful to me" (v. 2), the new Psalm begins with a resolute announcement of praise to God: "My heart is steadfast, O God... I will sing praises..." (*Ps* 107 [108],2). This praise replaces the lament in the opening lines of another Psalm (cf. *Ps* 59 [60],1-6), and thus becomes the basis of the following divine oracle (*Ps*

59 [60],8-10; *Ps* 107 [108],8-10) and of the supplication that surrounds it (*Ps* 59 [60],7.11-14; *Ps* 107 [108],7.11-14).

Hope and nightmare are blended to form the substance of the new prayer, the whole of which is intended to imbue confidence, even in the times of adversity which the entire community has experienced.

3. So the Psalm opens with a joyful hymn of praise. It is a morning song, accompanied by harp and lyre. (cf. Ps 107 [108],3). The message is clear. At the centre it has the divine "love" and "faithfulness" (cf. v. 5): in Hebrew, *bésed* and *'emèt* are typical words used to describe the loving fidelity of the Lord regarding the Covenant with his people. On the basis of this fidelity, the people are sure that God will never abandon them in the abyss of the void or of despair.

The Christian interpretation of this Psalm is particularly evocative. In v. 6, the Psalmist celebrates God's transcendent glory: "Be exalted (that is, "rise'), O God, above the heavens!". Commenting on this Psalm, Origen, the renowned third-century Christian writer, goes back to this sentence of Jesus: "And I, when I am lifted up from the earth, will draw all men to myself" (*Jn* 12,32), referring to his crucifixion, whose result is described in the affirmation of the next verse: "that your beloved may be delivered" (*Ps* 107 [108],7). Origin thus concludes: "What a marvellous meaning! The Lord was crucified and exalted so that his beloved might be delivered.... All we have asked for has come true: he has been lifted up and we have been delivered" (Origene-Gerolamo, *74 Omelie sul Libro dei Salmi,* Milan 1993, p. 367).

4. Let us now move on to the second part of Psalm 107 [108], a partial citation of Psalm 59 [60], as has been said. In the midst of the anguish of Israel, who feels that God is absent and remote ("have you not rejected us, O God?": v. 12), is raised the voice of the oracle of the Lord which echoes in the temple (cf. vv. 8-10). In this revelation, God is presented as the Judge and Lord of all the holy land, from the city of Shechem to the Vale of Succoth beyond the Jordan, from the eastern regions of Gilead and Manasseh to the central-southern regions of Ephraim and Judah, reaching even to the subjugated but foreign territories of Moab, Edom and Philistia.

The divine lordship over the promised land is then proclaimed in colourful martial or juridical imagery. If the Lord reigns, there is nothing to fear: we are not tossed here and there by the evil forces of fate or chaos. Even in the darkest of moments there is always a superior plan that governs history.

5. This faith kindles the flame of hope. God, in any case, will point to a way out, that is, a "fortified city" set in the region of Edom. This means that despite their hardship and his silence, God will reveal himself anew to sustain and guide his people. Effective help can come from him alone, not from external military alliances, that is, the power of armies (cf. v. 13). Only with him will freedom be won, and we will do "valiantly" (v. 14).

With St Jerome, let us remember the last lesson of the Psalmist, interpreted in a Christian key: "No one must despair of this life. You have Christ, and you are still afraid? He will be our strength, our bread, our guide" (*Breviarium in Psalmos,* Ps CVII: *PL* 26,1224).

Canticle   Is 61,10-62,5

I will greatly rejoice in the Lord,
my soul shall exult in my God;
for he has clothed me with the garments of salvation,
he has covered me with the robe of righteousness,
as a bridegroom decks himself with a garland,
and as a bride adorns herself with her jewels.

For as the earth brings forth its shoots,
and as a garden causes what is sown in it to spring up,
so the Lord God will cause righteousness and praise
to spring forth before all the nations.

For Sion's sake I will not keep silent,
and for Jerusalem's sake I will not rest,
until her vindication goes forth as brightness,
and her salvation as a burning torch.

The nations shall see your vindication,
and all the kings your glory;
and you shall be called by a new name
which the mouth of the Lord will give.

You shall be a crown of beauty
in the hand of the Lord,
and a royal diadem
in the hand of your God.

You shall no more be termed Forsaken,
and your land shall no more be termed Desolate;
but you shall be called My delight in her,
and your land Married;
for the Lord delights in you,
and your land shall be married.

For as a young man marries a virgin,
so shall your sons marry you,
and as the bridegroom rejoices over the bride,
so shall your God rejoice over you.

The rebirth and renewal of Jerusalem

1. The wonderful Canticle which the *Liturgy of Lauds* offers to us and which has just been proclaimed, begins like a *Magnificat:* "I will greatly rejoice in the Lord, my soul shall exult in my God" (*Is* 61,10). The text is set into the third part of the Book of the Prophet Isaiah, a section which scholars date to a later period when Israel, having returned from the exile in Babylon (sixth century BC), resumes life as a free people in the land of her fathers and rebuilds Jerusalem and the temple. Not for nothing is the holy city at the centre of the Canticle, as we shall see, and the horizon that is unfolding is bright and full of hope.

2. The Prophet introduces his Canticle by portraying the people reborn, spendidly attired like a bridal couple, ready for the great day of their wedding (cf. v. 10). This is immediately followed by the evocation of another symbol, an expression of life, joy and newness: the new shoots that spring up like sprouting plants (cf. v. 11).

The Prophets use the image of the new shoot in various forms to represent the messianic king (cf. *Is* 11,1; 53,2; *Zec* 3,8; 6,12). The Messiah is a fertile shoot that renews the world, and the Prophet explains the deep meaning of this vitality: "The Lord God will cause righteousness and praise to spring forth" (*Is* 61,11), so that the holy city will resemble a garden of righteousness, that is, of fidelity and truth, of justice and love. As the Prophet said a little earlier, "You shall call your walls Salvation, and your gates Praise" (*Is* 60,18).

3. The Prophet continues to raise his voice loudly: his tireless song is intended to portray the rebirth of Jerusalem, before which a new age is about to unfold (cf. *Is* 62,1). The city is pictured as a bride just before her wedding.

The spousal imagery which emerges vividly in this passage (cf. vv. 4-5) is one of the strongest images used in the Bible to exalt the bond of intimacy and the Covenant of love between the Lord and his chosen people. Its beauty which consists of "salvation", "justice" and "glory" (cf. vv. 1-2) will be so marvellous that it will be "a crown of beauty in the hand of the Lord" (cf. v. 3).

The crucial element will be the changing of the name, as happens in our day too when a girl marries. Taking a "new name" (v. 2) almost means taking on a new identity, undertaking a mission, radically changing one's life (cf. *Gn* 32,25-33).

4. The new name that will be taken by the bride Jerusalem, destined to represent the entire people of God, is illustrated in the contrast that the Prophet specifically accentuates: "You shall no more be termed Forsaken, and your land shall no more be termed Desolate; but you shall be called My delight is in her, and your land Married" (*Is* 62,4). The names that suggested the former situation of forsakenness and desolation, that is, the devastation of the city by the Babylonians and the drama of the Exile, are now replaced by the names of the rebirth and are terms of love and tenderness, celebration and happiness.

At this point full attention is focused on the Bridegroom. This is the great surprise: it is the Lord himself who will give Zion her new married name. The final declaration which sums up the theme of the song of love chanted by the people is astonishing above all: "As a young man marries a virgin, your Builder shall marry you, and as the bridegroom rejoices over the bride, so shall your God rejoice over you" (v. 5).

5. The song no longer sings of the marriage between a king and a queen, but celebrates the profound love which eternally unites God and Jerusalem. In his earthly bride, which is the holy nation, the Lord finds the same happiness which the husband experiences with his beloved wife.

The distant, transcendent God, the just judge, is now replaced by the God who is close and in love. This spousal symbolism would be transferred to the New Testament (cf. *Eph* 5,21-32) and taken up and developed by the Fathers of the Church. St Ambrose, for example, recalls that in this perspective, "the husband is Christ, the wife is the Church, a bride for her love and a virgin for her unsullied purity" (*Esposizione del Vangelo Secondo Luca: Opera Esegetiche* X/II, Milan-Rome 1978, p. 289).

He continues in another of his works: "The Church is beautiful. So the Word of God says to her, "Your beauty is unblemished, my friend, and in you there is no blame' (*Cantico* 4,7), for sin has overpowered me... Thus, the Lord Jesus - impelled by the desire for such a great love, by the beauty of her raiment and her grace, since in those who have been purified there is no longer any stain of sin - says to the Church, 'Place me as a seal upon your heart, as a seal upon your arm' (*Cantico* 8: 6), that is: you are adorned, O my soul, you are wholly beautiful, nothing do you lack! 'Place me as a seal upon your heart', so that your faith will be radiant in the fullness of the sacrament. And let your works shine out and show the image of God in whose image you were made" (*I Misteri,* nn. 49, 41: *Opera Dogmatiche,* III, Milan-Rome 1982, pp. 156-157).

Psalm 145

My soul, give praise to the Lord;
I will praise the Lord all my days,
make music to my God while I live.

Put no trust in princes,
in mortal men in whom there is no help.
Take their breath, they return to clay
and their plans that day come to nothing.

He is happy who is helped by Jacob's God,
whose hope is in the Lord his God,
who alone made heaven and earth,
the seas and all they contain.

It is he who keeps faith for ever,
who is just to those who are oppressed.
It is he who gives bread to the hungry,
the Lord, who sets prisoners free,

the Lord who gives sight to the blind,
who raises up those who are bowed down,
the Lord, who protects the stranger
and upholds the widow and orphan.

It is the Lord who loves the just
but thwarts the path of the wicked.
The Lord will reign for ever,
Sion's God, from age to age.

Praise the Lord, O my soul!

1. Psalm 145 [146] that we have just heard is an "alleluia", the first of five which complete the entire collection in the Psalter. The Jewish liturgical tradition formerly used this hymn as a morning song of praise; it culminates in the proclamation of God's sovereignty over human history. Indeed, the Psalm ends with the declaration: "The Lord will reign for ever" (v. 10).

From this follows a comforting truth: we are not left to ourselves, the events of our days are not overshadowed by chaos or fate, they do not represent a mere sequence of private acts without sense or direction. From this conviction develops a true and proper profession of faith in God, celebrated in a sort of litany in which the attributes of his love and kindness are proclaimed (cf. vv. 6-9).

2. God is the Creator of heaven and earth who faithfully keeps the covenant that binds him to his people; it is he who brings justice to the oppressed, provides food to sustain the hungry and sets prisoners free. It is he who opens the eyes of the blind, who picks up those who have fallen, who loves the just, protects the foreigner, supports the orphan and the widow. It is he who muddles the ways of the unjust and who reigns sovereign over all beings and over all ages.

These are 12 theological assertions which, with their perfect number, are intended as an expression of the fullness and perfection of divine action. The Lord is not a Sovereign remote from his creatures

but is involved   he One who metes out justice and
ranks himself o   /liest, of the victims, the oppressed,
the unfortunate

3. Man, therefc   cing a radical choice between two
contrasting pos   e there is the temptation to "trust in
princes" (cf. v   r criteria inspired by wickedness,
selfishness and   ; a slippery slope, a ruinous road, a
"crooked path ɛ   (cf. *Prv* 2,15), whose goal is despair.
    Indeed, the P_{H 5030A}   that man is a frail, mortal being, as
the very word _{RK LICENSING, LLC}   [ebrew, this word is used to signify
earth, matter, d_{KETING COMPANY, LLC / E IN U.S.A.}   ɛ constantly states - is like a palace
that crumbles [t_{mark.com}   l-7), a spider's web that can be torn
apart by the w   strip of grass that is green at dawn
but has withere____,_____ s 89 [90],5-6; 102 [103],15-16). When
death assails him, all his plans disintegrate and he returns to dust:
"When his breath departs he returns to his earth; on that very day his
plans perish" (*Ps* 145 [146],4).

4. However, there is another possibility open to man, and the Psalmist
exalts it with a beatitude: "Happy is he whose help is the God of
Jacob, whose hope is in the Lord his God" (v. 5). This is the path of
trust in God, eternal and faithful. The *amen,* which is the Hebrew
word for faith, precisely means being based on the steadfast solidity
of the Lord, on his eternity, on his infinite power. Above all, however,
it means sharing his choices, on which the profession of faith and
praise described above has shed light.

We must live in consistency with the divine will, offer food to the
hungry, visit prisoners, sustain and comfort the sick, protect and
welcome foreigners, devote ourselves to the poor and the lowly. In
practice this corresponds exactly to the spirit of the Beatitudes; it
means opting for that proposal of love which saves us already in this
life and will later become the object of our examination at the last
judgment, which will seal history. Then we will be judged on our
decision to serve Christ in the hungry, the thirsty, the foreigner, the
naked, the sick, the prisoner. "As you did it to one of the least of these
my brethren, you did it to me" (*Mt* 25,40): this is what the Lord will
say at that time.

5. Let us conclude our meditation ⟨　　　　　⟩ vith an idea for reflection which is offered to us by ⟨　　　⟩ n that followed.

When Origen, the great third-cen ⟨　　　⟩ verse 7 of our Psalm which says: "[the Lord] gives ⟨　　　⟩ y, the Lord sets the prisoners free", he finds in it an ⟨　　　⟩ o the Eucharist: "We hunger for Christ and he himse ⟨　　　⟩ read of heaven. Give us this day our daily bread' ⟨　　　⟩ ιese words are hungry; those who feel the need ⟨　　　⟩ ιgry". And this hunger is fully satisfied by the Sac ⟨　　　⟩ ιarist, in which man is nourished by the Body a ⟨　　　⟩ t (cf. Origene-Gerolamo, *74 Omelie sul Libro dei* ⟨　　⟩ pp. 526-527).

Thur

Of the Fourth Week

Psalm 142   vv. 1-11

Lord, listen to my prayer:
turn your ear to my appeal.
You are faithful, you are just; give answer.
Do not call your servant to judgment
for no one is just in your sight.

The enemy pursues my soul;
he has crushed my life to the ground;
he has made me dwell in darkness
like the dead, long forgotten.
Therefore my spirit fails;
my heart is numb within me.

I remember the days that are past:
I ponder all your works.
I muse on what your hand has wrought
and to you I stretch out my hands.
Like a parched land my soul thirsts for you.

Lord, make haste and answer;
for my spirit fails within me.

Do not hide your face
lest I become like those in the grave.

In the morning let me know your love
for I put my trust in you.
Make me know the way I should walk:
to you I lift up my soul.

Rescue me, Lord, from my enemies;
I have fled to you for refuge.
Teach me to do your will
for you, O Lord, are my God.
Let your good spirit guide me
in ways that are level and smooth.

For your name's sake, Lord, save my life;
in your justice save my soul from distress.

Penitential psalms

1. The last of the so-called "Penitential Psalms" in the seventh
supplication contained in the Psalter was just now proclaimed in Psalm
142 (cf. *Ps* 6; 31; 37; 50; 101; 129; 142). The Christian tradition has used
all of them to seek pardon from God for its sins. The text that we want
to examine today was particularly dear to St Paul, who detected in it a
radical sinfulness of every human creature: "for no man living is righteous
before you, (O Lord)" (v. 2). This thought is used by the Apostle as the
foundation of his teaching on sin and grace (cf. *Gal* 2,16; *Rm* 3,20).

The *Liturgy of Lauds* proposes to us this supplication as a
proposition of faith and an imploring of divine help at the beginning
of the day. The Psalm, in fact, has us say to God: "Let me hear in the
morning of your steadfast love, for in you I put my trust" (v. 8).

2. The Psalm begins with an intense and insistent invocation directed
to God, faithful to his promise of salvation offered to the people (cf.
v. 1). The person in prayer recognizes his unworthiness and therefore
humbly asks God not to act as a judge (cf. v. 2).

Then he traces a dramatic situation, similar to an earthly
nightmare, which he is battling; the enemy, who represents evil in
history and in the world, has led him to the threshold of death. He

has fallen, in fact, into the dust of the earth, which is probably an image of the grave; then there is the darkness which is the absence of the light, a divine sign of life; then finally, "the deaths of great time", that is, the long-gone dead (cf. v. 3), among which he seems to be already relegated.

3. The Psalmist's very being is devastated: he cannot even breathe and his heart seems like a piece of ice, incapable of continuing to fight (cf. v. 4). To the faithful, knocked down and trampled, only the hands are left free, which stretch towards the sky in a gesture that is, at the same time, one of imploring help and seeking assistance (cf. v. 6). The thought, in fact, recalls the past when God wrought marvels (cf. v. 5).

This spark of hope warms the ice of suffering and the test in which the person in prayer feels immersed and at the point of being swept away (cf. v. 7). The tension, however, remains ever strong; but a ray of light seems to appear on the horizon. We continue, then, to the other part of the Psalm (cf. vv. 7-11).

4. It opens with a new, pressing invocation. The faithful, feeling life almost ebbing away, raises his cry to God: "Make haste to answer me, O Lord! My spirit fails!" (v. 7). Then, he fears that God may be hiding his face and may be far away, abandoning and leaving his creature alone.

Indeed, the disappearance of the divine face plunges the man into desolation, into death itself, because the Lord is the giver of life. Trust in the Lord, who does not abandon, flowers precisely in this sort of extreme perspective. The person in prayer redoubles his supplications and supports them with a declaration of faith in the Lord: "for in you I put my trust... for to you I lift up my soul... I have fled to you... for you are my God...". He asks to be saved from his enemies (cf. vv. 8-10) and freed from anguish (cf. v. 11), but he also repeatedly makes another request that manifests a profound spiritual aspiration: "Teach me to do your will, for you are my God!" (v. 10a; cf. vv. 8b, 10b).

This admirable request we must make our own. We need to understand that the greatest good is the union of our will with the will of our heavenly Father, because only in this way are we able to receive in ourselves all his love, which brings us salvation and the fullness of life. If it is not accompanied by a strong desire of docility to God, our faith in him is not authentic. Thus, the person in prayer is aware of it and so he expresses this wish. His is therefore a true and proper profession of faith in God the Saviour, who removes the anguish and restores the taste for life, in the name of his "justice", namely, of his loving and salvific faithfulness (cf. v. 11). Starting with a very distressing situation, the person in prayer is led to hope, to joy and to light, thanks to a sincere union to God and to his will that is a will of love. This is the power of prayer, generator of life and of salvation.

5. Turning the gaze to the light of the morning of grace (cf. v. 8), St Gregory the Great, in his commentary of the seven Penitential Psalms, described this dawn of hope and of joy thus: "It is the day illuminated by that only truth which does not set, which the clouds do not darken and the rain does not obscure.... When Christ, our life, appears, and we begin to see God with open eyes, then every haze of darkness will flee, every puff of ignorance will dissolve, every cloud of temptation will be dissipated.... That will be the glorious and splendid day, prepared for all the elect by the One who has freed us from the power of darkness and has transferred us into the reign of his beloved Son.

"The morning of that day is the future resurrection.... On that morning, the faithfulness of the just will be brilliant, the glory will appear, the exaltation will be seen, when God will wipe away every tear from the eyes of the saints, when death will finally be destroyed, when the just will shine forth like the sun in the kingdom of the Father.

"On that day, the Lord will use his mercy, saying: 'Come, blessed of my Father' (*Mt* 25,34). Then, the mercy of God will be made manifest, which in the present life the human mind cannot conceive. The Lord has in fact prepared, for those who love him, that which eye has not seen, nor ear has heard, nor has entered the heart of man" (*PL* 79, coll. 649-650).

———— ✳ ————

Canticle   Is 66,10-14a

Rejoice with Jerusalem, and be glad for her,
all you who love her;
rejoice with her in joy,
all you who mourn over her,

That you may suck and be satisfied
with her consoling breasts,
that you may drink deeply with delight
from the abundance of her glory.

For thus says the Lord:
Behold, I will extend prosperity to her like a river,
and the wealth of the nations like an overflowing stream;
and you shall suck, you shall be carried upon her hip,
and dandled upon her knees.

As one whom his mother comforts,
so I will comfort you;
you shall be comforted in Jerusalem.
You shall see, and your heart shall rejoice;
your bones shall flourish like the grass.

Rejoice with Jerusalem!

1. The Canticle we have just heard is taken from the last page of the *Book of Isaiah*. It is a song of joy dominated by the maternal figure of Jerusalem (cf. 66,11), and then by God's own loving solicitude (cf. v. 13). Biblical scholars claim that this final section that opens onto a splendid and festive future is the testimony of a later voice, the voice of a Prophet who is celebrating the rebirth of Israel after the dark period of the Babylonian Exile. We are thus in the sixth century B.C., two centuries after the mission of Isaiah, the great Prophet under whose name the whole of this inspired work is placed.

We will now follow the joyful flow of this short Canticle, which begins with three imperatives which are indeed an invitation to happiness: "rejoice", "be glad" and "rejoice... in joy" (cf. v. 10). This is a shining thread that often runs through the last pages of the *Book of Isaiah*: the afflicted of Zion are comforted, crowned, covered with the "oil of gladness" (*Is* 61,3); the Prophet himself says: "I will greatly rejoice in the Lord, my soul shall exult in my God" (*ibid.*, v. 10); "as the bridegroom rejoices over the bride, so shall your God rejoice" over his people (*Is* 62,5). On the page before the Canticle which is the object of our song and of our prayer now, it is the Lord himself who shares in the happiness of Israel, about to be reborn as a nation: "Be glad and rejoice for ever in that which I create; for behold, I create

Jerusalem a rejoicing, and her people a joy. I will rejoice in Jerusalem, and be glad in my people" (*Is* 65,18-19).

2. The source of and reason for this inner exultation lie in the rediscovered vitality of Jerusalem, risen from the ashes of the ruins to which she had been reduced by the Babylonian armies. Indeed, mention is made of her "mourning" (66,10), now something in the past.

As is often the case in various cultures, cities are represented with feminine, indeed, maternal images. When a city is at peace it is like a protective and safe womb; indeed, it is like a mother who breastfeeds her children with tenderness and abundance (v. 11). In this light the entity which the Bible calls, using a female term, "the daughter of Zion", that is, Jerusalem, resumes her role as a city-mother who comforts, nourishes and delights her children, that is, her inhabitants. Onto this lively, tender scene descends the Lord's word that has the tone of a blessing (cf. vv. 12-14).

3. God makes use of other images linked to fertility: indeed, he speaks of rivers and streams, that is, water which symbolizes life, the flourishing of vegetation, the prosperity of the earth and its inhabitants (cf. v. 12). Jerusalem's prosperity, her "peace" (*shalom*), a generous gift of God, will assure her offspring a life surrounded by motherly tenderness: "they will be carried upon her hip, and dandled upon her knees" (*ibid.*), and this motherly tenderness will be the tenderness of God himself: "As one whom his mother comforts, so I will comfort you" (v. 13). Thus, the Lord uses a maternal metaphor to describe his love for his creatures.

We can also read an earlier passage in the *Book of Isaiah* which gives God a maternal profile: "Can a woman forget her sucking child, that she should have no compassion on the son of her womb? Even though these may forget, yet I will not forget you" (*Is* 49,15). In our Canticle the Lord's words to Jerusalem end by taking up the theme of inner vitality, expressed with another image of fertility and energy: that of new grass, an image applied to bones to portray the vigour of the body and of life (cf. *Is* 66,14).

4. At this point, as we contemplate the city-mother, it is easy to broaden our gaze to take in the silhouette of the Church, virgin and fertile mother. Let us conclude our meditation on the reborn

Jerusalem with a reflection by St Ambrose, inferred in his work *Le Vergini:* "Holy Church is immaculate in her spousal union: fruitful in giving birth, she is a virgin through her chastity, yet she is mother of the children she conceives. Thus, we are born from a virgin who has conceived, not by a human act but through the power of the Holy Spirit. We are therefore born of a virgin, not in physical travail but amid the rejoicing of angels. A virgin nourishes us, not with the milk of her body, but with what the Apostle talks about when he speaks of having breastfed the weak state of the adolescent people of God.

"What married woman has more children than holy Church? She is virgin through the holiness she receives in the sacraments and she is mother of peoples. Her fertility is also attested by Scripture which says: For the children of the desolate one will be more than the children of she who is married' (*Is* 54,1; cf. *Gal* 4,27); our mother has no husband but she has a bridegroom, for both the Church in the peoples and the soul in individuals - immune from any kind of infidelity, fruitful in the life of the spirit - not without modesty, espouse the Word of God as their eternal bridegroom" (I, 31: *SAEMO* 14/1, pp. 132-133).

Psalm 146

Praise the Lord for he is good;
sing to our God for he is loving:
to him our praise is due.

The Lord builds up Jerusalem
and brings back Israel's exiles,
he heals the broken-hearted,
he binds up all their wounds.
He fixes the number of the stars;
he calls each one by its name.

Our Lord is great and almighty;
his wisdom can never be measured.
The Lord raises the lowly;
he humbles the wicked to the dust.
O sing to the Lord, giving thanks;
sing psalms to our God with the harp.

He covers the heavens with clouds;
he prepares the rain for the earth,
making mountains sprout with grass
and with plants to serve man's needs.
He provides the beasts with their food
and young ravens that call upon him.

His delight is not in horses
nor his pleasure in warriors' strength.
The Lord delights in those who revere him,
in those who wait for his love.

Praise the Lord!

1. The Psalm just sung is the first part of a composition that also includes the next Psalm, n. 146 [147], that the original Hebrew had kept as one. It was the ancient Greek and Latin versions which divided the song into two different Psalms.

The Psalm begins with an invitation to praise God and then lists a long series of reasons to praise him, all expressed in the present tense. These are activities of God considered as characteristic and ever timely, but they could not be more different: some concern God's interventions in human life (cf. *Ps* 146 [147],3.6.11) and in particular for Jerusalem and Israel (cf. v. 2); others concern the created cosmos (cf. v. 4) and more specifically, the earth with its flora and fauna (cf. vv. 8-10).

Finally, in telling us what pleases the Lord, the Psalm invites us to have a two-dimensional outlook: of religious reverence and of confidence (cf. v. 11). We are not left to ourselves nor to the mercy of cosmic energies, but are always in the hands of the Lord, for his plan of salvation.

2. After the festive invitation to praise the Lord (cf. v. 1), the Psalm unfolds in two poetic and spiritual movements. In the first (vv. 2-6), God's action in history is introduced with the image of a builder who is rebuilding Jerusalem, restored to life after the Babylonian Exile (cf. v. 2). However, this great mason who is the Lord also shows himself to be a father, leaning down to tend his people's inner and physical wounds humiliated and oppressed (cf. v. 3).

Let us make room for St Augustine who, in the *Enarrationes in Psalmos 146* which he gave at Carthage in the year 412, commented on the sentence "the Lord heals the brokenhearted" as follows: "Those whose hearts are not broken cannot be healed.... Who are the brokenhearted? The humble. And those who are not brokenhearted? The proud. However, the broken heart is healed, and the heart swollen with pride is cast to the ground. Indeed, it is probable that once broken it can be set aright, it can be healed. 'He heals the brokenhearted, and binds up their wounds...'. In other words, he heals the humble of heart, those who confess, who are punished, who are judged with severity so that they may experience his mercy. This is what heals. Perfect health, however, will be achieved at the end of our present mortal state when our corruptible being is reinvested with incorruptibility, and our moral being with immortality" (cf. 5-8: *Esposizioni sui Salmi,* IV, Rome 1977, pp. 772-779).

3. God's action, however, does not only concern uplifting his people from suffering. He who surrounds the poor with tenderness and care towers like a severe judge over the wicked (cf. v. 6). The Lord of history is not impassive before the domineering who think they are the only arbiters in human affairs: God casts the haughty to the dusty ground, those who arrogantly challenge heaven (cf. *1 Sam* 2,7-8; *Lk* 1,51-53).

God's action, however, is not exhausted in his lordship over history; he is also the King of creation: the whole universe responds to his call as Creator. Not only does he determine the boundless constellations of stars, but he names each one and hence defines its nature and characteristics (cf. *Ps* 146 [147],4).

The Prophet Isaiah sang: "Lift up your eyes on high and see: who created these [the stars]? He who brings out their host by number, calling them all by name" (*Is* 40,26). The "hosts" of the Lord are therefore the stars. The Prophet Baruch continued: "The stars shone in their watches and were glad; he called them, and they said, "Here we are!'. They shone with gladness for him who made them" (*Bar* 3,34-35).

4. Another joyful invitation to sing praises (cf. *Ps* 146 [147],7) preludes the second phase of Psalm 146 [147] (cf. vv. 7-11). Once again God's creative action in the cosmos comes to the fore. In a territory where drought is common, as it is in the East, the first sign of divine love is the rain that makes the earth fertile (cf. v. 8). In this way the Creator prepares food for the animals. Indeed, he even troubles to feed the tiniest of living creatures, like the young ravens that cry with hunger (cf. v. 9). Jesus was to ask us to look at the birds of the air; "they neither sow nor reap nor gather into barns, and yet your heavenly Father feeds them" (*Mt* 6,26; cf. also *Lk* 12,24, with an explicit reference to "ravens").

Yet once again our attention shifts from creation to human life. Thus, the Psalm ends by showing the Lord stooping down to the just and humble (cf. *Ps* 146 [147],10-11), as was declared in the first part of our hymn (cf. v. 6). Two symbols of power are used, the horse and the legs of a man running, to intimate that divine conduct does not give in to or let power intimidate it. Once again, the Lord's logic is above pride and the arrogance of power, and takes the side of those who are faithful, who "hope in his steadfast love" (v. 11), that is, who abandon themselves to God's guidance in their acts and thoughts, in their planning and in their daily life.

It is also among them that the person praying must take his place, putting his hope in the Lord's grace, certain that he will be enfolded in the mantle of divine love: "The eye of the Lord is on those who fear him, on those who hope in his steadfast love, that he may deliver their soul from death, and keep them alive in famine.... Yea, our heart is glad in him, because we trust in his holy name" (*Ps* 32 [33],18-19.21).

Friday

Of the Fourth Week

Psalm 50 - See Friday of the first week (see p. 63 above)

Have mercy on me, O God!

1. For the fourth time during our reflections on the *Liturgy of Lauds,* we hear proclaimed Psalm 50 [51], the famous *Miserere*. Indeed, it is presented anew to us on the Friday of every week, so that it may become an oasis of meditation in which we can discover the evil that lurks in the conscience and beg the Lord for purification and forgiveness. Indeed, as the Psalmist confesses in another supplication, "O Lord... no man living is righteous before you" (*Ps* 142 [143],2). In the *Book of Job* we read: "How can man be righteous before God? How can he who is born of woman be clean? Behold, even the moon is not bright, and the stars are not clean in his sight; how much less man, who is a maggot, and the son of man, who is a worm!" (25,4-6).

These are strong, dramatic words that are intended to portray the full seriousness and gravity of the limitations and frailty of the human creature, his perverse capacity to sow evil and violence, impurity and falsehood. However, the message of hope of the *Miserere* which the Psalter puts on the lips of David, a converted sinner, is this: God can "blot out, wash and cleanse" the sin confessed with a contrite heart (cf. *Ps* 50 [51],2-3). The Lord says, through the voice of Isaiah, even if "your sins are scarlet, they shall be as white as snow; though they are red like crimson, they shall become like wool" (*Is* 1,18).

2. This time we will reflect briefly on the end of Psalm 50 [51], a finale that is full of hope, for the person praying knows that God has forgiven him (cf. vv. 17-21). On his lips is praise of the Lord, which he is on the point of proclaiming to the world, thereby witnessing to the joy felt by the soul purified from evil, hence, freed from remorse (cf. v. 17).

The person praying witnesses clearly to another conviction, making a link with the teaching reiterated by the Prophets (cf. *Is* 1,10-17; *Am* 5,21-25; *Hos* 6,6): the most pleasing sacrifice that rises to the Lord like a fragrance, a pleasant odour (cf. *Gn* 8,21), is not the holocaust of bulls and lambs, but rather of "the broken and contrite heart" (*Ps* 50 [51],19).

The Imitation of Christ, a text so dear to the Christian spiritual tradition, repeats this same recommendation of the Psalmist: "Humble repentance for sins is the sacrifice that pleases you, its fragrance far sweeter than the smoke of incense.... It is there that one is purified and every evil washed away" (cf. III 52.4).

3. The Psalm ends on an unexpected note in an utterly different perspective that even seems contradictory (cf. vv. 20-21). From the final supplication of a single sinner, it becomes a prayer for the rebuilding of the city of Jerusalem, which takes us from the time of David to that of the city's destruction centuries later. Moreover, having voiced the divine rejection of animal sacrifices in v. 18, the

Psalm proclaims in v. 21 that it is in these same burnt offerings that God will take delight.

It is clear that the last passage is a later addition, made at the time of the Exile and intended, in a certain sense, to correct or at least to complete the perspective of the Davidic Psalm on two points: on the one hand, it was not deemed fit that the entire Psalm be restricted to an individual prayer; it was also necessary to think of the grievous situation of the whole city. On the other hand, there was a desire to give a new dimension to the divine rejection of ritual sacrifices; this rejection could be neither complete nor definitive, for it was a cult that God himself had prescribed in the *Torah*. The person who completed the Psalm had a valid intuition: he grasped the needy state of sinners, their need for sacrificial mediation. Sinners cannot purify themselves on their own; good intentions are not enough. An effective external mediation is required. The New Testament was to reveal the full significance of this insight, showing that Christ, in giving his life, achieved a perfect sacrificial mediation.

4. In his *Homilies on Ezechiel,* St Gregory the Great shows a good understanding of the change of outlook that occurs between vv. 19 and 21 of the *Miserere.* He suggests an interpretation that we too can accept as a conclusion to our reflection. St Gregory applies v. 19, which speaks of a contrite heart, to the earthly life of the Church, and v. 21, which speaks of burnt offerings, to the Church in heaven.

Here are the words of that great Pontiff: "Holy Church has two lives: one that she lives in time, the other that she receives eternally; one with which she struggles on earth, the other that is rewarded in heaven; one with which she accumulates merits, the other that henceforth enjoys the merits earned. And in both these lives she offers a sacrifice: here below, the sacrifice of compunction, and in heaven above, the sacrifice of praise. Of the former sacrifice it is said: "The sacrifice acceptable to God is a broken spirit' (*Ps* 50 [51],19); of the latter it is written: 'Then will you delight in right sacrifices, in burnt offerings and in whole burnt offerings' (*Ps* 50 [51],21)... In both, flesh is offered, since the sacrifice of the flesh is the mortification of the body, up above; the sacrifice of the flesh is the glory of the resurrection in praise to God. In heaven, flesh will be offered as a burnt holocaust when it is transformed into eternal incorruptibility, and there will be no more conflict for us and nothing that is mortal, for our flesh will endure in everlasting praise, all on fire with love for him" (*Omelie su Ezechiele/2,* Rome 1993, p. 271).

Canticle   Tob 13,8-11.13-15

Let all men speak,
and give God thanks in Jerusalem.
O Jerusalem, the holy city,
he will afflict you for the deeds of your sons,
but again he will show mercy to the sons of the righteous.

Give thanks worthily to the Lord,
and praise the King of the ages,
that his tent may be raised for you again with joy.

May he cheer those within you who are captives,
and love those within you who are distressed,
to all generations for ever.

Many nations will come from afar
to the name of the Lord God,
bearing gifts in their hands,
gifts for the King of heaven.
Generations of generations
will give you joyful praise.

Rejoice and be glad
for the sons of the righteous,
for they will be gathered together,
and will praise the Lord of the righteous.

How blessed are those who love you!
They will rejoice in your peace.
Blessed are those who grieved
over all your afflictions;
for they will rejoice for you upon seeing all your glory,
and they will be made glad for ever.

Let my soul praise God the great King!

Give thanks worthily to the Lord

1. *The Liturgy of Lauds* has gathered among its Canticles a fragment of a hymn, that is placed as a seal on the history narrated in the biblical *Book of Tobit:* to which we listened a few moments ago. The rather long and solemn hymn is an expression typical of Judaic prayer and spirituality, which draws on other texts in the Bible.

The Canticle develops by means of a double invocation. Above all, what emerges is a repeated invitation to praise God (cf. vv. 3.4.7) for the purification he carries out is by means of exile. The "sons of Israel" are exhorted to welcome this purification with a sincere conversion (cf. vv. 6.8). If conversion will flower in the heart, the Lord will make the dawn of liberation rise on the horizon. It is precisely in this spiritual atmosphere that the Liturgy has chosen to set the Canticle it has taken from the broader context of *Tobit's* hymn in chapter 13.

2. The second part of the text intoned by the elderly Tobit, who throughout the Book is the protagonist with his son, Tobias, is an authentic and characteristic celebration of Zion. It reflects the impassioned nostalgia and the ardent love that is experienced by the Hebrew in the diaspora regarding the Holy City (cf. vv. 9-18) and this aspect also shines out from the passage that has been chosen as the morning prayer in the *Liturgy of Lauds.* Let us dwell on these two themes: the purification of sin through trial and the expectation of the encounter with the Lord in the light of Zion and of his holy temple.

3. Tobit presses sinners to convert and act with justice: this is the path to take to rediscover that divine love which gives serenity and hope (cf. v. 8).

Jerusalem's very history is a parable which teaches everyone what choice to make. God punished the city because he could not remain indifferent before the evil committed by his children. Now, however, seeing that many have converted and become faithful and righteous children, he will once again show his merciful love (cf. v. 10).

Throughout the Canticle of chapter 13 of *Tobit* this firm conviction is repeated often: the Lord "afflicts, and he shows mercy;... will afflict us for our iniquities; and again he will show mercy.... He will afflict you for the deeds of your sons, but again he will show mercy to the sons of the righteous" (vv. 2.5.9). God's punishment is a way to make sinners who are deaf to other appeals turn back to the right path. However, the last word of the righteous God remains a message of love and of forgiveness; he profoundly desires to embrace anew the wayward children who return to him with a contrite heart.

4. With regard to the elect people, divine mercy manifests itself with the reconstruction of the Temple of Jerusalem, carried out by God himself "so that his tent may be rebuilt in you with joy" (v. 10). Thus, Zion, the second theme, appears as a holy place on which not only the returning Hebrews converge, but also those on pilgrimage seeking God. And so, a universal perspective opens: the rebuilt Temple of Jerusalem, sign of the divine word and presence, will shine with a planetary light dispelling the darkness so that "many nations, the inhabitants of all the limits of the earth" (cf. v. 11), may begin marching, bearing their gifts and singing their joy at participating in the salvation that the Lord bestows in Israel.

Therefore the Israelites are marching with all peoples toward a single finality of faith and of truth. On them, the hymnist calls down a repeated blessing, saying to Jerusalem: "How blessed are those who love you! They will rejoice in your peace" (v. 14). Happiness is authentic when it is rediscovered in the light that shines from heaven on all who seek the Lord with a purified heart and a deep yearning for truth.

5. It is toward this Jerusalem, free and glorious, sign of the Church in the last stage of her hope, a prefiguration of Christ's Paschal sacrifice, that St Augustine turns with fervour in his book of *Confessions*.

Making reference to the prayer which he intends to raise in his "[inner] chamber", he describes for us "songs of love... between groaning with groanings unutterable, which in my wayfaring, made me remember Jerusalem, with heart lifted up towards it, Jerusalem my country, Jerusalem my mother, and You that rule over it, the Enlightener, Father, Guardian, Husband, the pure and strong delight, and solid joy, and all good things unspeakable". And he ends with a promise: "Nor will I be turned away, until You gather all that I am, from this dispersed and disordered estate, into the peace of that our most dear mother, where the first-fruits of my spirit be already (whence I am ascertained of these things), and You conform and confirm it forever, O my God, my Mercy" (cf. *Confessions*, 12.16.23).

———— ✵ ————

Psalm 147 - See Friday of the second week (see p. 143 above)

Praise the Lord, O Jerusalem!

1. The Psalm now offered for our reflection makes up the second part of the preceeding Psalm 146 [147]. However, the ancient Greek and Latin translations, followed by the Liturgy, considered it as an independent hymn, since its opening is clearly distinguishable from what goes before it. This beginning has also become famous because it has often been put to music in Latin: *Lauda, Jerusalem, Dominum.* These opening words comprise the typical invitation of psalmody to celebrate and praise the Lord: now Jerusalem, a personification of the people, is summoned to exalt and glorify her God (cf. v. 12).

Mention is made, first of all, of the reason for which the praying community must raise its praise to the Lord. Its nature is historic: it was he, the Liberator of Israel from the Babylonian exile, who gave security to his people by "strengthening the bars of the gates" of the city (cf. v. 13).

When Jerusalem had fallen under the assault of King Nebuchadnezzar's army in 586 B.C., the *Book of Lamentations* presents the Lord himself as the judge of Israel's sin, as he "determined to lay in ruins the wall of the daughter of Zion.... Her gates have sunk into the ground; he has ruined and broken her bars" (*Lam* 2,8.9). Now, instead, the Lord returns as the builder of the Holy City; in the restored temple he blesses his sons and daughters once again. Thus mention is made of the work carried out by Nehemiah (cf. 3,1-38), who restored the walls of Jerusalem, so that it would become again an oasis of serenity and peace.

2. Indeed, peace, *shalom,* is evoked without hesitation, as it is contained symbolically in the very name of Jerusalem. The Prophet Isaiah had already promised the city: "I will make your overseers peace and your taskmakers righteousness" (*Is* 60,17).

However, other than repairing the walls of the city, blessing and reconciling her in security, God offers Israel other essential gifts described at the end of the Psalm. Here, indeed, the gifts of Revelation, the Law and the divine regulations are recalled: "He declares his word to Jacob, his statutes and ordinances to Israel" (*Ps* 147,19).

In this way, the election of Israel and her sole mission among the peoples is celebrated: to proclaim to the world the Word of God. It is a prophetic and priestly mission, because "what great nation is there that has statutes and ordinances so righteous as all this law which I set before you this day?" (*Dt* 4,8). It is through Israel and, therefore, also through the Christian community, namely the Church, that the Word of God resounds in the world and becomes instruction and light for all peoples (cf. *Ps* 147,20).

3. So far, we have described the first reason to give praise to the Lord: it is a historical reason, one linked to the liberating and revealing action of God with his people.

There remains, however, another reason for exultation and praise: it is of a cosmic nature, connected to the divine creative action. The divine Word bursts in to give life to being. Like a messenger, it runs from one corner of the earth to the other (cf. *Ps* 147,15). And suddenly, there is a flowering of wonders.

Now winter arrives, its climatic phenomena painted with a touch of poetry: the snow is like wool because of its whiteness, the frost with its delicate particles is like the dust of the desert (cf. v. 16), the hail is like morsels of bread thrown to the ground, the ice congeals the earth and halts vegetation (cf. v. 17). It is a winter scene that invites one to discover the wonders of creation which will be taken up again in a very picturesque page of another book of the Bible, that of *Sirach* (43,18-20).

4. Behold, then, the reblossoming of springtime, always through the action of the divine Word: the ice melts, the warm wind blows and the waters flow (cf. *Ps* 147,18), repeating the perennial cycle of the seasons and therefore the same possibility of life for men and women.

Naturally, metaphorical readings of these divine gifts are not lacking. The "finest of wheat" makes one think of the immense gift of the Eucharistic bread. Indeed, Origen, the great Christian writer of the third century, identified that wheat as a sign of Christ himself and, in particular, of Sacred Scripture.

This is his commentary: "Our Lord is the grain of wheat that falls to the earth, and multiplies itself for us. But this grain of wheat is supremely copious. The Word of God is supremely copious, it encloses all delights in itself. All that you see, comes from the Word of God, in the same way as the Jews recount: when they ate the manna, it took on the taste in the mouth that each one desired. So also with the flesh of Christ, which is the word of the teaching, namely, understanding of the Sacred Scriptures, the greater our desire, the greater the nourishment we receive. If you are holy, you find refreshment; if you are a sinner, you find torment" (Origen-Jerome, *74 omelie sul libro dei Salmi* [74 Homilies on the Book of Psalms], Milan 1993, pp. 543-44).

5. The Lord, therefore, acts with his Word not only in creation but also in history. He reveals himself with the silent language of nature (cf. *Ps* 18 [19],2-7), but expresses himself in an explicit way through the Bible and his personal communication through the Prophets and fully through the Son (cf. *Heb* 1,1.2). They are two different but converging gifts of His love.

For this reason, our praise must rise to heaven each day. It is our gratitude which blossoms at dawn in the prayer of Lauds to bless the Lord of life and freedom, of existence and faith, of creation and redemption.

Saturday
———— ✠ ————
Of the Fourth Week

Psalm 91 - See Saturday of the second week (see p. 146 above)

Good versus evil

1. The Canticle just presented to us is the song of a man faithful to Holy God. It is in Psalm 91 [92] which, as the ancient title of the composition suggests, was used by Jewish tradition "for the Sabbath". The hymn opens with a general appeal to celebrate and praise the Lord in music and song. It seems to be a never-ending stream of prayer, for divine love must be exalted in the morning when the day begins, but it must also be declared during the day and through the hours of the night.

It was the reference to musical instruments that the Psalmist makes in the introductory invitation that moved St Augustine to meditate in his exposition on Psalm 91 [92]: "What does it mean, brothers, to sing praise with the psaltery? The psaltery is a musical instrument with strings. Our psaltery is our work. Those who do good work with their hands praise God with the psaltery. Those who confess with their lips, praise him with their singing! Song is on their lips! They praise him with their actions!... So who are those who sing? Those who delight in doing good. Indeed, singing is a sign of cheerfulness. What does the Apostle say? "God loves a cheerful giver' (*2 Cor* 9,7). Whatever you do, do it joyfully. Then you will be doing good and doing it well. On the other hand, if you are cast down while you work, even if good is done through you, it is not you who do it: you have your lute in your hands, you are not singing" (cf. *Esposizioni sui Salmi*, III, Rome 1976, pp. 192-195).

2. Through St Augustine's words we can enter the heart of our reflection and deal with the fundamental theme of the Psalm: good and evil. Both are scrutinized by the just and holy God, "on high for ever", who is eternal and infinite, who lets no human action escape him.

Thus, two opposite forms of conduct are repeatedly compared. In his conduct, the faithful person is devoted to celebrating the divine works and plumbing the depths of the Lord's thoughts, and on this path his life is radiant with light and joy. By contrast, the Psalmist outlines the dullness of the wicked person, incapable as he is of understanding the hidden meaning of human events. Ephemeral good fortune makes him arrogant, but in fact he is basically weak and doomed after his fleeting success to destruction and death. The Psalmist, using an interpretative key dear to the Old Testament, that is, retribution, is convinced that God will already reward the righteous in this life, giving them a happy old age, and that he will punish evildoers before long.

Actually, as Job affirmed and Jesus was to teach, history can never be so clearly interpreted. Thus, the Psalmist's vision becomes a plea to the just God "on high for ever", to enter into the sequence of human events, to judge them and make good shine forth.

3. The contrast between the righteous and the wicked is subsequently taken up once again by the person praying. On the one hand, there are the "enemies" of the Lord, the "evildoers", once again doomed to dispersal and destruction. On the other, the faithful appear in their full splendour, embodied by the Psalmist who describes himself with picturesque images taken from Oriental symbology. The righteous person has the irresistible strength of the wild ox and is ready to challenge any adversity; his glorious forehead is anointed with the oil of divine protection that becomes, as it were, a shield to defend the chosen one and guard him. From the heights of his strength and safety, the person praying sees the wicked hurled into the abyss of their ruin.

Psalm 91 [92] thus is replete with happiness, confidence and optimism: gifts that we must ask God for precisely in our time when the temptation of distrust and even despair can easily creep in.

4. At the end, in the atmosphere of profound peace that permeates it, our hymn casts a glance at the old age of the righteous and predicts that they will be equally serene. Even when these days loom on his horizon, the spirit of the praying person will still be vital, happy and active, and feel flourishing and fruitful like the palms and cedars planted in the courtyards of the temple of Zion.

The righteous are radicated in God himself, from whom they absorb the sap of divine grace. The life of the Lord nourishes them and makes them flourish and vigorous, that is, able to give to others and to witness to their own faith. The Psalmist's final words in this description of a just, hard-working life and an intense and active old age, are in fact linked to the declaration of the Lord's eternal fidelity. At this point, therefore, we can conclude by proclaiming the Canticle that is raised to the glory of God in the last Book of the Bible, *Revelation,* the book of the terrible struggle between good and evil, but also of hope in Christ's final victory: "Great and wonderful are your deeds, O Lord God the Almighty! Just and true are your ways, O King of the peoples!... For you alone are holy. All nations shall come and worship you, for your judgments have been revealed.... Just are you in these your judgments, you who are and were, O Holy One.... Yes, Lord God the Almighty, true and just are your judgments!" (cf. 15,3-4; 16,5.7).

Canticle Ezek 36,24-28

I will take you from the nations,
and gather you from all the countries,
and bring you into your own land.

I will sprinkle clean water upon you,
and you shall be clean from all your uncleannesses,
and from all your idols I will cleanse you.

A new heart I will give you,
and a new spirit I will put within you;
and I will take out of your flesh the heart of stone
and give you a heart of flesh.

And I will put my spirit within you,
and cause you to walk in my statutes
and be careful to observe my ordinances.

You shall dwell in the land
which I gave to your fathers;
and you shall be my people,
and I will be your God.

I will be your God!

1. The Canticle that has just echoed in our ears and hearts was composed by one of the great Prophets of Israel, Ezekiel, a witness of one of the most tragic ages the Jewish people lived through: the destruction of the Kingdom of Judea and its capital, Jerusalem, followed by the bitter exile in Babylon (sixth century B.C.). The passage that has become part of the Christian prayer of Lauds is an extract from chapter 36 of *Ezekiel*.

The context of this passage, transformed into a liturgical hymn, seeks to capture the deep meaning of the tragedy that the people lived in those years. The sin of idolatry had contaminated the land that the Lord had given to Israel as an inheritance. In the final analysis it was this more than anything else that was responsible for the loss of the homeland and dispersal among the nations. In fact, God is not indifferent to good and evil; he enters the history of humanity mysteriously with his judgment that sooner or later unmasks evil, defends its victims and points out the way of justice.

2. However, the goal of God's action is never the ruin, the pure and simple condemnation or elimination, of the sinner. It was the Prophet Ezekiel himself who cited these divine words: "Have I any pleasure in the death of the wicked, and not rather that he should turn from his way and live?... For I have no pleasure in the death of anyone; so return, and live" (18,22.23).

In this light we can understand the meaning of our Canticle that is filled with hope and salvation. After purification through trial and suffering, the dawn of a new era is about to break, as the Prophet Jeremiah had already announced, speaking of a "new covenant" between the Lord and Israel (cf. *Jer* 31,31-34). Ezekiel himself, in chapter 11 of his prophetic book, had proclaimed these divine words: "I will give them a new heart, and put a new spirit within them; I will take the stony heart out of their flesh, and give them a heart of flesh, that they may walk in my statutes and keep my ordinances and obey them; and they shall be my people, and I will be their God" (11,19-20).

In our Canticle (cf. *Ez* 36,24-28), the Prophet takes up this oracle and completes it with a marvellous explanation: the "new spirit" given by God to the children of his people will be his Spirit, the Spirit of God himself (cf. v. 27).

3. Thus, not only is a purification proclaimed, expressed in the sign of the water that washes away the stains on the conscience. There is not only the aspect of liberation from evil and sin (cf. v. 25), necessary though it may be. Ezekiel's message stresses another, far more surprising aspect: humanity is, in fact, destined to be born to new life. The first symbol is that of the "heart" which, in biblical language, suggests interiority, the personal conscience. God will tear from our breasts the "heart of stone" that is cold and hard, a sign of the persistence of evil. Into them he will put a "heart of flesh", that is, a source of life and love (cf. v. 26). The life-giving spirit that brought creatures to life in the creation (cf. *Gn* 2,7), will be replaced in the new economy of grace by the Holy Spirit, who sustains us, moves and guides us toward the light of truth and pours out "God's love... into our hearts" (*Rom* 5,5).

4. Thus will emerge that "new creation" which St Paul was to describe (cf. *2 Cor* 5,17; *Gal* 6,15), when the "old self" in us, the "sinful body", would pass away, so that "we might no longer be enslaved to sin" (*Rom* 6,6), but new creatures, transformed by the Spirit of the risen Christ: "You have put off the old nature with its practices and have put on the new nature, which is being renewed in knowledge after the image of its Creator" (*Col* 3,9-10; cf. *Rom* 6,6). The Prophet Ezekiel proclaims a new people which the New Testament would see as having been gathered together by God himself through the work of his Son. This community, possessing "a heart of flesh" and imbued with the "Spirit", would experience the living and active presence of God himself, who would enliven believers, acting in them with his efficacious grace. "All who keep his commandments abide in him", St John was to say, "and he in them. And by this we know that he abides in us, by the Spirit which he has given us" (*1 Jn* 3,24).

5. Let us end our meditation on the *Canticle of Ezekiel* by listening to St Cyril of Jerusalem who, in his *Third Baptismal Catechesis,* delineates in this prophetic passage the people of Christian Baptism.

"Through Baptism", he recalls, "all sins are forgiven, even the most serious transgressions". The Bishop therefore says to his listeners: "Have faith, Jerusalem, the Lord will remove your wickedness from you (cf. *Zep* 3,14-15). The Lord will cleanse you from your misdeeds...; he will sprinkle clean water upon you, and you shall be clean from all your uncleannesses' (*Ez* 36,25). The angels will encircle you rejoicing and they will soon sing: Who is that coming up from the wilderness', immaculate, and "leaning upon her beloved?' (*Sg* 8,5). In fact, it is the soul, formerly a slave and now free to address as her adopted brother her Lord, who says to her, accepting her sincere resolution, Behold, you are beautiful, beautiful!' (*Sg* 4,1).... Thus, he exclaims, alluding to the fruits of a confession made with a clear conscience,... may heaven deign that you all... keep alive the remembrance of these words and draw fruits from them, expressing them in holy deeds in order to present yourselves faultless before the mystical Bridegroom and obtain from the Father the forgiveness of your sins" (n. 16; *Le Catechesi,* Rome 1993, pp. 79-80).

Psalm 8 - See Saturday of the second week (see p. 153 above)

O Lord, our God!

1. In meditating on Psalm 8, a wonderful hymn of praise, we come to the end of our long journey through the Psalms and Canticles that make up the prayerful heart of the *Liturgy of Lauds*. In these catecheses, we have reflected on 84 biblical prayers whose spiritual intensity we have especially tried to emphasize, without overlooking their poetic beauty.

Indeed, the Bible invites us to start our day with a hymn that not only proclaims the marvels wrought by God and our response of faith, but celebrates them with "music" (cf. *Ps* 46 [47],8), that is, in a beautiful, luminous way, gentle and strong at the same time.

Psalm 8 is the most splendid example of all; in it, man, engulfed in night, feels like a grain of sand compared to infinity and the boundless space that arches above him, when the moon rises and the stars begin to twinkle in the vast expanse of the heavens (cf. v. 4).

2. In fact, in the middle of Psalm 8, a twofold experience is described. On the one hand, the human person feels almost overwhelmed by the grandeur of creation, "the work of the divine fingers". This curious phrase replaces the "works of the hands" of God (cf. v. 7), as if to suggest that the Creator had traced a drawing or an embroidery with the shining stars, casting them over the immensity of the firmament.

Yet on the other hand, God bends down to man and crowns him as his viceroy: "you crown him with glory and honour" (v. 6). Indeed, he entrusts the whole universe to this frail creature, so that he may draw from it knowledge and the means for his survival (cf. vv. 7-9).

The horizon of man's dominion over the other creatures is specified, as it were, recalling the opening page of *Genesis:* flocks, herds, the beasts of the field, the birds of the air, the fish of the sea were entrusted to man so that in giving them a name (cf. *Gn* 2,19-20), he might discover their profound reality, respect it and transform it through work, perfecting it so that it might become a source of beauty and of life. The Psalm makes us aware of our greatness, but also of our responsibility for creation (cf. *Wis* 9,3).

3. Reinterpreting Psalm 8, the author of the *Letter to the Hebrews* discovered in it a deeper understanding of God's plan for humankind. The human vocation cannot be restricted to the "here and now" of the earthly world; if the Psalmist says that God has put *all things* under man's feet, this means that he also wants him to subdue "the world to come" (*Heb* 2,5), the "kingdom that cannot be shaken" (12,28). In short, man's call is a "heavenly call" (3,1). God wants "[to bring] to glory" in heaven "many sons" (2,10). In order for this divine plan to take place, God had to trace out the life of "a pioneer" (cf. *ibid.*), in which the human vocation could find its first complete fulfilment. This pioneer is Christ.

The author of the *Letter to the Hebrews* remarked on this subject that the Psalm's words apply in a privileged way to Christ, that is, more specifically to him than to other men. In fact, the Psalmist uses the verb "to make less", saying to God: "you made him for a little while lower than the angels, you crowned him with glory and honour" (cf. *Ps* 8,6; *Heb* 2,6). For ordinary people this verb is inappropriate: they have not been "made lower" than the angels since they were never above them.

Instead, for Christ it is the right verb, because he was above the angels as the Son of God, and was made lower when he became man; then he was crowned with glory in his Resurrection. Thus, Christ fulfilled completely the vocation of man and, the author explains, he has done this "for every one" (*Heb* 2,9).

4. In this light, St Ambrose comments on the Psalm and applies it to us. He starts with the sentence that describes the "crowning" of man: "you crown him with glory and honour" (v. 6). He sees in that glory, however, the reward that the Lord keeps in store for us, when we shall have overcome the test of temptation.

These are the words of this great Father of the Church in his *Expositio Evangelii secundum Lucam* [Exposition of the Gospel according to Luke]: "The Lord has also crowned his beloved with glory and magnificence. That God who desires to distribute crowns, procures temptations: thus, when you are tempted, know that he is preparing a crown for you. Abolish the heroic fight of the martyrs and you will abolish their crowns; abolish their suffering and you will abolish their blessedness" (cf. IV, 41: *SAEMO* 12, pp. 330-333).

God weaves that "crown of righteousness" for us (*2 Tm* 4,8) as the reward for our fidelity to him which we were able to preserve, even when storms batter our heart and mind. But in all seasons he is attentive to his beloved creature and wants the divine "image" to shine perpetually in him (cf. *Gn* 1,26), so as to radiate a sign of harmony, light and peace in the world.

———— ✖ ————

Benedictus (Canticle of Zechariah)   Lk 1,68-79

Blessed be the Lord, the God of Israel!
He has visited his people and redeemed them.

He has raised up for us a mighty saviour
in the house of David his servant,
as he promised by the lips of holy men,
those who were his prophets from of old.

A saviour who would free us from our foes,
from the hands of all who hate us.
So his love for our fathers is fulfilled
and his holy covenant remembered.

He swore to Abraham our father to grant us,
that free from fear, and saved from the hands of our foes,
we might serve him in holiness and justice
all the days of our life in his presence.

As for you little child,
you shall be called a prophet of God, the Most High.
You shall go ahead of the Lord
to prepare his ways before him,

To make known to his people their salvation
through forgiveness of all their sins,
the loving kindness of the heart of our God
who visits us like the dawn from on high.

He will give light to those in darkness,
those who dwell in the shadow of death,
and guide us into the way of peace.

The Benedictus

1. Having reached the end of our long journey through the Psalms
and Canticles of the *Liturgy of Lauds,* let us pause to consider the
prayer that marks the Office of Lauds every morning. It is the
Benedictus, the Canticle intoned by Zechariah, the father of John the
Baptist, when the birth of that son changed his life, wiping away the

doubt that caused him to go mute, a serious punishment for his lack of faith and praise.

Now, instead, Zechariah can celebrate God who saves him, and he does so with this hymn, set down by Luke the Evangelist in a form that undoubtedly reflects the liturgical usage current in the original Christian community (cf. *Lk* 1,68-79).

The Evangelist himself describes it as a prophetic hymn, inspired by the breath of the Holy Spirit (cf. 1,67). Indeed, we have before us a benediction proclaiming the saving actions and liberation offered by the Lord to his people. Thus, it is a "prophetic" interpretation of history, the discovery of the intimate, profound meaning of all human events that are guided by the hidden but active hand of the Lord which clasps the more feeble and hesitant hands of men and women.

2. The text is solemn and, in the original Greek, is composed of only two sentences (cf. 68-75; 76-79). After the introduction, marked by the benediction of praise, we can identify in the body of the Canticle, as it were, three strophes that exalt the same number of themes, destined to mark the whole history of salvation: the covenant with David (cf. vv. 68-71), the covenant with Abraham (cf. vv. 72-75) and the Baptist who brings us into the new Covenant in Christ (cf. vv. 76-79). Indeed, the tension of the whole prayer is a yearning for the goal that David and Abraham indicate with their presence.

It culminates in one of the last lines: "The day shall dawn upon us from on high..." (v. 78). This phrase, which at first sight seems paradoxical with its association of "dawn" and "on high", is actually full of meaning.

3. Indeed, in the original Greek, the "rising sun" is *anatolè,* a word which in itself means both the light of the sun that shines on our planet and a new shoot that sprouts. Both these images have messianic value in the biblical tradition.

On the one hand, Isaiah reminds us, speaking of the Emmanuel, that "the people who walked in darkness have seen a great light; those who dwelt in a land of deep darkness, on them has light shined" (*Is* 9,1). On the other, referring once again to the king-Emmanuel, he describes him as the "shoot from the stump of Jesse", that is, from the house of David, a shoot upon which the Spirit of the Lord was to rest (cf. *Is* 11,1-2).

With Christ, therefore, appears the light that enlightens every creature (cf. *Jn* 1,9) and makes life flourish, as John the Evangelist was to say, combining the two realities: "in him was life, and the life was the light of men" (1,4).

4. Humanity that was engulfed "in darkness and in the shadow of death" is illumined by this dazzling revelation (cf. *Lk* 1,79). As the Prophet Malachi had announced: "For you who fear my name, there will arise the sun of justice with its healing rays" (3,20). This sun "guides our feet into the way of peace" (*Lk* 1,79).

So let us move on, taking that light as our reference point; and may our faltering steps which, during the day, often stray to dark and slippery paths, be sustained by the light of the truth that Christ spreads in the world and in history.

At this point, let us listen to a teacher of the Church, one of her Doctors, the Englishman Venerable Bede (seventh-eighth centuries). In his *Homily for the Birth of St John the Baptist* he commented on the Canticle of Zechariah as follows: "The Lord... has visited us as a doctor visits the sick, because to heal the deep-rooted sickness of our pride, he gave us the new example of his humility; he redeemed his people, for at the price of his blood he set us free when we had become servants of sin and slaves of the ancient enemy.... Christ found us lying 'in darkness and in the shadow of death', that is, oppressed by the long-lasting blindness of sin and ignorance.... He brought to us the true light of his knowledge, and banishing the darkness of error, he has shown us the sure way to the heavenly homeland. He has directed the steps of our actions to make us walk on the path of truth, which he has pointed out to us, and to enable us to enter the home of eternal peace, which he has promised us".

5. Lastly, drawing from other biblical texts, the Venerable Bede concluded, giving thanks for the gifts received: "Given that we are in possession of these gifts of eternal bounty, dear brethren... let us also praise the Lord at all times (cf. *Ps* 33 [34],2), for "he has visited and redeemed his people'.

May praise be always on our lips, let us cherish his memory and in turn, proclaim the virtue of the One who has "called you [us] out of darkness into his marvellous light' (*1 Pt* 2,9). Let us ceaselessly ask his help, so that he may preserve in us the light of the knowledge that he brought to us, and lead us onwards to the day of perfection" (*Omelie sul Vangelo,* Rome, 1990, pp. 464-465).

Index

——— ❈ ———

(Page references in bold refer to catechesis on the psalm or canticle.)